ROUTLEDGE LIBRARY EDITIONS:
NUCLEAR SECURITY

I0028043

Volume 9

THE ARMS RACE AND ARMS CONTROL 1984

THE ARMS RACE AND ARMS CONTROL 1984

STOCKHOLM INTERNATIONAL PEACE
RESEARCH INSTITUTE

R Routledge
Taylor & Francis Group

LONDON AND NEW YORK

First published in 1984 by Taylor & Francis Ltd

This edition first published in 2021
by Routledge
2 Park Square, Milton Park, Abingdon, Oxon OX14 4RN

and by Routledge
52 Vanderbilt Avenue, New York, NY 10017

Routledge is an imprint of the Taylor & Francis Group, an informa business

© 1984 Stockholm International Peace Research Institute

British Library Cataloguing in Publication Data
A catalogue record for this book is available from the British Library

ISBN: 978-0-367-50682-7 (Set)
ISBN: 978-1-00-309763-1 (Set) (ebk)
ISBN: 978-0-367-51420-4 (Volume 9) (hbk)
ISBN: 978-1-00-305379-8 (Volume 9) (ebk)

Publisher's Note
The publisher has gone to great lengths to ensure the quality of this reprint but points out that some imperfections in the original copies may be apparent.

Disclaimer
The publisher has made every effort to trace copyright holders and would welcome correspondence from those they have been unable to trace.

The Arms Race and Arms Control 1984

sipri

Stockholm International Peace Research Institute

SIPRI is an independent institute for research into problems of peace and conflict, especially those of disarmament and arms regulation. It was established in 1966 to commemorate Sweden's 150 years of unbroken peace.

The Institute is financed by the Swedish Parliament. The staff, the Governing Board and the Scientific Council are international.

Governing Board

Rolf Björnerstedt, Chairman (Sweden)
Egon Bahr (FR Germany)
Francesco Calogero (Italy)
Tim Greve (Norway)
Max Jakobson (Finland)
Karlheinz Lohs
 (German Democratic Republic)
Emma Rothschild (United Kingdom)
The Director

Director

Frank Blackaby (United Kingdom)

sipri

Stockholm International Peace Research Institute
Bergshamra, S-171 73 Solna, Sweden
Cable: Peaceresearch, Stockholm
Telephone: 08-55 97 00

The Arms Race and Arms Control 1984

sipri

Stockholm International Peace Research Institute

Taylor & Francis
London and Philadelphia
1984

UK	Taylor & Francis Ltd, 4 John St, London WC1N 2ET
USA	Taylor & Francis Inc., 242 Cherry St, Philadelphia, PA 19106-1906

British Library Cataloguing in Publication Data

The Arms race and arms control.—1984
    1. Arms control—Periodicals
    2. Arms race—Periodicals
    I. Stockholm International Peace Research
Institute
    327.1'74'05   JX1974

    ISBN 978–0–367–51426–6
    ISSN 0265-1807

Library of Congress Cataloging Number

LC 83-641034

Typeset by The Lancashire Typesetting Co. Ltd, Bolton.

PREFACE

This book is SIPRI's third short annual report on what is going on in the world military sector, and on the success or failure of the attempts to curb what is happening there. Why is such a report needed?

It is needed because we have here a process that has got out of control—dangerously out of control. Nuclear weapons provide the most obvious example. The size of the world stockpile of nuclear weapons is such that the use of only a small part of it would produce a planetary disaster. Yet all the five nuclear powers—the United States and the Soviet Union in particular—are engaged in massive programmes of developing and deploying new nuclear weapons. At the moment, there are no negotiations anywhere about these matters.

The military seek to exploit for military purposes every new scientific development which comes their way. Thus the world is on the edge of an immensely expensive technological arms race in outer space—first, with the development of weapons to shoot down satellites, and then with the development of systems of defence against ballistic missiles. In these matters too, no effective negotiations are going on.

The acceleration of the arms race is not simply a technological struggle between the United States and the Soviet Union. Third World countries are also acquiring more sophisticated weapons, enthusiastically supplied to them by industrial countries which then deplore the conflicts in which these weapons are used.

There are many strong forces making for the continuation of the dangerous course on which the world now seems set. One of the few forces on the other side is that of public opinion. That is why as many people as possible should know something about what is going on. To this end, this paperback presents the more immediately relevant chapters from *World Armaments and Disarmament, SIPRI Yearbook 1984*, whose full contents are listed at the back of the book.

April 1984
Frank Blackaby
Director

CONTENTS

World Armaments and Disarmament, SIPRI Yearbook 1984:
Contents List

GLOSSARY

Acronyms

ABM	Anti-ballistic missile	ICBM	Intercontinental ballistic missile
ALCM	Air-launched cruise missile	INF	Intermediate-range nuclear force
ASAT	Anti-satellite		
ASBM	Air-to-surface ballistic missile	IRBM	Intermediate-range ballistic missile
ASW	Anti-submarine warfare	ISMA	International Satellite Monitoring Agency
AWACS	Airborne warning and control system		
		LRTNF	Long-range theatre nuclear force
BMD	Ballistic missile defence		
BW	Biological weapon	MAD	Mutual assured destruction
C³I	Command, control, communications and intelligence	MARV	Manoeuvrable re-entry vehicle
		M(B)FR	Mutual (balanced) force reduction
CBM	Confidence-building measure	MIRV	Multiple independently targetable re-entry vehicle
CBW	Chemical and biological warfare		
CD	Committee on Disarmament (from 1984: Conference on Disarmament)	MRV	Multiple (but not independently targetable) re-entry vehicle
		NPT	Non-Proliferation Treaty
CDE	Conference on Disarmament in Europe	OPANAL	Agency for the Prohibition of Nuclear Weapons in Latin America
CEP	Circular error probable		
CSBM	Confidence- and security-building measure	PNE(T)	Peaceful Nuclear Explosions (Treaty)
CSCE	Conference on Security and Co-operation in Europe	PTB(T)	Partial Test Ban (Treaty)
		R&D	Research and development
CTB	Comprehensive test ban	RV	Re-entry vehicle
CW	Chemical weapon	RW	Radiological weapon
DC	Disarmament Commission	SALT	Strategic arms limitation talks
ENMOD	Environmental modification	SAM	Surface-to-air missile
ERW	Enhanced radiation (neutron) weapon	SCC	Standing Consultative Commission (US–Soviet)
FBS	Forward-based systems	SLBM	Submarine-launched ballistic missile
FOBS	Fractional orbital bombardment system	SLCM	Sea-launched cruise missile
		SRBM	Short-range ballistic missile
GLCM	Ground-launched cruise missile	SSBN	Ballistic missile-equipped, nuclear-powered submarine
IAEA	International Atomic Energy Agency	START	Strategic arms reduction talks
		TTBT	Threshold Test Ban Treaty

Anti-ballistic missile (ABM) system	Weapon system for intercepting and destroying ballistic missiles.
Anti-satellite (ASAT) system	Weapon system for destroying, damaging or disturbing the normal function of, or changing the flight trajectory of, artificial Earth satellites.
Atomic weapon	Explosive device in which the main part of the explosive energy released results from the fission of the nuclei of heavy atoms such as uranium-235 or plutonium-239.
Ballistic missile	Missile which follows a ballistic trajectory (part of which may be outside the Earth's atmosphere) when thrust is terminated.
Battlefield nuclear weapons	*See:* Theatre nuclear weapons.
Binary chemical weapon	A shell or other device filled with two chemicals of relatively low toxicity which mix and react while the device is being delivered to the target, the reaction product being a super-toxic chemical warfare agent, such as nerve gas.
Biological weapons (BW)	Living organisms or infective material derived from them, which are intended for use in warfare to cause disease or death in man, animals or plants, and the means of their delivery.
Chemical weapons (CW)	Chemical substances—whether gaseous, liquid or solid—which might be employed as weapons in combat because of their direct toxic effects on man, animals or plants, and the means of their delivery.
Circular error probable (CEP)	A measure of missile accuracy: the radius of a circle, centred on the target, within which 50 per cent of the weapons aimed at the target are expected to fall.
Committee on Disarmament (CD)	Multilateral arms control negotiating body, based in Geneva, which is composed of 40 states (including all the nuclear weapon powers) and called the Conference on Disarmament from 1984. The CD is the successor of the Eighteen-Nation Disarmament Committee, ENDC (1962–69), and the Conference of the Committee on Disarmament, CCD (1969–78).
Conference on Disarmament in Europe (CDE)	Conference on confidence- and security-building measures and disarmament in Europe, the first stage of which opened in Stockholm, Sweden, in January 1984.
Conference on Security and Co-operation in Europe (CSCE)	Conference of the European states and the USA and Canada, which on 1 August 1975 adopted a Final Act (also called the Helsinki Declaration), containing, among others, a Document on confidence-building measures and certain aspects of security and disarmament.
Conventional weapons	Weapons not having mass destruction effects. *See also:* Weapons of mass destruction.
Counterforce attack	Nuclear attack directed against military targets.
Countervalue attack	Nuclear attack directed against civilian targets.
Cruise missile	Unmanned, self-propelled, guided weapon-delivery vehicle which sustains flight through aerodynamic lift and can fly at very low altitudes following the contours of the terrain. It can be air-, ground- or sea-launched and deliver a conventional or nuclear warhead with high accuracy.
Disarmament Commission (DC)	A subsidiary, deliberative organ of the UN General Assembly for disarmament matters, composed of all UN members.
Enhanced radiation weapon (ERW)	*See:* Neutron weapon.
Enriched nuclear fuel	Nuclear fuel containing more than the natural content of fissile isotopes.
Enrichment	*See:* Uranium enrichment.
Eurostrategic weapons	*See:* Theatre nuclear weapons.

Fall-out	Particles contaminated with radioactive material as well as radioactive nuclides, descending to the Earth's surface following a nuclear explosion.
First-strike capability	Capability to destroy within a very short period of time all or a very substantial portion of an adversary's strategic nuclear forces.
Fission	Process whereby the nucleus of a heavy atom splits into lighter nuclei with the release of substantial amounts of energy. At present the most important fissionable materials are uranium-235 and plutonium-239.
Flexible response	Reaction to an attack with a full range of military options, including a limited use of nuclear weapons.
Fractional orbital bombardment system (FOBS)	System capable of launching nuclear weapons into orbit and bringing them back to Earth before a full orbit is completed.
Fuel cycle	*See:* Nuclear fuel cycle.
Fusion	Process whereby light atoms, especially those of the isotopes of hydrogen—deuterium and tritium—combine to form a heavy atom with the release of very substantial amounts of energy.
Genocide	Commission of acts intended to destroy, in whole or in part, a national, ethnical, racial or religious group.
Ground zero	The point on the Earth's surface at which a nuclear weapon is detonated or, for airburst, the point on the Earth's surface directly below the point of detonation.
Helsinki Declaration	*See:* Conference on Security and Co-operation in Europe (CSCE).
Intercontinental ballistic missile (ICBM)	Ballistic missile with a range in excess of 5 500 km.
Intermediate-range nuclear force (INF)	*See:* Theatre nuclear weapons. (US–Soviet negotiations on INF were adjourned *sine die* in November 1983.)
International Nuclear Fuel Cycle Evaluation (INFCE)	International study conducted in 1978–80 on ways in which supplies of nuclear material, equipment and technology and fuel cycle services can be assured in accordance with non-proliferation considerations.
Kiloton (kt)	Measure of the explosive yield of a nuclear weapon equivalent to 1 000 tons of trinitrotoluene (TNT) high explosive. (The bomb detonated at Hiroshima in World War II had a yield of some 12–15 kilotons.)
Launcher	Equipment which launches a missile. ICBM launchers are land-based launchers which can be either fixed or mobile. SLBM launchers are missile tubes on submarines.
Launch-weight	Weight of a fully loaded ballistic missile at the time of launch.
Long-range theatre nuclear force (LRTNF)	*See:* Theatre nuclear weapons.
Manoeuvrable re-entry vehicle (MARV)	Re-entry vehicle whose flight can be adjusted so that it may evade ballistic missile defences and/or acquire increased accuracy.
Medium-range nuclear weapons	*See:* Theatre nuclear weapons.
Megaton (Mt)	Measure of the explosive yield of a nuclear weapon equivalent to one million tons of trinitrotoluene (TNT) high explosive.
Multiple independently targetable re-entry vehicles (MIRV)	Re-entry vehicles, carried by one missile, which can be directed to separate targets (as distinct from—multiple but not independently targetable re-entry vehicles—MRVs).
Mutual assured destruction (MAD)	Concept of reciprocal deterrence which rests on the ability of the nuclear weapon powers to inflict intolerable damage on one another after surviving a nuclear first strike. *See also:* Second-strike capability.

Mutual reduction of forces and armaments and associated measures in Central Europe	Subject of negotiations between NATO and the Warsaw Treaty Organization, which began in Vienna in 1973. Often referred to as mutual (balanced) force reduction (M(B)FR).
Neutron weapon	Nuclear explosive device designed to maximize radiation effects and reduce blast and thermal effects.
Nuclear fuel cycle	Series of steps involved in preparation, use and disposal of fuel for nuclear power reactors. It includes uranium ore mining, ore refining (and possibly enrichment), fabrication of fuel elements and their use in a reactor, reprocessing of spent fuel, refabricating the recovered fissile material into new fuel elements and disposal of waste products.
Nuclear weapon	Device which is capable of releasing nuclear energy in an explosive manner and which has a group of characteristics that are appropriate for use for warlike purposes. The term denotes both the thermonuclear and atomic weapons.
Nuclear weapon-free zone (NWFZ)	Zone which a group of states may establish by a treaty whereby the status of total absence of nuclear weapons to which the zone shall be subject is defined, and a system of verification and control is set up to guarantee compliance.
Peaceful nuclear explosion (PNE)	Application of a nuclear explosion for such purposes as digging canals or harbours or creating underground cavities.
Plutonium separation	Reprocessing of spent reactor fuel to separate plutonium.
Radiological weapon (RW)	Device, including any weapon or equipment, other than a nuclear explosive device, specifically designed to employ radioactive material by disseminating it to cause destruction, damage or injury by means of the radiation produced by the decay of such material, as well as radioactive material, other than that produced by a nuclear explosive device, specifically designed for such use.
Re-entry vehicle (RV)	That part of a strategic ballistic missile designed to carry a nuclear warhead and to re-enter the Earth's atmosphere in the terminal phase of the trajectory.
Second-strike capability	Ability to survive a nuclear attack and launch a retaliatory blow large enough to inflict intolerable damage on the opponent. *See also:* Mutual assured destruction.
Standing Consultative Commission (SCC)	US–Soviet consultative body established in accordance with the SALT agreements.
Strategic arms limitation talks (SALT)	Negotiations between the Soviet Union and the United States, held from 1969 to 1979, which sought to limit the strategic nuclear forces, both offensive and defensive, of both sides.
Strategic arms reduction talks (START)	Negotiations between the Soviet Union and the United States, initiated in 1982, which seek to reduce the strategic nuclear forces of both sides. Adjourned *sine die* in December 1983.
Strategic nuclear forces	ICBMs, SLBMs and ASBMs (not yet deployed) as well as bomber aircraft of intercontinental range.
Tactical nuclear weapons	*See:* Theatre nuclear weapons.
Terminal guidance	Guidance provided in the final, near-target phase of the flight of a missile.
Theatre nuclear weapons	Nuclear weapons of a range less than 5 500 km. Often divided into long-range—over 1 000 km (for instance, so-called eurostrategic weapons), medium-range, and short-range—up to 200 km (also referred to as tactical or battle-field nuclear weapons). For the USSR, weapons of a range exceeding 1 000 km (but less than 5 500 km) are medium-range. The USA uses the term 'intermediate' to denote weapons of a range both above and below 1 000 km (but not short-range).

Thermonuclear weapon	Nuclear weapon (also referred to as hydrogen weapon) in which the main part of the explosive energy release results from thermonuclear fusion reactions. The high temperatures required for such reactions are obtained with a fission explosion.
Throw-weight	'Useful weight' of a ballistic missile placed on a trajectory toward the target.
Toxins	Poisonous substances which are products of organisms but are inanimate and incapable of reproducing themselves. Some toxins may also be produced by chemical synthesis.
Uranium enrichment	The process of increasing the content of uranium-235 above that found in natural uranium, for use in reactors or nuclear explosives.
Warhead	That part of a missile, torpedo, rocket or other munition which contains the explosive or other material intended to inflict damage.
Weapons of mass destruction	Nuclear weapons and any other weapons which may produce comparable effects, such as chemical and biological weapons.
Weapon-grade material	Material with a sufficiently high concentration either of uranium-233, uranium-235 or plutonium-239 to make it suitable for a nuclear weapon.
Yield	Released nuclear explosive energy expressed as the equivalent of the energy produced by a given number of tons of trinitrotoluene (TNT) high explosive. *See also:* Kiloton and Megaton.

Introduction

FRANK BLACKABY

The purpose of this introduction is to provide a general overview of what is going on in the world military sector, and to report on the progress—or lack of progress—in attempts at control. The general picture of 1983, and the prospects for 1984, are sombre. Substantial rearmament programmes—particularly in the nuclear weapon field—are going ahead. The arms control negotiations dealing with these weapons are still in suspense (March 1984). The problem for 1984 is one of limiting the damage caused by the events of 1983.

Indeed there was virtually no progress anywhere in arms control in 1983. There was stalemate at the Vienna talks on force reductions in Europe. At the Conference on Disarmament in Geneva, the only negotiations which showed any sign of movement were those on chemical weapons; however, final agreement is clearly a long way off.

This introduction concentrates on nuclear weapon issues: the negotiations about eurostrategic and intercontinental weapons; nuclear explosions and a comprehensive test ban; and peace movements and the various proposals for raising the nuclear threshold in Europe. A section follows on the militarization of space, and the absence of negotiations in this sphere.

Rearmament programmes also show up in the figures for world military expenditure; this introduction reports on trends in military spending and in the arms trade. It discusses developments in chemical weapons—in evidence on allegations of use, and in the Geneva negotiations and gives a short report on the Conference on Confidence and Security-Building Measures which began in Stockholm in January 1984.

I. Nuclear weapons

Nuclear weapons in Europe

At the beginning of 1983, there seemed to be a slim chance of some agreement at Geneva before new intermediate-range nuclear missiles were deployed in Europe. Hopes faded during the year. The negotiations broke down on 23 November 1983.

The US position was that there should be some measure of equality between Soviet land-based intermediate-range nuclear weapons targeted on western Europe and US weapons, stationed in Europe, which could reach the Soviet Union. This equality could be either at zero or some other number. Initially the United States had demanded parity, not just with Soviet warheads targeted on Europe, but with all Soviet intermediate land-based warheads, including those on missiles deployed in eastern Siberia. As a late concession, the United States agreed not to include the missiles located in the Far East, and also agreed to discuss aircraft.

The Soviet Union's final position was that it was willing, in exchange for no new deployment on the US side, to reduce the number of missile launchers targeted on western Europe to a figure of 140 (or possibly 120)—leading to a rough equivalence with the number of French and British warheads targeted on the Soviet Union. It also tentatively floated this offer in a form which did not mention French and British forces. This would bring the number of Soviet warheads targeted on western Europe below the figure which existed before the SS-20s were deployed. It offered to dismantle the missiles which would be removed, and to freeze the number in eastern Siberia. The assessment in *SIPRI Yearbook 1983*—that the Soviet Union would not be willing to go much beyond this offer—proved correct.

The matter of nuclear-capable aircraft with a combat radius of 1 000 km or more was left unresolved. Soviet figures show NATO having more such aircraft than the Soviet Union; US figures show the opposite. However, according to the US chief negotiator, the differences had been narrowed before the talks broke down.

The negotiations provided a good case history of the many fallacies which have bedevilled so many arms control negotiations since the end of World War II. There was the central fallacy that there is some military need for parity in nuclear weapon deployment. There is no such military need: each side already has far more nuclear weapons than it could conceivably use without producing a planetary disaster. The demand for parity is a political, not a military demand. There is the fallacy that, if new weapons are deployed, this will make the other side more malleable at the conference table. Certainly in these negotiations the opposite appears to be true. There is the 'myth of the last move': that, after some new deployments, the game will stop and some alleged disparity will be rectified. The game does not stop: new moves produce countermoves.

At the turn of 1983/84, nine Pershing II missiles were declared operational in the Federal Republic of Germany (Schwäbisch-Gmünd), and the first flight of cruise missiles (16) was operational in Britain (Greenham Common). In Italy, the first cruise missile flight was scheduled to be operational in March 1984. In FR Germany (Hasselbach), cruise missile deployment is not due until 1986. In Belgium and the Netherlands, the sites for eventual cruise missile deployment have been designated (Florennes and Woensdrecht, respectively). However, it is still uncertain whether the two governments will accept deployment. NATO's December 1979 decision envisages a total deployment of 572 missiles. If East–West relationships remain tense, the number could ultimately be greater.

On the Soviet side, an unspecified number of SS-22 missiles are being deployed in the German Democratic Republic and in Czechoslovakia, manned by Soviet troops. New SS-23 missiles are likely to follow, replacing old Scud systems. The declared moratorium on the deployment of SS-20 missiles within striking range of Europe has been lifted. The Soviet Union, in explicit response to the short flight time of the Pershing II missile, is reported to be deploying submarine-launched ballistic missiles nearer than before to the US coastline; this may be followed by the deployment of new sea-launched cruise missiles.

The new deployment of land-based missiles in Europe may indeed seem small, compared with the total stock of nuclear weapons or with other new deployments—the USA proposes to deploy some 8 000 cruise missiles on bombers, ships and submarines, most of them with nuclear warheads. However, the European deployments are more important than their numbers may suggest. The Soviet Union sees the Pershing II as a particularly dangerous weapon, because it is considered accurate enough, and with a long enough range, to destroy Soviet command centres. Its flight time is short: so the Soviet Union could be tempted to move towards pre-delegation of firing authority, and even to consider 'launch-on-warning', which—given the risk of false warnings—would be very dangerous. The same thing could happen on the side of the United States, if it also becomes threatened by Soviet warheads which are accurate and have short flight times. Forward-based systems are growing, creating very unstable situations.

The political consequences of the new deployments are also unsettling. There is now no consensus on defence policies between the government and the main opposition party in either FR Germany or Britain. In eastern Europe, there is little doubt that many inhabitants of the GDR and Czechoslovakia are unhappy about additional nuclear-capable missiles, manned by Soviet forces, deployed on their territory.

Those in the West who have regarded the new deployment of inter-mediate-range missiles as a 'victory' for the West and a 'defeat' for the Soviet Union have failed to understand the idea of common security. Security can only be obtained in the long run by policies and practices which increase the feeling of security of both parties. Any step which makes a potential enemy feel more insecure is a backward step, which simply stirs up more trouble for the future. In the long run, security for one side cannot be obtained by deployments which reduce the feeling of security on the other side.

Intercontinental nuclear weapons

The competition in intercontinental nuclear weapons is intensifying: there are formidable weapon developments in train. As usual, much more is known about US plans than about Soviet plans. However, so far as advanced military technology is concerned, the United States has tended to lead the Soviet Union.

The United States is upgrading its strategic nuclear weapon deployment right across the board. To justify its programme, it has used in particular the 'window of vulnerability' argument—that Soviet land-based missiles are now powerful and accurate enough to eliminate in a first strike virtually all US land-based missiles. The implication is that the Soviet Union has acquired some kind of strategic superiority, and the US government finds this unacceptable.

There are many reasons for doubting whether this window of vulnerability exists. To attempt a first strike of this kind would be an act of incredible folly. First of all, it assumes a degree of accuracy and reliability for the Soviet intercontinental ballistic missile (ICBM) force which is entirely implausible. Second, there is no way in which the Soviet Union could effectively attack both US bomber bases and land-based missiles; either there would be sufficient warning time for the bombers to take off, or the attack on airfields would enable US missiles to be launched before they were hit. Third, there would be the likelihood that the United States would use its largely invulnerable submarine-launched ballistic missile force in retaliation.

The US programme includes the building of a new ballistic missile submarine fleet, and the development of a new missile for that fleet (the Trident II (D5)) which is expected to be accurate enough to attack Soviet missiles in their silos. The proposed land-based missile—the MX—would also have that capacity. Cruise missiles are accurate enough to destroy hardened targets as well. It appears that the USA wishes to be in a position to threaten Soviet land-based missiles in the same way that, it suggests, the Soviet Union threatens US land-based missiles.

In the longer term, there is a possibility that the USA might move away from the large land-based missiles with multiple warheads to smaller land-based missiles, probably mobile, with single warheads. There appears to be some belated recognition that missiles with multiple warheads are destabilizing, since a single missile on one side can threaten a number of missiles on the other. However, this would not be a return to the simple 'mutually assured destruction' doctrine of the 1960s: for it is proposed that the new land-based missile with a single warhead (the Midgetman) should also have the power and accuracy to attack Soviet missiles in their silos.

The forward plans of the Soviet Union are not published: they can only be inferred. There are certainly attempts to match new US deployments. The Soviet Union is probably developing cruise missiles with capabilities similar to those of the US missiles, some of them to be deployed on platforms at sea, close to the extensive US coastlines. The USSR has an ambitious construction programme for ballistic and cruise missile-carrying submarines. It is also seeking to develop new solid-fuelled missiles. It has been testing one new ICBM (US code-name Plesetsk-4), an ICBM which the Soviet Union claims is a modification of the SS-13 (US code-name Plesetsk-5), and a new submarine-launched ballistic missile, the SS-NX-20. There will quite probably be an increase in the total number of Soviet intercontinental nuclear warheads which is at least equivalent to the expected US increase.

Both the USA and the USSR declare that the sole purpose of their nuclear weapons is deterrent: that a nuclear war cannot be won, and therefore must never be fought. However, both sides are proceeding to develop and deploy weapons far beyond the requirements of mutually assured destruction. Each, it seems, believes in the political value of nuclear weapons—that an apparent inferiority (even if it has no military meaning) is damaging, and that consequently an apparent military superiority is politically beneficial. If it becomes generally accepted that the nuclear weapon states are right in believing that nuclear weapons provide political power in international affairs, then it is hard to see how, in the long run, the number of nuclear weapon states can remain as limited as it is now.

Negotiations

The negotiations about intercontinental nuclear weapons—at present in suspense—confront a number of problems. Like the negotiations about eurostrategic weapons, they are bedevilled by the demand for parity. Given the different mix of weapons, with their varying capacities, it is very hard to negotiate agreements if that demand is pressed beyond the requirement for some very rough measure of overall equivalence. With nuclear weapons at their present levels, there is no military need for parity: certainly no need for it in any sub-category of nuclear weapons. There is no military use that could be made of margins of superiority, as measured by one or other of the measuring rods of nuclear weapon stocks.

There is a further complication now, arising from US allegations that the Soviet Union has been failing to comply with a number of treaties, or with undertakings it gave to respect the provisions of treaties signed but not ratified. These allegations have been met by Soviet counter-allegations. Almost all were based on suppositions or other, rather loose, grounds. These matters could have been clarified through existing consultation procedures. The fact that this route has not been sufficiently used testifies to the propagandistic nature of the mutual recriminations.

Further, once a party has made a public allegation of this kind, it has put itself in the position of a prosecuting counsel: that is, it is interested in evidence which supports the allegation, and not interested in evidence which rebuts it. This has been seen in the case of the allegations of Soviet involvement in the use of toxins in Laos, Afghanistan and Kampuchea. The US State Department tends to pour scorn on any evidence that might suggest a natural origin for the phenomena it reports, since it is now committed to the accusation.

It is probably true that the US and west European governments feel themselves under some public pressure not to appear too belligerent. Now that the deployments of new missiles in western Europe are under way, the tone of Western speeches and public statements has changed. The speeches now emphasize the need for dialogue; references to limited nuclear war are replaced by statements that nuclear war cannot be won. It is, of course, not difficult to change the tone of speeches. It is much harder for the electorate to establish whether or not there has been any change in the negotiating stance, or in strategic or military doctrine.

Before the negotiations about intercontinental nuclear weapons were suspended, the gap between the positions taken by the USA and the USSR still seemed wide. The USA was still primarily concerned with the threat from heavy Soviet missiles—the SS-18s and SS-19s: its negotiating strategy was to find ways of reducing in particular the number of these missiles, by a limit on total throw-weight, or by a ceiling on the number of land-based launchers. The Soviet Union was more interested in overall limits, with freedom to mix. It conceded that warheads and not just launchers should be counted; it wished to bring in discussion of bombers and cruise missiles from the start of the negotiations. This point the USA conceded.

In the USA, a number of influential members of the Congress were not satisfied with the Administration's negotiating stance; they indicated that they would only continue to support the MX programme if there were a change. One of their requirements was that the Administration should in some form adopt the 'build-down' proposal: the basic idea is that two old nuclear warheads should be eliminated for each new warhead deployed (though the ratio of old to new could be varied). In this way modernization would be accompanied by a reduction rather than an increase in the total number of warheads. The Administration agreed to put forward the proposal of a working party on this idea at Geneva. When the negotiations were broken off, the Soviet Union had not accepted the idea.

Negotiations are now suspended, while new deployments of nuclear weapons, both in Europe and elsewhere, are not. It is doubtful whether there is now much point in keeping the negotiations on eurostrategic weapons separate from those on intercontinental nuclear weapons. There are a great many overlaps between the weapons discussed in the two separate forums. The land-based cruise missiles are basically the same missiles as those which the United States intends to deploy at sea. It seems logical for the Soviet Union to wish to negotiate about all US nuclear warheads which could land on its territory, wherever they are fired from. Further, if the negotiations encompass all weapons with ranges of 1 000 km or more, this should make it more possible to accommodate in some way Soviet concern about French and British nuclear warheads.

The danger is that such negotiations would take a great many years, and in the mean time there would be no check to new nuclear weapon developments. Some interim check is badly needed: it would have to be relatively simple. One such suggestion is that of the Independent Commission on Disarmament and Security Issues (the Palme Commission): "We urge the Soviet Union and the United States to declare reciprocally a one-year pause on deployment of nuclear weapons to open the way for the resumption of talks."

The Western peace movements: the nuclear threshold

Insofar as their objective was to prevent the deployment in western Europe of Pershing II and cruise missiles, the west European peace movements failed. However, insofar as their objective was to persuade people to their point of view, the movements have had considerable success. In a number of countries a majority of the population seems—judging from opinion polls—to sympathize with some of the movements' main aims. Further, in both Britain and FR Germany the main opposition parties declared their opposition to the deployment of missiles at the end of 1983.

In the USA, the pressure from the various peace movements—in particular the nuclear freeze movement—has also had some political effect. On many armament and arms control issues, the majority of members of Congress have been more sympathetic to arms control issues than the Administration. For example, in spite of the Administration's requests in successive years, appropriations for the production of new binary chemical weapons have been turned down.

A number of research programmes were under way in 1983 to examine in greater detail the possible effects of nuclear war. One main suggested conclusion was that previous studies had not taken sufficient account of the effects of smoke and other residues from burning cities and forests. The use of only a small proportion of the world's stockpiles of nuclear weapons, it was suggested, could produce a 'nuclear winter'. The question follows: if the use of a small proportion of the stockpile could produce this effect, what justification could there be for its total size?

A broad consensus has emerged on the need to raise the nuclear threshold in Europe—and the peace movements can claim a good deal of credit for this change. NATO has announced the withdrawal of 1 400 nuclear weapons from Europe over the coming 5–6 years, including atomic demolition mines and warheads on Nike–Hercules missiles. These weapons would have to be used at the beginning of a conflict, before NATO's ability to stop a conventional attack by conventional means had been tested. With the introduction of new long-range theatre nuclear forces, further nuclear weapons are to be removed on a one-for-one replacement basis. These measures suggest that NATO's nuclear posture may slowly be moving towards 'no-early-use'.

However, there are at the same time developments which point in the other direction. The production of neutron warheads, meant for deployment in Europe, is continuing. (Altogether US nuclear weapon production is now of the order of 2 000 warheads a year.) Nuclear munitions still have considerable support among the armed services. The current modest trend towards denuclearization may still be reversed. In eastern Europe there are indications that in addition to missile modernization the Soviet Union is also storing nuclear weapons 'on the spot'. These weapons may include nuclear artillery shells.

No-first-use

There is a strong case for the peace movements to concern themselves with the issue of no-first-use of nuclear weapons. NATO's doctrine of flexible response, implying possible first use of nuclear weapons, has come under attack from a number of sources—from the churches, from international lawyers, from high ranking military officers and from leading politicians, including former members of the US and British administrations. There is a powerful argument for the West to prepare itself for a no-first-use commitment through changes in military force posture, and for a Soviet demonstration of the seriousness of its declared intent never to be the first to use nuclear weapons, through redeployment of its forces.

To be meaningful, a no-first-use declaration would have to be accompanied—or preferably preceded—by a withdrawal of battlefield nuclear weapons from areas adjacent to the East–West border in Europe. It could be followed by the removal of nuclear weapons from the territories of all European countries which do not themselves possess them. In the conventional field, perceived discrepancies in military strength might be eliminated through negotiation of a mutually acceptable balance of forces at a level lower than the present one.

In trying to redress the perceived conventional weapon imbalance, NATO has predominantly chosen the rearmament route. Recently, one main emphasis has been on exploiting emerging technologies for striking deep into enemy territory as a method of defence. The proponents of 'deep strike' claim that new conventional technologies offer a rather cheap way of raising the nuclear threshold. Sceptics emphasize the vulnerability of some of the new technologies, and the west European allies have voiced concern about the costs involved.

The arms control implications of many deep-strike technologies are potentially serious. They could prove destabilizing by enhancing the incentives for pre-emption on both sides, especially if combined with such offensive operational doctrines as the US AirLand Battle on the Western side and the operational manoeuvre groups on the Eastern side. If, instead, some of the deep-strike technologies were used in combination with less offensive defence postures, such as disengagement zones, they could perhaps enhance confidence and security in Europe.

Nuclear explosions

According to preliminary figures, there were 50 nuclear explosions carried out in 1983: 27 by the Soviet Union, 14 by the USA, 7 by France, and 1 each by Britain and China. However, this may not be a complete list. The United States does not announce all its tests. The Soviet Union does not announce any, and the information comes from the seismic detection systems in other countries. Thirteen of the Soviet explosions—those which took place outside the known weapon test sites—were possibly for civil engineering purposes. However, all nuclear explosions can provide some information of military value.

The French tests have come under increasing criticism from states in the South Pacific, as well as from non-governmental organizations active in the protection of the environment, since the tests are conducted on the other side of the world from France itself. These tests are on the Mururoa atoll in the Pacific Ocean.

Comprehensive test ban

It is now 20 years since the USA, the USSR and the UK signed a treaty whose preamble stated that they were seeking to achieve the discontinuance of all test explosions of nuclear weapons for all time, and were determined to continue negotiations to this end. However, it appears that an agreement on a comprehensive test ban is now much further away than it was in 1980, when the trilateral negotiations were discontinued. The major obstacle is the attitude of the US government, which has decided to regard such a measure as a long-term goal of its policy rather than a high-priority objective of arms control efforts, as most countries do. The USA has also

9

failed to ratify two other treaties concerning nuclear explosions, both of which it signed some years ago: the Threshold Test Ban Treaty (signed in 1974) and The Peaceful Nuclear Explosions Treaty (signed in 1976).

During the 1983 session of the Committee on Disarmament at Geneva, Sweden tabled a full draft treaty for a comprehensive test ban. However, the working group established in this area was given a mandate which did not include the elaboration of an actual treaty; its task was only to discuss and define issues relating to verification and compliance.

II. Military space programmes

Outer space has, of course, been militarized for a long time, in that the bulk of the activity in space is for military purposes. Two recent developments threaten a great deal more military activity in the future than in the past.

The first development concerns anti-satellite (ASAT) weapons. The Soviet Union has, over a number of years, conducted tests with an anti-satellite device—essentially intercepting one satellite with another. It has, however, not admitted that these were anti-satellite tests—indeed, it has not admitted that it has any military space programmes at all. The USA has been developing a rather more sophisticated anti-satellite weapon—a missile launched from an F-15 aircraft. The first test of this air-launched system was conducted in January 1984. (Until 1975 the USA had deployed a land-based ASAT system at Kwajalein atoll in the Pacific Ocean.) If there is no treaty banning these weapons, then we can expect the development of weapons which can attack satellites in high orbits—the present systems can only attack low-orbit satellites; we can also expect the exploration of defensive measures—hardened satellites, and the deployment of spare satellites to replace any which might be attacked.

There is a link between this first development and the second—President Reagan's proposal, in a notable speech on 23 March 1983, in which he appealed to the US scientific community to work towards solving the problems of defence against ballistic missiles. The development of defence against ballistic missiles is not the problem of developing one particular weapon: it involves developing and perfecting a whole set of systems.

The expansion of the US research and development programme—which was already considerable—is now beginning. (As usual, there are only Western reports of the Soviet research and development efforts, some suggesting that they have been of comparable size to those of the USA up to now.) The US proposed programme has come under substantial criticism, particularly from scientists in the arms control community. The criticism is on three main grounds. First, they doubt whether effective systems can be developed, even with enormous expense. Even then, there could be a number of ways for new offensive developments in nuclear delivery systems to negate these defensive systems. Second, before such systems were deployed, there would have to be an abrogation (or re-negotiation) of the Anti-Ballistic Missile Treaty, and also the Partial Test Ban Treaty. Third, if either side were to develop what it believed to be a successful system, then fears of an attempted first strike might be better based than they are now.

Arms control in outer space

It has been found impossible, in the Committee on Disarmament at Geneva, to set up a working group to negotiate a treaty on arms control in outer space. The non-aligned countries, China and the Soviet Union wanted a working group with a mandate for undertaking negotiations for "the conclusion of an agreement or agreements". The United States and other Western countries agreed only to a mandate restricted to identifying issues relevant to the prevention of an arms race in outer space. Somewhat reluctantly, the non-aligned countries, *faute de mieux*, went along with this limited suggestion. However, at the time of writing (March 1984) the Soviet Union has not done so.

The Soviet Union, in 1983, submitted a new draft treaty in this field. It also declared a unilateral moratorium on the launching of any anti-satellite weapons, for as long as other states refrained from deploying such weapons.

Any agreement seems very distant. The USA argues that it needs to catch up with Soviet deployment; and an inter-agency study has concluded that it would be impossible to verify such an accord. The USA also probably considers that any prohibition of anti-satellite weapons would prevent the eventual deployment of an anti-ballistic missile system. If weapons which could attack satellites were banned, this would prevent the deployment of weapons which could attack ballistic missiles—for any weapon which could attack a ballistic missile could also attack a satellite.

However, there is pressure in the US Congress for negotiations on anti-satellite weapons. This has been expressed in a resolution which calls for the President to "endeavour in good faith to negotiate a mutual and verifi-able ban on anti-satellite weapons" before the Administration can proceed with testing an anti-satellite weapon against a target in space.

III. Chemical weapons

While there was no progress in negotiations about a comprehensive test ban, or a ban on anti-satellite weapons, there was some progress in 1983 in negotiations about chemical weapons.

The negotiations were helped by the fact that the US Congress eventually turned down the Administration's request for appropriations for the production of new binary chemical weapons. (The Soviet Union continues its policy of saying nothing whatever about its production or stocks of chemical weapons.)

At the negotiations, the Committee on Disarmament has accepted that the objective is complete disarmament. That would be a most impressive achievement, which would augur well for success elsewhere. For success in the chemical weapon negotiations, verification and other confidence-building measures of an exceptionally innovative kind will be needed, because of the peculiarities of chemical weapon technology and of the industrial base which supports it. If these complex problems can be solved, it should be possible to solve other simpler ones.

The gap between the US and Soviet positions is still wide: a document from the Committee sets out the state of agreement and disagreement on more than 100 issues on which consensus must be reached. However, this and other documents do serve to set out the outer bounds within which a potentially valuable compromise might be negotiated.

In the interim before a chemical weapons convention is agreed upon (which may indeed be a very long interim) the UN General Assembly has been concerning itself with establishing a mechanism for investigating allegations of the use of chemical or biological weapons. In October 1983 an expert group submitted a report, with detailed recommendations on the way in which such an investigation should be conducted: the work of the group was extended by a General Assembly resolution. A complaint was received by the Secretary-General, from Iran, that Iraq had used chemical weapons. The expert group which he appointed has reported that mustard gas and nerve gas have been used in Iran. The Security Council has condemned their use, without naming the culprit. The USA has banned the export of certain chemicals to both countries. Both countries are parties to the Geneva Protocol.

The other allegations of the use of chemical weapons have been the US allegations concerning Yellow Rain in Afghanistan and South-East Asia. A number of academics concerned themselves with this question during 1983. What has become clearer is that most (and maybe all) publicly disclosed evidence pointing to the use of toxic weapons in these countries does not in fact exclude the possibility of natural causation for the reported death and disease.

It is most important that the UN should be enabled to set up an efficient fact-finding mechanism. This would help to deter possible violations, and should also discourage ill-considered charges.

IV. Military expenditure and the arms trade

In the past two years (using provisional figures for 1983) the rise in the volume of world military spending is estimated at about 5 per cent per year—well above the post-war trend.

A good deal of this acceleration is explained by the US rearmament programme: the volume rise in the rest of the world, excluding the USA, was 3 per cent during the past two years. After the end of the war in Viet Nam, military spending in the USA came down, and then levelled off between 1975 and 1979. Since 1979, with the rearmament programme initiated by President Carter, and intensified by President Reagan, the volume increase in US military spending has averaged 7.5 per cent per year. In the post-war period, accelerations of this kind have previously only happened when the United States was engaged in an actual war—at the time of the Korean or Viet Nam wars.

The trend in the Soviet Union is always a matter for conjecture; the official rouble figure for 1983 was slightly lower than that for 1979, which seems highly implausible. During 1983 the CIA reduced its estimate of the trend of Soviet military spending, and now puts the volume trend from 1976 to 1981 at 2 per cent per year. Their preliminary estimates for 1982 indicate a continuation of that trend.

Other NATO countries—apart from Britain—have not followed the US example. British military spending has been influenced not only by a determination to fulfil NATO goals but also by the Falklands/Malvinas war. Identifiable extra costs for the war and subsequent garrison have recently been estimated at $4.7 billion to the end of fiscal year 1986/87, but this may not be the full picture. Economic constraints are beginning to tell. Over a long period up to 1980, in most Western countries, military spending was a falling share of central government expenditure. In many countries the fall has now slowed down or stopped, and in some—the United States and Britain, for example—it has begun to rise.

In a period of fluctuating exchange-rates, it is not easy to produce a sensible figure for the total of world military expenditure. The SIPRI estimate for world military spending in 1983, *at 1980 prices and exchange-rates*, is $600–650 billion. If one applies to that figure the US rate of inflation between 1980 and 1983, it produces a figure of $750–800 billion.

Whereas world military spending has been rising fast, the arms trade in major weapons has not. Since 1980 the trend has flattened out and, on provisional figures, shows some decline. The main reason is undoubtedly economic. Third World countries are extensively in debt, and are in no position to continue massive purchases of major weapons. A recent study has concluded that about a quarter of the accumulated Third World debt can be explained by weapon imports. A number of OPEC countries which accounted for a good part of the increase in arms sales since the early 1970s have faced reduced export earnings.

On the supplier side, the Soviet Union and the United States account for a third each of total exports of major weapons; the Soviet share has been declining, while the trend for US arms exports is rising. Facing domestic arms procurement cut-backs, many supplier countries have intensified their marketing efforts in order to increase their arms export revenues. Some governments which might, possibly, have wished to constrain their arms sales on political grounds have found the economic pressures too strong. The arms market is becoming more of a buyer's market; thus, for example, Iraq and Iran have had little difficulty in obtaining a continued re-supply of weapons. Had it been possible to organize an effective arms embargo on those two countries, the war could have been brought to a halt.

V. The Stockholm Conference

The conference at Stockholm—the first phase of the Conference on Confidence- and Security-Building Measures and Disarmament in Europe—is in its early stages. It began, perhaps, with some excessive expectations of what it might accomplish, to some extent because a number of foreign ministers attended the meeting and met for discussions.

The proposals from the NATO group of countries were presented early. They consist essentially of proposals for an intensified process of informamation exchange and notifications—*inter alia* a yearly exchange of information on the location and command organization of military formations; an annual forecast of military activities; notification of movements of troops as well as manoeuvres; and a certain number of permitted inspections to determine the non-threatening nature of notified activities. The NATO countries argue that this proposal is fully in line with the restricted mandate for the first phase of the conference, as set out in the final document of the conference in Madrid.

At the time of writing, the Soviet Union had not tabled proposals. However, judging from the opening speech of the Soviet Foreign Minister, the Soviet Union gives priority to such items as a pledge of no-first-use of nuclear weapons, a pledge of mutual non-use of conventional and nuclear military force, and nuclear and chemical weapon-free zones. It remains to be seen how these matters could be dealt with in this first phase of the conference.

Appendix A

Public opinion and nuclear weapons

EYMERT DEN OUDSTEN
The assistance of Connie de Boer of the POLLS Archives at the University of Amsterdam is gratefully acknowledged.

Superscript numbers refer to the list of notes and references at the end of the appendix.

This appendix briefly summarizes some of the developments in public opinion about nuclear weapons during 1983.[1] The material is based on opinion polls. It is, of course, well known that answers to opinion polls can vary with the wording of the question: on a number of the subjects discussed below, the question was put, by various organizations, in a variety of different ways. On some subjects, therefore, the conclusions are reasonably robust and give a good indication of the way in which, for instance, a vote in a referendum might have gone.

Missile deployment in FR Germany and Britain

In the Federal Republic of Germany, the question was generally put in some variation of the following form: "If there is no agreement at Geneva, should the Pershing II and cruise missiles be deployed?" However the question was asked, there was a significant margin of opinion against deployment. The margin increases somewhat when the words "new" and "American" are included in the description of the missiles. It decreases somewhat when the SS-20 is mentioned, and also when there is a reference to the NATO dual-track decision. However, there was no case in which the answers to the question showed a majority in favour of deployment.

In Great Britain, the question was usually put in the form: "Do you think that Britain should or should not allow cruise missiles to be based here?" Sometimes the words "new" and "American-controlled" were added. With one exception, there was a majority against deployment. The exception was a poll taken in June 1983, about the time of the general election. On this occasion the proposition was: "Great Britain should ban cruise missiles from being stationed in Great Britain", without any reference to the missiles being US missiles or under US control. By October, there was once again a majority against deployment.

In Britain, an overwhelming majority of the respondents want joint control of the missiles. When the question was put: "If American missiles are based in this country, should they be under the joint control of the

Figure A1. Federal Republic of Germany: replies concerning the deployment of cruise and Pershing II missiles

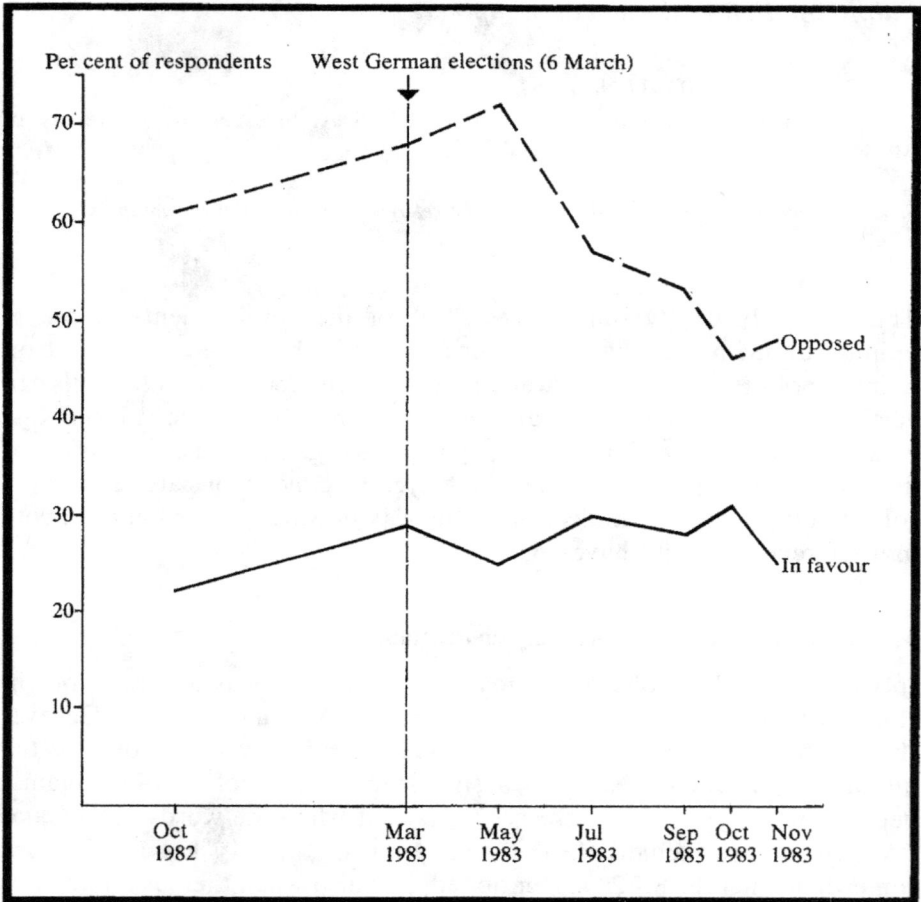

Sources: October 1982, SINUS; March 1983, INFAS; May 1983, Forschungsgruppe Wahlen; July 1983, INFAS; September 1983, INFAS (the third possibility, "negotiate further", has been divided into two-thirds against and one-third for, according to a similar question in March 1983); October 1983, Allensbach; and November 1983, Gallup.

British and American governments or under the sole control of the American government?", 93–95 per cent of the respondents opted for joint control.[2]

Threat perceptions and the fear of war

In October 1983 the Atlantic Institute for International Affairs (AIIA) and a number of national newspapers sponsored a poll, executed by Louis Harris with over 10 000 respondents in nine countries. A similar poll had

Figure A2. Great Britain: replies concerning the deployment of cruise missiles

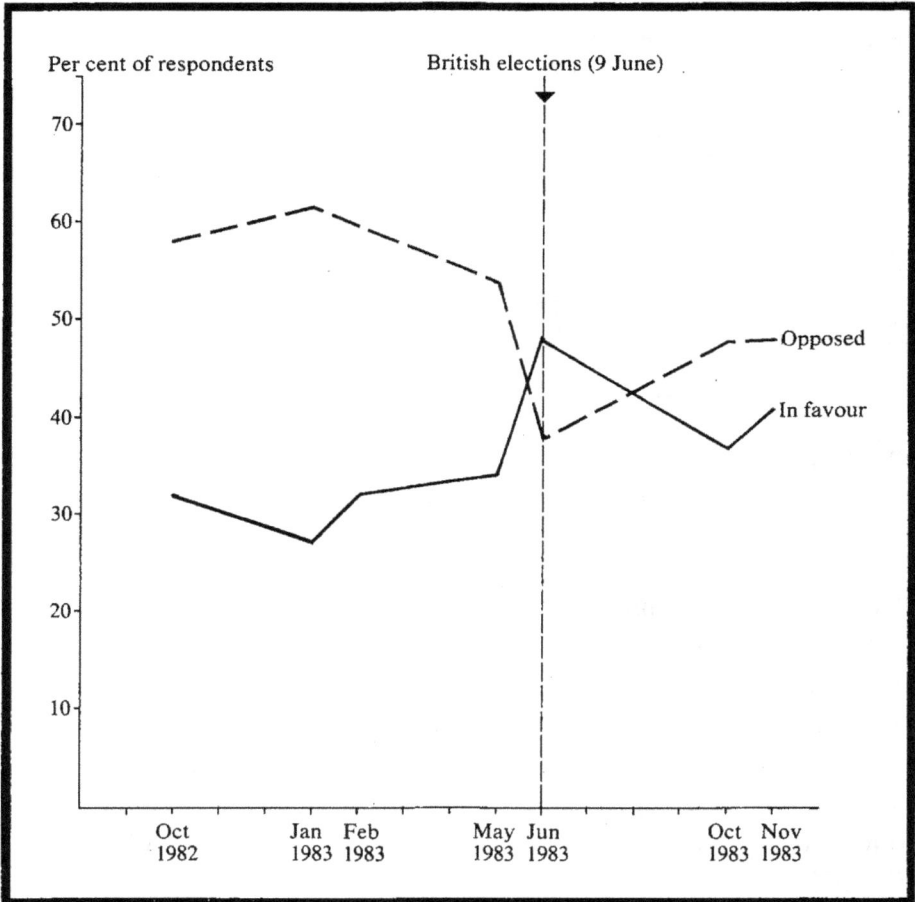

Sources: October 1982, Gallup; January 1983, MORI; February 1983, Gallup; May 1983, Marplan; June 1983, NOP; October 1983, Marplan; November 1983, Gallup.

been taken in September 1982. During 1983, in almost all countries where the poll was taken there was an increasing fear of war and an increasing concern with nuclear weapons. The evidence is in the replies to the question: "Which of the following are your greatest concerns for yourself and your country today?", with a list of some 10 items, including un-employment, inflation, and so on. Between September 1982 and October 1983, in all the countries surveyed except Norway and Spain, there was an increase in the percentage of respondents who listed "the threat of war" and "nuclear weapons" among their greatest concerns. The most startling

17

Table A1. "The threat of war" and "nuclear weapons" among "your greatest concerns for yourself and your country"

Figures are the percentage of respondents naming them.

	The threat of war		Nuclear weapons	
	Sep 82	Oct 83	Sep 82	Oct 83
FR Germany	25	28	32	38
France	42	44	18	26
Italy	37	36	40	38
Japan	36[a]	42	28[a]	34
The Netherlands	32	37	49	49
Norway	36	37	38	40
Spain	42	39	27	30
United Kingdom	28	31	28	29
United States	23	45	18	37
Weighted average[b]	31	42	30	35

[a] March 1983.
[b] Weighted by population.

Source: AIIA/Harris/*International Herald Tribune* polls, September 1982 and October 1983.

change was in the United States, where the percentage doubled for both categories (see table A1).

The use and possession of nuclear weapons

There have been a number of enquiries which attempt to elicit the views of respondents about the use of nuclear weapons. The tables below present some of the results, in which the respondents were asked to indicate which statement most closely approximated to their views.

Except in the United States, there is support for the view that the use of nuclear weapons is not acceptable, not even in response to a nuclear weapon attack. In Britain and France, countries with an independent nuclear deterrent, some 25 per cent of the population take this view. FR Germany, which does not have nuclear weapons of its own, follows with 30 per cent. The remaining five countries have a near or full majority taking this position.

The use of nuclear weapons against a non-nuclear attack has lost almost all support, except in the United States. In the four countries where the questions were asked both in 1981 and 1983, support for this policy fell by more than half between these two years; it is now well below 10 per cent (and only 14 per cent in the United States). The implication is clearly that a policy of no-first-use commands wide support.

A separate set of questions approaches the same subject in a rather different way, asking questions not about the use of nuclear weapons, but

Table A2. Replies to the question: "In the current debate over East–West nuclear weapons, which of the following best expresses your personal view about what the West should do?" (October 1983)

(1) Give up all nuclear weapons regardless of whether the Soviet Union does.

(2) Introduce no more nuclear weapons, even if the Soviet Union does.

(3) Introduce just enough nuclear weapons to create a balance between East and West until an acceptable agreement can be found.

(4) Introduce more nuclear weapons than the Soviet Union has introduced, in order to establish and maintain nuclear superiority.

(5) No answer/no opinion.

Figures are the percentage of respondents.

	(1)	(2)	(1)+(2)	(3)	(4)	(5)
FR Germany	23	18	41	39	1	19
France	16	13	29	47	6	18
Italy	35	10	45	30	2	23
Japan	22	20	42	21	4	33
The Netherlands	25	20	45	38	2	15
Norway	15	21	36	55	3	6
Spain	55	12	67	16	2	15
United Kingdom	17	12	29	62	4	5
United States	4	8	12	63	20	5
Weighted average[a]	18	13	31	45	9	15

[a] Weighted by population.

Source: AIIA/Harris Poll, October 1983.

Table A3. Replies to the question: "Which of the following statements most closely approximates to your own attitude towards nuclear weapons?"

(1) The use of nuclear weapons is not acceptable under any circumstances, not even when attacked by nuclear weapons.

(2) Nuclear weapons should be used if we are attacked with nuclear weapons.

(3) If we are attacked with non-nuclear weapons, we should be justified in using nuclear weapons to end the war quickly.

(4) No answer/no opinion.

Figures are the percentage of respondents.

	(1)		(2)		(3)		(4)	
	Jul 81	Oct 83	Jul 81	Oct 83	Jul 81	Oct 83	Jul 81	Oct 83
FR Germany	29	31	37	42	17	4	17	23
France	44	27	32	52	17	8	8	13
Italy	42	47	39	28	12	5	8	20
Japan	–	58	–	18	–	3	–	21
The Netherlands	–	42	–	36	–	4	–	18
Norway	–	48	–	45	–	4	–	3
Spain	–	61	–	24	–	2	–	13
United Kingdom	24	24	47	61	19	8	10	7
United States	–	14	–	66	–	14	–	6
Weighted average[a]		33		46		8		13

[a] Weighted by population.

Source: AIIA/Harris Poll, October 1983 (for the data from October 1983); Crespi, L., 'West European Perceptions of the US', paper presented at the Convention of the International Society of Political Psychology, June 1982, table 4 (for the data from July 1981).

about their possession. Outside the United States, these questions show a fairly wide measure of support (though only in one case a majority) for unilateral nuclear disarmament or a unilateral nuclear weapon freeze. The one country where there is some support for the idea of nuclear superiority is the United States, with about one-fifth of the respondents in favour of nuclear superiority; and there is very little support in the USA for any unilateral action.

Notes and references

[1] These and other developments are more fully discussed in the following articles: Capitanchik, D. and Eichenberg, R., 'Defense and public opinion', *Chatham House Papers* (Royal Institute of International Affairs), 1983; Eichenberg, R., 'The myth of hollanditis', *International Security*, Vol. 8, No. 2, Fall 1983, pp. 143–59; Everts, P., 'Public opinion, the churches and foreign policy: studies of domestic factors in the making of Dutch foreign policy', Ph.D. thesis at Leiden University, Netherlands, 1983; *IISS Conference on Defense and Consensus: The Domestic Aspects of Western Security*, Adelphi papers 182, 183 and 184 (IISS, London, 1983); Crespi, L., 'US standing in west European public opinion, some long term trends', *USICA Report no. R-13-82* (US International Communication Agency), July 1982; Fiske, S., Fischhoff, B. and Milburn, M. (eds), Special on 'Images of Nuclear War', *Journal of Social Issues*, Vol. 39, No. 1, 1983; Lumsden, M., 'Nuclear weapons and the new peace movement', in SIPRI, *World Armaments and Disarmament, SIPRI Yearbook 1983* (Taylor & Francis, London, 1983), chapter 6, pp. 101–28; Russett, B. and Deluca, D., 'TNF: public opinion in western Europe', *Political Science Quarterly*, summer 1983, pp. 179–214.

[2] National Opinion Polls, May/June 1983 (95 per cent); MORI, January 1983 (93 per cent).

1. Nuclear weapons

SVERRE LODGAARD and FRANK BLACKABY

The tables on Soviet and US strategic nuclear weapon capability are based on material prepared by FRANK BARNABY; the section on US and Soviet forward plans draws heavily on material prepared by the Center for Defense Information, Washington.

Superscript numbers refer to the list of notes and references at the end of the chapter.

I. Introduction

This chapter begins by reviewing Soviet and US nuclear weapon system programmes. As with any statistics of military capabilities, there is much more material on US than on Soviet forward plans. It then reports on some of the debates on these issues in the United States, and in particular on the discussion of the conclusions of the Scowcroft Commission. Finally, it turns to the question of arms control negotiations. At the time of writing there are no negotiations, and it is wholly uncertain when they might be resumed. In the long run, the choice is between a resumption and an unending arms race in nuclear weapon systems. It is useful, therefore, to set out some of the considerations relevant to their resumption.

II. Soviet nuclear weapon programmes

Material on possible future Soviet developments in nuclear weapon technology continues to come mainly from the United States: the Soviet Union still does not publish its forward plans.

Intercontinental nuclear weapon systems

The Soviet Union's current intercontinental ballistic missile (ICBM) arsenal is made up of 550 SS-11s, 60 SS-13s, 150 SS-17s, 308 SS-18s and 330 SS-19s (see table 1.1). Future developments are unlikely to lead to any increase in the total number of missile launchers—the number has fallen since the mid-1970s. In the absence of an arms control agreement, the trend will probably be towards an increased number of warheads, solid-fuelled rather than liquid-fuelled missiles, and improvements in accuracy and survivability.

B

Table 1.1. Soviet strategic nuclear weapon capability at the end of 1983

Delivery vehicle	First deployed	Range (km)	Number deployed[a]	Warheads per vehicle	Yield per warhead (Mt)	Total warheads	Total delivery capability (Mt)
Land-based ICBMs							
SS-11 Mod 1	1966	10 500	250	1	1	250	250
Mod 3	1973	8 800	300	3	0.3	900	270
SS-13	1968	10 000	60	1	0.6	60	36
SS-17 Mod 1[b]	1975	10 000	130	4	0.75	520	390
Mod 2	1977	11 000	20	1	6	20	120
SS-18 Mod 2[c]	1977	11 000	115	8	0.9	920	828
Mod 3[d]	1979	16 000	23	1	20	23	460
Mod 4	1982	11 000	170	10	0.5	1 700	850
SS-19 Mod 2	1979	10 000	20	1	10	20	200
Mod 3	1982	10 000	310	6	0.55	1 860	1 023
Sub-total			*1 398*			*6 273*	*4 427*
Sea-based SLBMs							
SS-N-5[e]	1964	1 200	9	1	1	9	9
SS-N-6 Mod 2	1973	3 000	128	1	1	128	128
Mod 3	1974	3 000	256	2	0.2	512	102
SS-N-8 Mod 2	1972[f]	9 100	292	1	0.8	292	234
SS-N-17	1977	3 900	12	1	1	12	12
SS-N-18 Mod 2[g]	1978	8 000	64	1	0.45	64	29
Mod 3[h]	1980	6 500	160	7	0.2	1 120	224
SS-N-20	1982	8 300	20	9[i]	0.5[j]	180	90
Sub-total			*941*			*2 317*	*828*
Strategic bombers							
Tu-95 Bear	1956	10 000+[k]	100	2[m]	2[m]	200	400
Mya-4 Bison	1956	10 000+[k]	45	2[m]	2[m]	90	180
Sub-total			*145*			*290*	*580*
Total			**2 484**			**8 880**	**5 835**

[a] As of September 1983. All numbers are approximations, especially divisions between different models.
[b] Being replaced by Mod 3 from 1982, possibly with 4 × 2 Mt MIRV.
[c] Being replaced by Mod 4.
[d] Replacing Mod 1.
[e] SALT-accountable.
[f] First deployment of shorter-range Mod 1.
[g] Being replaced by Mod 3.
[h] Replacing Mod 1 (with 3 RVs) and Mod 2.
[i] Maximum number, loading varying from 6 to 8.
[j] SIPRI estimate.
[k] Depending on mission profile and weapon load.
[m] Average.

Most of the SS-17s, -18s and -19s have multiple independently targetable warheads; that phase of modernization is probably virtually complete. However, all these missiles, except the SS-13 (which seems to have been a relatively unsuccessful missile), are fuelled by liquids that are highly toxic and volatile. Preparing them for launching is time consuming, and the rockets require an intricate set of pumps and circuits in order to regulate the fuel flow.

The United States concluded more than 30 years ago that liquid fuels were too dangerous and unreliable and developed solid propellants. There is little doubt that the Soviet Union would like to make the shift to solid fuels. To quote Dr John Kincaid, who helped design most of the basic rocket motors now used by the US ballistic missile-equipped strategic nuclear submarines (SSBNs): "Whoever thinks the Soviets have stuck with liquids because they chose to do things that way does not know what they are talking about. No one would mess around with liquids if they did not have to."[1]

The Soviet Union is now testing a solid-fuelled ICBM, denoted the SS-X-24, which could become a mobile ICBM carrying up to 10 warheads. However, up to September 1983 there were reported to have been seven failures out of ten tests of this missile; normally at least a dozen successful tests are needed before deployment.[2] It is also suggested that fifth-generation SS-18s and SS-19s are being developed, but have not yet been tested.

The Soviet Union will probably continue to replace older submarines and launchers in its submarine-launched ballistic missile force. (The SALT I agreement, as extended, allows the Soviet Union 62 modern hulls with 950 launchers.) The first Typhoon Class submarine has completed its sea trials and has moved to port facilities on the north coast of the Kola peninsula: a second Typhoon has been launched at the Severodvinsk shipyard. These new submarines are each equipped with 20 launchers for the SS-NX-20 solid-fuelled ballistic missile. The Soviet Union conducted some initial unsuccessful tests with this missile, which is said to have 6–9 warheads and a range of 8 300 km.

The Soviet Union's long-range bomber force consists of 145 aircraft that are 25 years old. There are Western reports of the development of a new strategic bomber, designated Blackjack A by NATO. There are also Western reports of new air-launched cruise missiles: one designated in the West AS-X-15, with a range of 2 700 km, which could be deployed on Backfire or Blackjack bombers; and another, designated BL-10, a high-altitude supersonic cruise missile, with a range of some 3 500 km, which could be carried by old Tu-95 Bear bombers operating from stand-off carriers.[3]

Long-range theatre nuclear weapon systems

LRTN missiles

After the breakdown of the Geneva long-range theatre nuclear forces (LRTNF) talks, the Soviet Union lifted the moratorium on deployment of SS-20 missiles directed at Europe. More SS-20s are therefore likely to be deployed in the European part of the USSR, to avoid the impression that the moratorium was an empty gesture. Nevertheless, the SS-20 programme

Table 1.2. Long-range theatre nuclear missiles

Country	Missile designation	Year first deployed	Range (km)	CEP (m)	Warheads	Inventory[a] A	B	Programme status
USSR	SS-4 Sandal	1959	1 800	2 400	1 × Mt	240	} 455	SS-4/SS-5 phasing out; the USSR has stated that there are no SS-5s left
	SS-5 Skean	1961	3 500	1 200	1 × Mt			
	SS-20	1976/77	5 000	400	3 × 150-kt MIRV 1 × ?[b]	378	...	According to NATO, by the end of 1983 there were 243 within range of Europe
	SS-N-5 Serb	1963	1 200	n.a.	1 × Mt	39	18	3 on each Golf II submarine, 6 of which have been deployed in the Baltic since 1976
USA	Pershing II	1983	1 800	40	10–50 kt[c]	9		108 launchers to be deployed by 1985
	GLCM	1983	2 500	50	200 kt[d]	32[e]		464 missiles to be deployed by 1988
UK	Polaris A-3	1967	4 600	800	3 × 200-kt MRV	64		On 4 SSBNs, being replaced by the Chevaline system[f]
	Trident II (D5)[g]	(1990s)	10 000	250	8 × 355-kt MIRV	0		Replacing the Polaris/Chevaline system from the 1990s, with 64 launchers on 4 submarines
France	SSBS S-3	1980	3 000	n.a.	1 × 1-Mt	18		On 5 SSBNs
	MSBS M-20	1977	3 000	n.a.	1 × 1-Mt	80		
	MSBS M-4	(1985)	4 000	n.a.	6 × 150-kt MRV	0		On the 6th SSBN; total programme, including retrofits: 96 (by 1992)

[a] A: US figures as of January 1984. B: Soviet figures as of 1 June 1983. Approximately two-thirds of the missiles are assumed to be within striking range of Europe.

[b] Some SS-20 missiles are equipped with a single warhead and may therefore have intercontinental range.

[c] Selectable yield.

[d] The W 84 warhead with a selectable yield, of which 200 kt is likely to be the highest.

[e] Includes 16 missiles at Greenham Common, and 16 missiles at Comiso scheduled to be operational by March 1984.

[f] Probably with three warheads. Six warheads (MRV), each of 50 kt, have also been indicated.

[g] Range and yield are based on the likely US choice of warheads. Since the UK will supply its own charges, it may choose force specifications which differ from that of the USA.

Table 1.3. US strategic nuclear weapon capability at the end of 1983

Delivery vehicle	First deployed	Range (km)	Number deployed[a]	Warheads per vehicle	Yield per warhead (Mt)	Total warheads	Total delivery capability (Mt)
Land-based ICBMs							
Minuteman II	1966	12 500	450	1	1.2	450	540
Minuteman III	1970	14 000	250	3	0.17	750	128
Minuteman III (Mk 12A)	1979	14 000	300	3	0.335	900	302
Titan II	1963	12 000	45[b]	1	9	45	405
Sub-total			*1 045*			*2 145*	*1 375*
Sea-based SLBMs							
Poseidon (C3)	1971	4 000[c]	304	10[d]	0.04	3 040	122
Trident I (C5)	1979	7 400[c]	264	8[e]	0.1	2 112	211
Sub-total			*568*			*5 152*	*333*
Strategic bombers[f]							
B-52	1956	10 000+[g]	241[h]	24[i]			
Bombs				4	2[j]	964	1 928
SRAM[k]		160[m]		20[n]	0.170	1 020	173
ALCM[o]		2 500		12[p]	0.2	384[q]	77
Sub-total			*241*			*2 368*	*2 178*
Total			**1 854**			**9 665**	**3 886**

a As of September 1983.

b Titan ICBMs are being withdrawn at a rate of about one every 30–45 days; retirement is planned to be completed in September 1987.

c With maximum number of MIRVs.

d Average number, maximum is 14.

e Average number, maximum is 10.

f In addition, there are 60 FB-111A medium bombers in service.

g Depending on model, mission profile and weapon load.

h 151 B-52Gs and 90 B-52Hs are operational. In addition, there are 31 B-52Ds being phased out, some 40 B-52G/Hs for training and in active reserve, plus more than 180 B-52s in inactive storage at Davis-Monthan AFB, Arizona.

i Maximum weapon load: 4 bombs and 20 SRAMs.

j Average yield.

k Short-Range Attack Missile.

m At high altitude.

n Maximum number (8 internally, 12 externally loaded).

o Air-Launched Cruise Missile (AGM-86B).

p Present configuration, all externally loaded. Later modifications will allow 8 internally loaded, for a total of 20.

q 2 squadrons each with 16 B-52Gs are operational.

Figure 1.1. Maximum range of SS-22 and SS-23 missiles from positions in Czechoslovakia and the German Democratic Republic

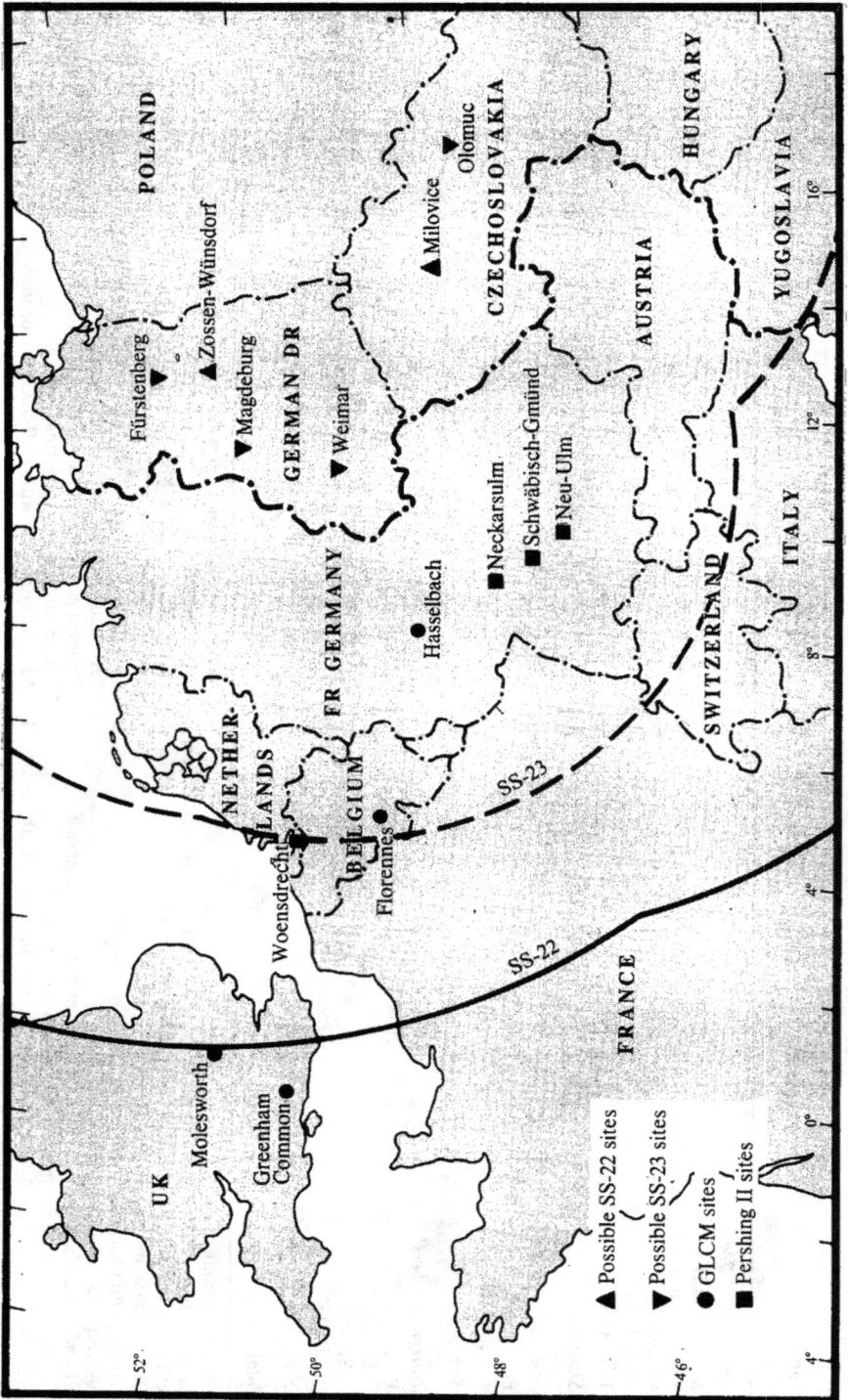

26

seems nearly completed. According to NATO, a total of 378 systems are now deployed, along with reload missiles. At the time the talks broke down and the moratorium was lifted, 243 launchers were deployed within striking range of western Europe (see table 1.2).[4]

Recent SS-20 deployments have been in eastern Siberia. There seem to be three base complexes in that area: at Novosibirsk (east of 80°), and at Drowjanaja and Olowjanaja on the Mongolian border east of Baikal. Altogether, 135 launchers have been deployed, and preparations for another 9 launchers are being made (according to the USA). The number of warheads on LRTN missiles in the area has increased greatly, possibly by a factor of three since the deployment of SS-20s started.

This Asian deployment of SS-20s, together with the build-up of other Soviet forces in the Far East, has led to increased concern in China, Japan and some other east Asian countries. Thus, in the statement issued after the ninth 'summit' meeting at Williamsburg, USA in May 1983 there was a specific reference to the need to consider both Asian and European deployments of SS-20s together: "Our nations are united in efforts for arms reductions . . . . The security of our countries is indivisible and must be approached on a global basis".[5] The Foreign Ministry of South Korea is reported as suggesting, on the question of deployment of SS-20s in north-east Asia, that the United States should afford Asia as much interest as it affords Europe in arms limitation talks with the USSR.[6] The Foreign Ministers of China and Japan, at a meeting in New York on 29 September 1983, agreed to "exchange information" on the Soviet SS-20s, while recognizing that their presence in Asia "constitutes a great threat" to the region.[7] China reportedly intended to add the reduction of SS-20s in the Far East to the other three conditions for improvement of Chinese–Soviet relations.[8]

In Europe, new theatre nuclear missiles are being deployed in the German Democratic Republic and Czechoslovakia. Marshal Ogarkov is reported as saying that "their range is sufficient for reaching most of the areas of the position of the American missiles being deployed in the countries of Western Europe".[9] Marshal Ogarkov further said that these were not deployments that would have occurred in any case: "They were not planned in advance and were necessitated only by the introduction of new American missiles into Europe".[9] These seem to be references to the SS-22, the successor to the SS-12 Scaleboard, which was not previously deployed outside the USSR. With a maximum range of about 900 km it is on the verge of reaching the cruise missile sites in Britain and would cover much of France (see figure 1.1), but it cannot reach Comiso in Italy.

If the objective was to put political and military pressure on FR Germany, then the SS-23 missile in particular—due to succeed the Scud—might have been appropriate. With a range of about 500 km, it would cover virtually all of FR Germany from positions in the GDR and Czechoslovakia. By the beginning of 1984, some SS-23s might have been fielded in the USSR. However, it was not known to be operational with Soviet forces in any of the east European countries.

Soviet leaders have also referred to additional naval deployments of nuclear weapons. Mr Andropov said, on 24 November 1983, "Since by deploying its missiles in Europe the United States increases the nuclear threat to the Soviet Union, the corresponding Soviet systems will be deployed with due account for this circumstance in ocean areas and in seas."[10] This may refer to sea-launched cruise missiles. The new SS-NX-21 cruise missile with a maximum range of about 3 000 km is likely to be deployed on Victor 3 Class submarines, and possibly also on converted Yankee Class submarines (nine have been converted from SSBNs to general-purpose submarines). The missile may be fitted into existing torpedo tubes on the Victor 3, which has 18 such tubes. Andropov's statement may refer to forward basing of existing cruise missile submarines as well, such as the Echo II type, whose missiles have a range of about 500 km. Also, in the beginning of 1984, some Delta II Class SSBNs moved south of the GIUK (Greenland–Iceland–United Kingdom) gap, sending another political message of Soviet counteraction to US missile deployments in Europe.[11]

In addition to the sea-based SS-NX-21, the Soviet Union has flight-tested another three types of cruise missile. Those which are air-launched have already been described. The ground-launched cruise missile (SSC-X-4) is similar in design and operational characteristics to the US GLCMs being deployed in western Europe.

LRTN aircraft

The deployment of Soviet LRTN aircraft has been undramatic over the past two years (compare *SIPRI Yearbook 1982*, tables 1.3–1.7). The Soviet Air Force still maintains a force of around 400 obsolescent Tu-16 Badger and Tu-22 Blinder aircraft in the bomber role, with a similar number for other missions (such as anti-shipping, electronic warfare, intelligence and aerial refuelling). The fleet of modern Tu-22M Backfires is increasing at a steady rate of 30 per year; at present there are some 210 available, of which 100 are assigned to naval aviation. A little less than one-third are deployed in the Far East.

As a result of the major reorganization of Soviet air forces, the modern Su-24 Fencer fighter-bombers have been transferred from frontal aviation to the new "aviation armies of the Soviet Union", which have replaced strategic aviation (the bomber force).[12] There are more than 600 Su-24s in service, with production continuing at a rate of some 60 per year.

III. US nuclear weapon programmes

The present inventory of United States intercontinental nuclear weapon systems is set out in table 1.3. There are very substantial programmes now in progress for upgrading these systems, with new weapon developments for all three legs of the strategic triad—on land, on sea and in the air.

Some 15 major programmes are under way (see table 1.4). All have so far received Congressional approval. The one programme which has had some appreciable difficulties in Congress, and which could still be aborted, is the MX programme (discussed below).

This section briefly reports on the status of the main programmes.

Submarine-launched ballistic missiles

The first two Ohio Class submarines with Trident missiles are now on patrol; a third was commissioned in June 1983, and a fourth in February 1984. This class has 24 missile tubes (as compared with 16 for the Lafayette Class equipped with Poseidon missiles), capable of carrying a larger missile than its predecessor. The eventual Trident programme will probably be for 20–25 submarines.

The first eight Ohio Class submarines will be fitted with the Trident I (C4) missile; this missile has now been retrofitted into 12 Lafayette Class submarines. The new Trident II (D5) missile, now under development, should be installed in the ninth Ohio Class submarine, scheduled for delivery in December 1988. Throughout the period 1989–96 the first eight Ohio Class submarines will be retrofitted with the D5 missile. The D5 missile will have much greater throw-weight than the C4; it will be able to carry 10 warheads, and is expected in addition to have the accuracy which would make it effective in attacking Soviet silos.

Long-range bombers

The bomber programme is linked with the development of cruise missiles. The later versions of the B-52 bomber are being equipped with air-launched cruise missiles. Sixty-four B-52G bombers—four squadrons—have each been fitted with 12 cruise missiles: eventually 105 B-52G bombers will be converted in this way. The air-launched cruise missile has a range of some 2 500 km, so that the bomber does not need to penetrate enemy defences. The missile carries a 200-kiloton warhead, and is highly accurate. In addition, 90 B-52Hs will carry 20 missiles, 12 externally and 8 internally. Further, there is a programme for 100 B-1B bombers: the first 16 are due

Table 1.4. Major US nuclear weapon system programmes

Weapon system	Number	First year operational	Money spent FY 1984 ($ bn)	Money requested for FY 1985 ($ bn)	Number requested for FY 1985	Money proposed for FY 1986 ($ bn)	Unit cost ($ mn)	Estimated total cost ($ bn)[a]	Remarks
MX missile	223	1986	10.9	5.0	40	3.8	123	27.4	100 deployed by 1989, balance test and spares
Trident submarine	20–25	1982	15.2	2.0	1	1.9	1 600	31–39	Cost for first 15 submarines: $23.6 bn
Trident I missile	595	1979	8.0	0.164	0	0.109	19	11.2	For 12 backfitted submarines and first 8 Trident submarines with 211 test and spares
Trident II missile	740	1989	2.2	2.3	0 (R&D)	3	50	37.6	For 15 submarines; for 20–25 submarines cost would be $45–53 bn
B-1B bomber	100	1986	18.4	8.2	34	6	400	40	90 operational aircraft will be deployed at four bases
Stealth bomber	132	Early 1990s	?	1	0 (R&D)	?	?	40–50?	Classified programme; one estimate $6.3 bn for FYs 1984–88
B-52 bomber modifications	263	Ongoing	2.8	0.596		0.461	20 per aircraft	5.8	Radar, engines, avionics and other improvements
Air-launched cruise missile	1 739	1982	4	0.155	0	?	2.7	4.7	Production cancelled at 1 739 of original 4 348
Ground-launched cruise missile	565	1983	2.2	0.707	120	0.733	6.3	3.6	464 for Europe, 1983–88
Sea-launched cruise missile	4 068	1984	2.6	0.670	180	0.593	2.8	11.5	Total is for all versions; includes 74 for R&D, 758 for nuclear attack

Advanced cruise missile	2 600	1987/88	?	?	0 (R&D)	?	5–7	7	Classified programme; figures are estimates
Pershing II missile	380	1983	1.8	0.472	93	0.521	7.0	2.7	108 for FR Germany, 1983–85
C³I	Many programmes	Ongoing	?	9	–	?	–	40–50	Hundreds of programmes
Air defence	Many programmes	Ongoing	0.400+	0.396	various	0.489	–	7.8	Radar, F-15 aircraft, AWACS aircraft
Midgetman missile	1 000	1992	0.345	0.465	0 (R&D)	0.482	38–70	38–70	20-year costs could be $107 bn

ᵃ Does not include DoE costs for nuclear warheads and bombs which normally are an additional 10–20 per cent of the weapon system cost.

Source: Based on a table in The Defense Monitor, Vol. 12, No. 7, p. 9; table updated as of February 1984 on the basis of FY 1985 budget figures.

to go into operation late in 1986. Eventually they will also become cruise missile carriers after their penetration role has been taken over by the advanced technology (Stealth) bomber, which is still in the research and development stage: the operational date is given as 1991. Meanwhile the Air Force is incorporating some of the 'stealth' technology into the B-1B programmes.

Cruise missiles

The US cruise missile programme is a massive one, covering air, land and sea versions. The present programme is for some 8 000 of the three different varieties. Rapid advances are being made in cruise missile technology.

For the *air-launched cruise missile* (ALCM), the original plan was to build 4 348 of the first version. However, the decision has now been taken to limit the purchase of this first version to 1 739, and thereafter to go directly to the second version—the advanced cruise missile. If the total still remains the same, the implication is that some 2 600 of the advanced version will be procured, but it is possible that fewer may be bought. Information about this advanced version is classified; it could have up to three times the range of the first version, greater accuracy, increased speed and some stealth characteristics.

The *ground-launched cruise missile* (GLCM) is the weapon which is now being installed in western Europe. The first flight of 16 missiles is already operational at Greenham Common, UK. Another flight will be operational at Comiso, Italy in March 1984. In the next five years, 464 of these missiles are due to be deployed: the total procurement envisaged is 565. In Belgium and the Netherlands, the designated cruise missile sites are at Florennes (in Namur) and Woensdrecht (in Nord Brabant) respectively. The deployments are scheduled to begin in 1985 at Florennes and at the end of 1986 at Woensdrecht. So far, neither Belgium nor the Netherlands has made a political decision to accept deployment. In FR Germany, cruise missiles will be deployed at Hasselbach, in Rheinland-Pfalz.

The *sea-launched cruise missile* (SLCM) programme is a mixed programme of short-range (450 km) anti-ship missiles, medium-range (2 500 km) nuclear land-attack missiles, and medium-range conventional land-attack missiles—in all some 4 000 missiles for use on some 76 surface ships and 80 submarines by the early 1990s. The 450-km range anti-ship missile, with a conventional warhead, has already been installed on one attack submarine, and was due to be installed on a destroyer in March 1984. The 2 500-km range nuclear land-attack missile is scheduled to be deployed on attack submarines and surface ships in June 1984. The conventional land-attack version appears to be at an earlier stage of development.

32

This programme appears to have gone ahead without much consideration for the arms control problems which it poses. The conventional and nuclear models are indistinguishable and the missile is compact. Once large numbers of these sea-launched missiles are deployed—and the Soviet Union, which has had cruise missiles of shorter range at sea for a long time, may soon deploy the SS-N-21—then nearly every type of ship could become a potential nuclear attack platform.

Long-range theatre nuclear weapon systems

While the first GLCMs were being installed at Greenham Common, the first Pershing II missiles were installed in FR Germany. Both were declared operational by the turn of 1983/84. Over the next three to four years, 108 Pershing II launchers are due to be deployed in the Schwäbisch-Gmünd–Neu Ulm–Neckarsulm area. At the end of 1982, the West German government turned down a US suggestion to deploy one reload missile per launcher. Tentative plans now call for having only enough disassembled spare parts on hand to ensure that 108 missiles are operational at any time. However, it is not clear whether the US government actually dropped the reload option: the momentum of euromissile deployments and the tense relationship between East and West may still lead to the fielding of reload missiles. The original production programme was for 380 missiles.

The range of the Pershing II remains a matter of dispute, with the United States claiming that it could not reach Moscow, and the Soviet Union claiming that it could. To extend its range from 1 800 km (the official Western figure) to 2 500 km (the official Soviet estimate) poses no big technical problem. For instance, the range of a ballistic missile can be significantly increased by using fuel with a higher energy content per unit. It will probably be hard to allay Soviet suspicions that the Pershing II could be used against the command, control, communications and intelligence (C^3I) installations around the Soviet capital.

Whereas the Pershing II replaces the Pershing IA with the US forces in FR Germany on a one-for-one basis, no decision has been made so far to replace the 72 Pershing IAs operated by West German forces on a double-key basis with Pershing IBs. The Pershing IB has about the same range as the Pershing IA, but is terminally guided (like the Pershing II).

As with the WTO deployments, NATO deployments in the aircraft sector have been undramatic over the past two years. The F-111s remain the backbone of the US Air Force long-range interdiction force: of the 250 still in service, some 150 are deployed in Britain. In addition, the US Strategic Air Command has 60 FB-111 medium bombers in service. With necessary modifications and upgrading, the F/FB-111 force could remain in the US inventory throughout the 1990s. To complement the F-111s in the long-range strike mission, the USAF plans to modify 400 aircraft from its F-15 or F-16 programmes into a longer-range 'E' version.

Any statement of long-range theatre nuclear systems in Europe must include those deployed by France and Britain. There has been no significant change in present or proposed intermediate-range missile deployment (table 1.2). In the aircraft sector, the British Vulcan bombers have been retired from a nuclear role. The French plan to convert the Mirage IV to air-to-surface (ASMP) missile carriers. Eighteen such carriers are planned under the 1984–88 programme, together with 70 Mirage 2000N and 50 Super Etendard ASMP carriers. The Tornado programme is well under way; this aircraft is nuclear-capable and has a range well in excess of 1 000 km. More than 300 of the interdiction strike (IDS) version have been delivered to the British, West German and Italian air forces (out of a total of 532 planned).

The MX missile

Over a long period US government defence spokesmen have pointed to a 'window of vulnerability'—a situation in which Soviet land-based missiles could achieve an effective first strike against US land-based missiles. The Soviet Union was in a position to do this, it was argued, because the bulk of its missiles were land-based, with warheads powerful enough and accurate enough to destroy US silos. There are many reasons for thinking that an attempt at a first strike of this kind would be a totally irrational act, inviting the destruction of the Soviet Union. The window of vulnerability was, however, one of the main arguments used for the massive upgrading of US nuclear weaponry.

The Administration, however, faced a problem in explaining how the MX missiles would help to close this window of vulnerability. It is a much larger missile than the Minuteman, with more throw-weight and greater accuracy. It could, therefore, threaten Soviet silos in the same way that Soviet SS-18s can threaten US silos. The difficulty was that the MX is as vulnerable as the Minuteman missile. How could a missile which was itself vulnerable help to close the window of vulnerability?

In the long history of the MX missile, a number of different basing modes have been suggested. Under the Carter Administration, the proposal was for a 'race track' type of deployment, with the missiles being shuttled from one hole to another. A later proposal—under the Reagan Administration—went to the other extreme: the missiles would be deployed together, in a 'dense pack' mode, and would not be vulnerable because of the 'fratricide' effect of incoming missiles attacking them. The Administration failed to win Congressional approval for this latter idea. It therefore agreed to set up a commission not only to consider the problem of the basing of land-based missiles, but also to review the strategic modernization programme as a whole. This commission, chaired by a retired general, General Brent Scowcroft, was set up in January 1983, and reported in April.

IV. The Scowcroft Commission

The Scowcroft Commission had as senior counsellors representatives of previous administrations—for instance, Harold Brown, Henry Kissinger and James Schlesinger. It had a wide remit—"the strategic modernization program of the United States"—and it certainly had in mind to produce a report which might have bipartisan support. It is noticeable that the Commission could not bring itself to refer to the MX missile as the 'Peacekeeper' missile, the label which the Administration had invented.

The Commission usefully disposed of the window of vulnerability, by pointing out that the Soviet Union could not eliminate both US ICBMs and bomber and submarine bases simultaneously. This is because the Soviet Union would have to use different weapon systems to attack the bombers and the ICBMs. To attack the bombers, they would have to use the system which arrives promptly—submarine-launched missiles from submarines close offshore. However, these missiles are not accurate enough to destroy US ICBM silos, which would have to be attacked by Soviet ICBMs with a 30-minute flight time. If the Soviet Union tried a simultaneous *launch* of submarine-launched ballistic missiles (SLBMs) and ICBMs, the detonation of the SLBM warheads would precede the arrival of the Soviet ICBMs by 15 minutes—and US ICBMs could be launched before they were destroyed. (The Commission notes that this would be 'launch-under-attack', not 'launch-on-warning'.) If on the other hand the Soviet Union fired its missiles in such a way that the SLBMs and ICBMs would *arrive* together, the early warning of the firing of the Soviet ICBMs would give time for the bombers to take off before they were destroyed.

The Commission, although it briefly discussed—and endorsed—most other parts of the programme, concentrated on the land-based missile question. It recommended that in the longer run the United States should move away from heavy multi-warhead land-based missiles towards small single-warhead ICBMs: "looking towards deployment probably in the early 1990s. We suggest a single-warhead missile in order to reduce the value of the target, making it unremunerative to attack and, thus, enhancing the stability of the force—and small in order to open up . . . the opportunities for survivable basing almost certainly to include mobile basing."[13] The Commission thus recognized that the whole move towards

35

multiple warheads was a mistake—and vindicated the position of those senators who in 1970 had argued for a mutual pause in the flight testing of MIRVed ICBMs with an eye towards banning them. For much the same reasons, the Commission recommended that research begin on smaller ballistic missile-carrying submarines, carrying fewer missiles than the Trident.

However, although the Commission declared its interest in arms control, its prime concern seemed to be with reducing the vulnerability of US missiles; at the same time it endorsed programmes which would increase the vulnerability of Soviet missiles. Thus it prescribed a hard-target kill capacity for the Midgetman missile: "It should have sufficient accuracy and yield to put Soviet hardened military targets at risk";[14] and it endorsed the cruise missile and the Trident II (D5) submarine-launched missile programmes—all these missiles could attack Soviet missiles in their silos. This broad endorsement of missile programmes with a hard-target kill capacity raises some questions about the chairman's claim that: "We are proposing new directions, both in ICBM forces and arms control. That new departure, fundamentally, is to integrate strategic force programs with arms control and to move both in the direction of stability".[13]

Further, the Commission—in a recommendation which brought a great deal of critical scrutiny in Congress—argued for the immediate deployment of about 100 MX missiles in existing Minuteman silos. It justified this somewhat contrary-looking recommendation on three grounds: first, to demonstrate US will and cohesion—in effect a fear that a decision now not to deploy would be taken as a sign of weakness; next, "in order to reduce the substantial imbalance in the capability of US ICBM forces compared to those of the Soviet Union. The Soviets can, with their ICBM forces, put our forces and other critical targets at risk in a way that the United States cannot begin to match"; and finally, "the MX is essential to induce the Soviets towards negotiations".[13]

Congressional advocates of arms control were more impressed by the arguments for eventual single-warhead missiles than by the arguments for the MX. The argument about the need to demonstrate US will could be used as justification for very foolish decisions. The second argument seems to imply a belief that Soviet ICBMs can put US strategic forces 'at risk' in a meaningful way, whereas elsewhere in the report the Commission argues powerfully that this is not the case. The final 'bargaining chip' argument has been used so often for deployments that were never subsequently reversed that it has fallen into disrepute.

The Administration has indicated that, in exchange for not deploying the MX, they would expect the Soviet Union to "forego their heavy and medium ICBMs".[15] This is hardly a serious negotiating position.

Congress, Scowcroft and arms control negotiations

Members of the Senate used the debate over the MX missile to attempt to force changes in the Administration's arms control stance. In May 1983, 19 senators wrote to the President: one paragraph of their letter reads as follows:

We wish to emphasize that our support for releasing fiscal year 1983 funds does not represent a consensus on the need to deploy 100 MX missiles in Minuteman silo launchers. Rather, yesterday we effected our part of an agreement with your Administration to proceed with [a] military controversial program in exchange for a strong commitment to proceed seriously and immediately with a reformulation of the U.S. START proposal, a meaningful guaranteed builddown proposal, development of a more survivable, small single-warhead ICBM and creation of a bi-partisan, durable arms control panel.[16]

The build-down proposal is one of a number of arms control suggestions put forward in the US Congress. Many senators and representatives had clearly concluded that the Administration's negotiating position at Geneva was inadequate. Further, they saw the prospect, in the absence of any strategic arms control agreement, of an increase in the number of US strategic warheads from 9 500 to around 15 000, presumably matched by an equivalent increase on the Soviet side.

The build-down proposal was particularly promoted in Congress by Senators Cohen, Nunn and Perry and, in the House of Representatives, by Messrs Aspin, Gore and Dicks. The aim of the proposal is to permit modernization of the strategic forces, but at the same time to bring about a reduction in the number of warheads. The basic proposal—subsequently elaborated—is that the Soviet Union and the United States should each agree to eliminate two nuclear warheads from its strategic forces for each new warhead deployed.

The threat of opposition to the MX missile was sufficient to make the Administration agree to incorporate the build-down proposal into the Geneva strategic arms reduction talks (START) in some way. On 4 October 1983 the President announced that he was instructing the START delegation to propose to the Soviet side the setting up of a working group to discuss build-down. The proposal specifically includes:

1. A provision which links reductions to modernization using variable ratios which identify how many existing nuclear warheads must be withdrawn as new warheads of various types are deployed. According to press reports the ratios call for a 2:1 build-down of MIRVed ICBMs, a 3:2 build-down of SLBM warheads, and a 1:1 replacement of single-warhead ICBMs.

2. A provision calling for a guaranteed annual 5 per cent reduction if there is no new deployment.

(Whichever of these provisions produced the greater reduction would govern.)

3. A provision which addresses the build-down and trade-off of bombers and ALCMs, in which the USA has an advantage, for Soviet advantages in ICBMs.

4. The appointment of R. James Woolsey as member-at-large to join the US delegation.

The Administration also agreed to keep the Scowcroft Commission in being for possible future recommendations.

Critics of the build-down proposal argue that it permits the very process which arms control negotiations should be primarily concerned to stop—the technological modernization of weapons. Further, it could lead to an unstable situation if the introduction of new MIRVed missiles led to the withdrawal of single-warhead missiles. The proponents argue that it would produce a big improvement on the situation which would otherwise occur: that it would in fact encourage the deployment of single-warhead missiles, since these would not require reductions in the total missile stock: and that the proposal offers the prospect of a bipartisan approach to arms control.

There is no evidence as yet of any Soviet interest in the proposal.

V. Negotiations

The positions at the moment of breakdown

On 15 November 1983 the British government announced the arrival of cruise missiles at Greenham Common. On 22 November the *Bundestag* reaffirmed its support for deployment of cruise and Pershing missiles in FR Germany. On 23 November the Soviet Union discontinued the talks on long-range theatre nuclear forces, and on 8 December the Soviet government also suspended the strategic arms reduction talks without agreeing on a date for resumption.

At START, the main distinction between the negotiating positions of the United States and the Soviet Union was this: the United States was particularly concerned with the threat from Soviet heavy land-based missiles and wanted an agreement which would lead to a sizeable reduction in their number. In addition to the reduction of warheads and launchers, this could be through special provisions limiting total throw-weight. However, in the course of the negotiations the United States adjusted its position, seeking not to regain equality in throw-weight but a reduction in the disparity. Initially, the United States proposed that the first stage of an agreement should not include bombers or cruise missiles: later it agreed to their inclusion. The Soviet Union wanted an agreement on the lines of the SALT I or SALT II agreements, primarily setting overall numerical limits significantly lower than the limits set by SALT II, allowing each side freedom to mix as it thought best. It agreed, in the course of the negotiations, to use warheads as well as launchers as primary counting units. It also indicated a willingness to consider verification measures which apparently went beyond those it was willing to consider in SALT II.[17]

At the LRTNF talks, the United States demanded numerical equality between warheads on Soviet land-based missiles within range of western Europe, and warheads on US missiles stationed in Europe which could reach the USSR. Various figures—from the initial 0 up to 420—were suggested. It is unclear what portion of the total number of SS-20s the USA wanted to include in a European deal: the USSR had indicated that all missiles west of 80° East could be taken into account. As in START, the Soviet Union eventually agreed to take both warheads and launchers into consideration, and offered to reduce the number of SS-20 launchers to 140 (420 warheads, reload capabilities not included) and eliminate all remaining SS-4s and SS-5s in exchange for no new deployment in western Europe. That would have brought the number of warheads on Soviet LRTN missiles targeted on Europe below the number which existed before the SS-20 deployments began. The parties agreed that decommissioned SS-20s should not be redeployed further east, and that the number of Soviet LRTN missiles in eastern Siberia should be frozen. The parties also agreed to bring LRTN aircraft into the deal, and—according to the US negotiator—the final positions on aircraft were not very far apart.[18]

An interesting exchange took place over the possibility of equal reductions, in existing and prospective deployments, of 572 warheads on both sides. Such a reduction would bring the number of Soviet SS-20 launchers down to about 120 (or a little more than that) in exchange for no new deployments in western Europe—still an approximate equivalent of the British and French forces, but without using that as the rationale for the accord. In the immediate aftermath of the breakdown, the two chief negotiators gave very different accounts of the origin of this proposal.[19]

These are brief summaries of the positions when the talks broke down. Obviously, it is important that negotiations should begin again; but there will be another failure unless the major powers define their national security objectives in ways which make arms control possible.

Security policy and arms control

Nuclear superiority

For arms control to succeed, its provisions must be compatible with national security policies. The prime objective of arms control is to reduce the risk of nuclear war. If the superpowers, as an integral part of their security policies, make preparations for fighting and winning a nuclear war, and if they are bent on trying to achieve some kind of nuclear superiority, then arms control negotiations are a waste of time. Negotiations can only have some reasonable chance of success if the nuclear powers accept that nuclear weapons have one use and one use only—to deter their use by others.

The leaders of both superpowers have stated that nuclear wars cannot be won and therefore must never be fought. However, the defence guidance documents in the United States, setting guidelines for the armed forces for the next five years, tell a rather different story. If deterrence fails, they indicate that the goal is to "prevail" in a nuclear war, and to be able to terminate the war on conditions favourable to the United States.[20] On both sides, the procurement policies in the nuclear weapon field do not seem to match the statements of the leaders.

Political advantage

Both superpowers also appear to believe that an appearance of inferiority in nuclear weapons brings great political damage. It follows that they believe—though they do not say this—that an appearance of superiority brings great political advantage. Thus, the former head of the Arms Control and Disarmament Agency, Eugene Rostow, has said, "The present state of the nuclear balance is a pervasive and insidious political force deeply affecting political attitudes throughout the West",[21] and again on another occasion, "The nuclear weapon is primarily a political, not a military force—a potent political force, generating currents of opinion which are transforming our world . . . I believe the risk of nuclear war is far less today than the risk that the unity of the West will be destroyed and the West reduced to neutrality by psychological and political pressures emanating from the nuclear balance."[22]

If, as Rostow suggests, there was indeed a political wound from the alleged Soviet superiority in land-based missiles, it was a self-inflicted wound. Instead of constantly referring to a non-existent window of vulnerability, US spokesmen could simply have pointed out that a land-based missile superiority, if it existed, had no military value. Then there would be no cause for political consequences of any kind. The political effect, such as it is, was created by the same people who then proceeded to stress its importance.

All that it is necessary to do with a superiority which is militarily meaningless is, first, to point out that this is so and, second, to invoke the concept of sufficiency, not parity. Then there would be no reason for political consequences to arise from a militarily meaningless number.

The view that apparent nuclear superiority or inferiority is of great political importance is a very dangerous one. The consequence is an unending arms race in nuclear weapons. Further, the lesson will not be lost on the non-nuclear nations—that nuclear weapons, in the judgement of the United States and the Soviet Union, yield political dividends. The political importance that the major powers ascribe to nuclear weapons is a prescription for proliferation. All efforts to obtain unilateral advantage are at odds with arms control.

Reshaping the political relationship

When both sides are engaged in qualitative and quantitative developments of their nuclear weapons, they inevitably begin to think in terms other than those of basic deterrence: they look for some additional return from their investments in their weapons. In the Soviet Union, military considerations have always been important in foreign policy: so there is a natural tendency to seek a preponderance wherever possible. In the United States, there is a fixed belief that the Soviet Union will be forced to make concessions if it is confronted by an ambitious rearmament programme in the United States. There is no evidence that this tactic had any success in the past, and it is even less likely to be successful now. However, it is a view which still seems to be held as tenaciously as ever.

Arms build-ups often give rise to the doctrines which justify them. Military, industrial and technological forces have been combining to push doctrines away from basic deterrence and towards a belief that political and military gains can be obtained from some advantage in nuclear weapons. The prospects for arms control are poor so long as these beliefs hold sway.

The issue of compliance with arms control obligations has been turned into political polemics; this is another practice that has to be abandoned. The objective should be to clarify questionable behaviour, making full use of existing consultation mechanisms to that end—"not to exploit these concerns in order to further poison relations, repudiate existing agreements or, worse still, terminate arms control altogether".[23]

Security policy and arms control: the European dilemma

In Europe, the nuclear weapon policies which are now being pursued suffer from one fundamental flaw and one serious myth. The flaw concerns the role of nuclear weapons in national defence. Once the nuclear threshold is crossed, it is extremely hard to imagine that the use of nuclear weapons would be limited to selective employment in the battle area, or that fire-breaks would be observed which would limit collateral damage. Nuclear warfighting is not a meaningful form of defence. It is not surprising that NATO has never agreed on what to do next if an initial use of nuclear weapons, to show resolve, fails to stop hostilities.[24] Security policies should no longer be based on a nuclear response to a conventional attack. For the European states, the policy of extended deterrence is profoundly untenable.

The myth is that cruise and Pershing missiles will provide a link to US strategic intercontinental nuclear forces, and that the United States will be prepared to launch nuclear strikes against the Soviet Union in defence of western Europe. The coupling is rather the other way around: the new missiles make it virtually certain that western Europe will be drawn into any strategic war between the two superpowers (for a comprehensive discussion, see *SIPRI Yearbook 1982*, pages 25–32).

Instead of seeking technological fixes to sustain the myth, the west European members of NATO would do better to recognize the compelling logic of strategic parity between the two superpowers: the nuclear umbrella, originally meant to defend Europe, is gone. It makes no sense to ask the United States for a reassurance that it cannot possibly give. In a nuclear war, acts of irrationality may no doubt occur, and forward deployment of cruise and Pershing missiles may make Soviet decision makers more uncertain of the Western response to a WTO thrust westwards. But for the west European states it is hardly prudent defence planning to stake their national security on the assumption that, in time of war, the US authorities will abandon prudence and reason and risk committing suicide on their behalf.

The structure of resumed negotiations

Combining START and LRTNF

The basic requirement of successful negotiations is that the objectives of arms control policy and security policy should be compatible. However, the structure of the two sets of talks will also have to be reviewed: the present structure could hardly survive. Arms control negotiations should reflect military realities: the military reality is that many different types of nuclear weapons, located in different places, could be used for destroying any particular target. It is not very sensible, therefore, for arms control to constrain some of these options but not others. For instance, from the Soviet point of view, a land-based cruise missile launched from Britain or Italy towards Soviet territory is essentially in the same category as an air-launched or a sea-launched cruise missile fired from a US bomber or submarine, and it is not easy to see why they should be dealt with in separate negotiations. The division between START and the LRTNF talks was always somewhat arbitrary.

The growing deployment of forward-based systems also makes this separation less sensible. Just as weapons with an intercontinental range can be used over shorter distances, so systems with ranges less than 5 500 km (the traditional criterion for a strategic system) can be used for strategic missions if they are forward based. The correlation between range and mission is weak.

Negotiations about sub-categories of nuclear weapons are always prone to circumvention. The sea-based cruise missile is a case in point: it was included neither in START nor in the LRTNF talks. Also, in an amalgamated set of negotiations it would be easier to deal with the vexed question of French and British forces, and trade-offs because of geographical asymmetries, technological differences and differences in force structure would be easier to negotiate. The balance of the argument is for treating intercontinental and theatre nuclear systems in one negotiation.

The lower end of the range spectrum

The LRTNF talks were mainly concerned with systems having a maximum range somewhere between 1 000 and 5 500 km. However, non-circumvention rules for weapons of shorter range were considered. When forward based, such systems can cover many targets otherwise covered by LRTNFs. For instance, SS-22s in the GDR and Czechoslovakia can cover about 80 per cent of the nuclear weapon targets in western Europe, and SS-23s almost 50 per cent. A merged negotiation would also encounter this problem. One possibility would be to keep the 1 000-km limit and negotiate non-circumvention rules, through geographical limitations on deployment. Another solution, even better from the point of view of arms control, would be to lower the limit of the negotiations to 200 km—that is, to include everything except the short-range theatre nuclear forces.

The missile systems currently considered by NATO for deep-strike missions have ranges clearly in excess of 200 km (see chapter 5). Nuclear as well as conventional options are being considered for these weapons. It would therefore be an advantage to include them in the negotiations. A limit on nuclear warheads which included them would give both sides an incentive to deploy conventional munitions for these missions.

For shorter-range nuclear weapons, the disengagement option, as a technique of constraint, is perhaps more promising. If this were to be combined with negotiations covering all other nuclear weapons, then in principle the entire range would be covered.

Overall step-by-step reductions

If overall limits were negotiated, this would make it easier for trade-offs between asymmetric force positions, leaving both sides to mix force components as they wished. It should only be necessary to fix limits for a few dimensions of nuclear weapon capability: deliverable warheads would be the main unit of account.

The nuclear balance is not delicate. For basic deterrence, all that is required is sufficiency—enough nuclear weapons to survive a first strike and inflict severe damage on the other side. There is no military need for parity. There is no rational military use which could be made of some margin of superiority, measured by one or other of the yardsticks used. The search for parity is part of the problem, not a route to a solution.

It follows that there is a wide range of possible agreements which would enhance the security of both superpowers. One such agreement would be a deep, say 50 per cent, cut in the limits set by the SALT II agreement. However, a slower step-by-step approach may be easier to negotiate. "Experience teaches that negotiations with the Russians can proceed only if limitations accepted at one stage serve as a basis for stricter constraints at the next."[25]

Destabilizing technologies

More important than overall reductions are curbs on destabilizing technologies, for example, technologies that may be taken to serve nuclear first-strike purposes. Improved accuracies and anti-submarine warfare capabilities have such destabilizing effects. Effective ballistic missile defences deployed in outer space would also be destabilizing if they could ever be made to work. Even if only proposed, they could set in motion the development of countermeasures on the other side.

The increase in accuracy, which gives ballistic as well as cruise missiles and other stand-off weapons high counterforce potential (i.e., a potential to destroy the nuclear forces of the adversary), is particularly disturbing. It is true that the vulnerability to these weapons of ICBMs in hardened silos has been exaggerated: but this vulnerability is widely believed. The short flight time of forward-based missiles is also destabilizing: it encourages pre-delegation of authority to fire under attack. It could lead either of the superpowers to consider seriously a policy of launch-on-warning (although, in view of the uncertainties of such a system, it is hard to believe that either of them would in fact adopt it).

These developments lead to a greater risk of war by technical error and pressure for pre-emption in time of crisis. Some forward-based systems will, moreover, be targeted on enemy C^3I centres. If they were used for this function in war, the result could be a totally uncontrolled nuclear attack from the other side.

The Pershing II missile combines many of these destabilizing characteristics. It is the first ballistic missile with a terminal guidance system, the CEP[26] being a few tens of metres, and the flight time is only 12 minutes over a distance of 1 800 km. For strategic uses against Soviet territory, it will probably be targeted on C^3I installations and other targets deemed time-urgent (such as quick-reaction alert aircraft, missiles and submarines in port). It is mobile and therefore difficult to destroy unless pre-empted at base. However, Soviet deployments in the GDR and Czechoslovakia could provide area coverage of the Schwäbisch-Gmünd–Neu Ulm–Neckarsulm region, and so make it vulnerable. The temptation to pre-empt would increase on both sides.

Mainly because of their long flight time, the cruise missiles are less destabilizing. Still, they constitute another serious challenge to arms control, not least because of the verification problems that they raise. For some years, US plans for deployment of cruise missiles have indicated a leap forward in the number of deliverable strategic warheads. Air- and ground-launched cruise missiles are being deployed, while the first nuclear sea-based missiles are due to become operational on general-purpose submarines in the second half of 1984. Recently, the Soviet Union has also flight-tested long-range cruise missiles with terrain guidance technologies. Limits are therefore urgently needed. A complete ban on sea-launched cruise missiles is essential for effective verification of future agreements.

The role of forward-based systems in superpower force postures is increasing: witness the forward deployment of ballistic missiles in eastern and western Europe, huge cruise missile acquisitions for deployment world-wide, and submarines patrolling closer to foreign shores.

As one superpower increases its forward-based deployment, the other follows suit. Thus the Soviet Union deploys new missiles in eastern Europe, and threatens to deploy near the US coastline missiles which "will be comparable with the new American missiles in flight time to targets, nuclear yield and accuracy".[27] Long open coastlines with naval bases and many important airfields near the sea make the United States vulnerable to this counter-strategy.

This move towards forward-based systems is a very dangerous one, and it should be a high priority in resumed negotiations to find a way of restraining and reversing it.

The role of European countries

Nuclear weapons are also used as important means of political control. New US missiles in western Europe and new Soviet missiles in eastern Europe strengthen the grip of the major powers in their respective parts of the continent; and in the nature of things the major powers themselves may well be reluctant to give up the political leverage which they believe these deployments provide.

The initiative, therefore, for some halt and reversal to the competition in nuclear weapons may well have to come from Europe itself. Europeans have powerful reasons for concern: some 10 000 nuclear weapons are deployed on European soil for use in time of war. It is in this part of the world that public opinion against nuclear arms is most strongly voiced.

During the LRTNF talks, the European members of NATO formed a Special Consultation Group advisory to the United States. In a resumed negotiation, the claim for a European say would be particularly strong if the negotiations were to cover all nuclear weapons down to the 200-km threshold. Countries in other parts of the world where nuclear weapons above this range are deployed, or certain countries which consider themselves targets for such weapons, should also be involved. At the LRTNF talks, NATO proposed an overall ceiling with regional sub-ceilings. That might be a reasonable approach for new negotiations, with mechanisms for more direct third party participation.

The need for some interim measure

It does not seem likely that negotiations on nuclear arms control will be resumed soon—and when they do resume, they will probably take a long time. In the meantime, deployments of new nuclear weapons on new platforms will be going ahead. That is why it is very important that there should be some interim measure, setting some cap on nuclear arsenals.

In January 1984, at a combined meeting of the Palme and Brandt Commissions in Rome, the Palme Commission proposed a one-year moratorium on nuclear weapon deployments. The Commission urged "the Soviet Union and the United States to declare reciprocally a one-year pause on deployment of nuclear weapons to open the way for the resumption of talks". The statement went on to say, "This moratorium would create more favourable conditions and facilitate agreement on new principles to guide negotiations for significant qualitative limitations and quantitative reductions of nuclear weapons."[28] For Europe, such a moratorium would be sensible because it would provide another chance for agreed restraints on euromissiles. However, acceptance of the final Soviet offer in Geneva, to cut Soviet forces targeted on Europe by half, would have been better.

The statement did not specify how far down the range the moratorium should apply. However, it would seem that battlefield nuclear weapons could be exempted. On the NATO side, the number of these weapons is being reduced in any case, making a moratorium less relevant for this category of weapon: and the best way to deal with them is by a disengagement agreement rather than a moratorium.[29]

The argument may be presented that a moratorium would in some sense be of more benefit to the Soviet Union than to the United States. The United States is proposing to deploy a number of nuclear-tipped cruise missiles this year; the Soviet cruise missile programme is not that far advanced. On the other hand, any new Soviet ICBM deployments would be halted; the United States is not due to deploy new ICBMs in 1984. Both sides would have to stop bomber programmes and modernization at sea. The Soviet moratorium on deployment of SS-20s would be reinstated. Soviet deployment of SS-22s in the GDR and Czechoslovakia would be halted at a very early stage, and in western Europe, no further cruise or Pershing II missile would be added to the 41 now deployed.

A moratorium would not damage security on either side. The question is whether the superpowers are willing to stop their struggle for margins of superiority and apparent associated political advantage. The moratorium proposal is a test of their willingness to do so.

Notes and references

[1] *United States–Soviet Relations*, Hearings before the Committee on Foreign Relations, US Senate, 98th Congress, first session on Arms Control Resolutions, Part 2 (US Government Printing Office, Washington, D.C., 1983), p. 93.

[2] Getler, M., *Washington Post*, 16 September 1983.

[3] Robinson, C. A., 'Soviets test new cruise missile', *Aviation Week & Space Technology*, 2 January 1984.

[4] Official US figure. There may be one reload missile fielded per launcher.

[5] Statement at Williamsburg summit meeting, 29 May 1983.

[6] *Korea News Review*, 8 October 1983.

[7] Jiji Press, 29 October 1983.

[8] The three conditions are: reduction of forces along the Chinese–Soviet border (including Mongolia); an end to military support to Viet Nam in its war against Kampuchea; and withdrawal of Soviet troops from Afghanistan.

[9] Marshal Ogarkov, statement at a press conference, Moscow, 5 December 1983, quoted by TASS.

[10] TASS press release, 25 November 1983.

[11] See *Washington Post*, *Washington Times* and *Wall Street Journal*, all of 27 January 1984.

[12] Urban, M. L., 'Major re-organization of Soviet air forces', *International Defence Review*, Vol. 16, No. 6, 1983, p. 756.

[13] Statement by Lt. Gen. Brent Scowcroft, in *Committee on Armed Service*, House of Representatives, 98th Congress, 1st session, Part 2, Strategic Programs (US Government Printing Office, Washington, D.C., 1983), p. 63.

[14] Report of the President's Commission on Strategic Forces, April 1983, p. 15.

[15] Note 1, p. 15.

[16] Note 1, pp. 44 and 45.

[17] Speech by Edward Rowny before the Commonwealth Club of California, 27 January 1984.

[18] Nitze, P. H., 'The American negotiator's view of the Geneva talks', *New York Times*, 20 January 1984.

[19] Nitze (note 18); and Kvitsinsky, Y., 'The Soviet negotiator blames America', *New York Times*, 13 January 1984.

[20] *New York Times*, 30 May 1982.

[21] Note 1, p. 191.

[22] Note 1, p. 210.

[23] Harriman, A. W., 'Three years of Reagan: "nuclear irresponsibility" ', *New York Times*, 3 January 1984.

[24] For an overview and assessment of the debate on no-first-use, see Blackaby, F., Goldblat, J. and Lodgaard, S., *No-First-Use*, SIPRI (Taylor & Francis, London, 1984).

[25] Smith, G. C., Warnke, P. C. and Rhinelander, J. B., 'The road back to the negotiating table', *New York Times*, 29 December 1983.

[26] Circular error probable, a measure of missile accuracy: the radius of a circle, centred on the target, within which 50 per cent of the weapons aimed at the target are expected to fall.

[27] Kvitsinsky (note 19).

[28] Statement by the International Commission on Disarmament and Security Issues (ICDSI, the Palme Commission) following a joint meeting of ICDSI and the International Commission on International Development Issues (ICIDI, the Brandt Commission) in Rome, 20–22 January 1984.

[29] NATO has announced the withdrawal of 1 400 nuclear warheads from western Europe over the coming 5–6 years, comprising atomic demolition mines and warheads for Nike-Hercules air defence missiles. For a presentation and discussion of nuclear disengagement options in Europe, see Lodgaard, S. and Thee, M. (eds), *Nuclear Disengagement in Europe*, SIPRI (Taylor & Francis, London, 1983).

2. Nuclear explosions

RAGNHILD FERM

Superscript numbers refer to the list of notes and references at the end of the chapter.

I. Explosions in 1983

According to preliminary data, 50 nuclear explosions were carried out in 1983, all underground. Of these the United States conducted 14, the Soviet Union 27 and France 7. The United Kingdom and China conducted only one explosion each (see appendix 2A).

Fourteen of the 27 Soviet explosions took place at the known weapon test sites—12 at Semipalatinsk in the eastern part of Kazakhstan, and 2 on Novaya Zemlya. The remaining 13 were conducted outside these sites and are therefore presumed to have served non-weapon purposes. Six of these explosions, conducted on 24 September 1983, took place at five-minute intervals, which may be an indication that they were used in an engineering project. Indeed, in the area north of the Caspian Sea where they took place, large underground chambers may be needed for storage of natural gas. According to the data compiled by SIPRI, the Soviet Union has carried out 62 'peaceful' nuclear explosions during the past 10 years, while the United States has not conducted any explosion of that kind since 1973.

In all, as many as 1 440 nuclear explosions have been carried out since 1945, and it is noteworthy that the average number of explosions per year has increased considerably since the signing of the 1963 Partial Test Ban Treaty (PTBT), which prohibited atmospheric tests but allowed testing underground.

The figures given in this chapter may not be entirely accurate. Official information is either lacking or incomplete, because of the usual secretiveness of the military establishments. Certain states are reluctant even to reveal their capabilities to detect nuclear explosions, or to help others improve such capabilities. Some may also fear unfavourable public reaction to announced tests. Moreover, there is a trend in nuclear testing to reduce the size of explosions; in the case of very weak events, it is impossible to distinguish, through seismological methods alone, between chemical and nuclear explosions.

Appendix 2A

Nuclear explosions, 1983 (preliminary data)

Note

1. The following sources were used in compiling the list of nuclear explosions:

(a) US Department of Energy,

(b) Hagfors Observatory of the Research Institute of the Swedish National Defence, and

(c) press reports.

2. Events marked with an asterisk * may be part of a programme for peaceful uses of nuclear energy in view of their location outside the known weapon testing sites.

3. m_b (body wave magnitude) indicates the size of the event; the data have been provided by the Hagfors Observatory of the Research Institute of the Swedish National Defence.

Date (GMT)	Latitude (deg)	Longitude (deg)	Region	m_b
USA				
11 Feb	37.051 N	116.045 W	Nevada	
17 Feb	37.163 N	116.063 W	Nevada	
26 Mar	37.301 N	116.460 W	Nevada	5.3
14 Apr	37.073 N	116.046 W	Nevada	6.1
5 May	37.012 N	116.089 W	Nevada	4.7
26 May	37.103 N	116.006 W	Nevada	
9 Jun	37.158 N	116.089 W	Nevada	4.9
3 Aug	37.119 N	116.089 W	Nevada	
11 Aug	37 N	116 W	Nevada	
27 Aug	37 N	116 W	Nevada	
1 Sep	37.273 N	116.355 W	Nevada	5.5
21 Sep	37.210 N	116.210 W	Nevada	
22 Sep	37.106 N	116.049 W	Nevada	
16 Dec	37 N	116 W	Nevada	5.3
USSR				
1 Feb	47 N	48 E	W Kazakhstan*	4.3
24 Feb	47 N	48 E	W Kazakhstan*	4.3
25 Feb	47 N	48 E	W Kazakhstan*	4.2
2 Mar	47 N	48 E	W Kazakhstan*	4.1
30 Mar	50 N	78 E	E Kazakhstan	5.0
12 Apr	49.815 N	78.222 E	E Kazakhstan	5.0
30 May	49.740 N	78.210 E	E Kazakhstan	
12 Jun	49.894 N	78.964 E	E Kazakhstan	
24 Jun	50 N	78 E	E Kazakhstan	5.0
10 Jul	51.327 N	53.286 E	S Ural Mountains*	
10 Jul	51.336 N	53.290 E	S Ural Mountains*	
10 Jul	51.357 N	53.301 E	S Ural Mountains*	
28 Jul	50 N	78 E	E Kazakhstan	5.0

18 Aug	73.373 N	54.839 E	Novaya Zemlya	
11 Sep	49.801 N	78.244 E	E Kazakhstan	
24 Sep	46.773 N	48.300 E	N of Caspian Sea*	5.4
24 Sep	46.763 N	48.281 E	N of Caspian Sea*	5.2
24 Sep	46.872 N	48.214 E	N of Caspian Sea*	5.2
24 Sep	46.748 N	48.299 E	N of Caspian Sea*	5.4
24 Sep	46.772 N	48.267 E	N of Caspian Sea*	5.5
24 Sep	46.758 N	48.257 E	N of Caspian Sea*	5.5
25 Sep	73.341 N	54.501 E	Novaya Zemlya	6.4
6 Oct	49.933 N	78.833 E	E Kazakhstan	
26 Oct	49.883 N	78.856 E	E Kazakhstan	
20 Nov	50 N	78 E	E Kazakhstan	6.4
29 Nov	50 N	78 E	E Kazakhstan	5.5
26 Dec	50 N	78 E	E Kazakhstan	5.7

UK

22 Apr	37.112 N	116.022 W	Nevada

France

19 Apr	21.864 S	138.941 W	Mururoa
25 May	21.912 S	138.936 W	Mururoa
28 Jun	21.815 S	138.950 W	Mururoa
20 Jul	22 S	139 W	Mururoa
4 Aug	22 S	139 W	Mururoa
3 Dec	22 S	139 W	Mururoa
7 Dec	22 S	139 W	Mururoa

China

6 Oct	41.552 N	88.741 E	Lop Nor	5.9

3. World military expenditure

ELISABETH SKÖNS and RITA TULLBERG

The section on US military expenditure is based on material provided by DAVID JOHNSON, Center for Defense Information, Washington, D.C.

Superscript numbers refer to the list of notes and references at the end of the chapter.

I. Introduction

In 1982 the rate of growth in world military spending, at 6.1 per cent, was extraordinarily rapid. The estimated rise in 1983 was smaller, but it is still well above the long-term trend of 2.9 per cent for the past 10 years. When comparing the period 1979–83 with 1975–79, the volume increase has accelerated from 2.4 per cent per year on average to 3.3 per cent.

The acceleration is due to the extremely rapid rate at which the United States is investing resources for military ends. This can be seen if US military spending is excluded from the world total. The trend then becomes reversed. The rate of growth in military expenditure for all other countries combined has almost halved from 3.3 per cent per year for the period 1975–79 to 1.7 per cent over the period 1979–83.

Military expenditure rates in other regions of the world have, however, also been both high and accelerating. In the Middle East, Oceania and South America there has been a marked acceleration. In South Asia military expenditure has grown at continuously high rates; in the Far East (excluding China) growth rates are also very high, although they have been substantially lower in recent years.

There are, however, examples of average growth rates for 1979–83 which are below 3 per cent per year. These are Europe—NATO, the WTO as well as the neutral and non-aligned countries—the African continent and China, the latter having reduced its military expenditure by an average of more than 9 per cent per year during this period.

There exist no indisputable data on Soviet military expenditure trends. Since the Soviet Union persistently refuses to publish any credible figures, its military spending has long been the subject of more or less ingenious estimation techniques and guesses. The US Central Intelligence Agency estimates, which are the most widely quoted, have recently been revised for the period since 1976. Soviet arms procurement costs are now estimated to have been roughly constant since 1976, compared to the previous estimates showing a 4 per cent real increase per year. The estimates for total Soviet military spending have thereby been reduced to a 2 per cent trend from the previous estimates of 3–5 per cent. Although the higher estimates, especially for procurement, have been a major argument for the initiation of the current US military build-up and for the conclusion that the policy of detente towards the Soviet Union had failed, the revision seems to have been largely ignored.

World military expenditure in 1983 has, according to SIPRI estimates, reached US $750–800 billion, at current prices.[1] This massive diversion of resources for military consumption is a growing problem for most countries. In industrial market economies, military spending is being maintained, in the face of high budget deficits, at the expense of other government programmes. In the Soviet Union, military spending already absorbs a high share of national product and aggravates the shortage of labour. In most Third World countries, which have to import their weapons, debt problems are becoming acute. Even oil exporters are no longer completely free from financial constraints in the current situation of a weakened demand for oil.

II. NATO

There has been a dramatic rise in NATO military expenditures in recent years. The acceleration from a real growth rate of 4 per cent in 1981 to 6 per cent in 1982 and 8 per cent in 1983 is of course mainly a reflection of the extraordinary rate of rearmament in the United States. In 1983 the real increase in US military expenditure according to the NATO definition was 11.3 per cent, the steepest rise since 1967.

The disparity between military spending in the USA and other NATO countries has, as expected, increased considerably over the past year (figure 3.1). What was less expected, however, is that the combined military expenditures of the latter show a substantial rise for 1983. With 1983 growth rates of 3.9 per cent for NATO Europe and 3.3 per cent for Canada, the average increase in non-US NATO military spending exceeds for the first time the 3 per cent volume target to which all NATO members committed themselves in 1978. However—so far as NATO Europe is concerned—the picture changes radically when the figure for the UK is excluded. For the rest of NATO Europe, the 1983 volume increase was only 1.6 per cent.

The growth rates in table 3.1 are based on NATO standardized military expenditure data which have been deflated using consumer price indices, in order to obtain a trend for the opportunity cost of military expenditures. Prices for military purchases do not necessarily move in line with average consumer prices. Since the value of the dollar has risen considerably during recent years, prices for arms imports have increased rapidly. Thus, the

Figure 3.1. NATO military expenditure, 1950–83

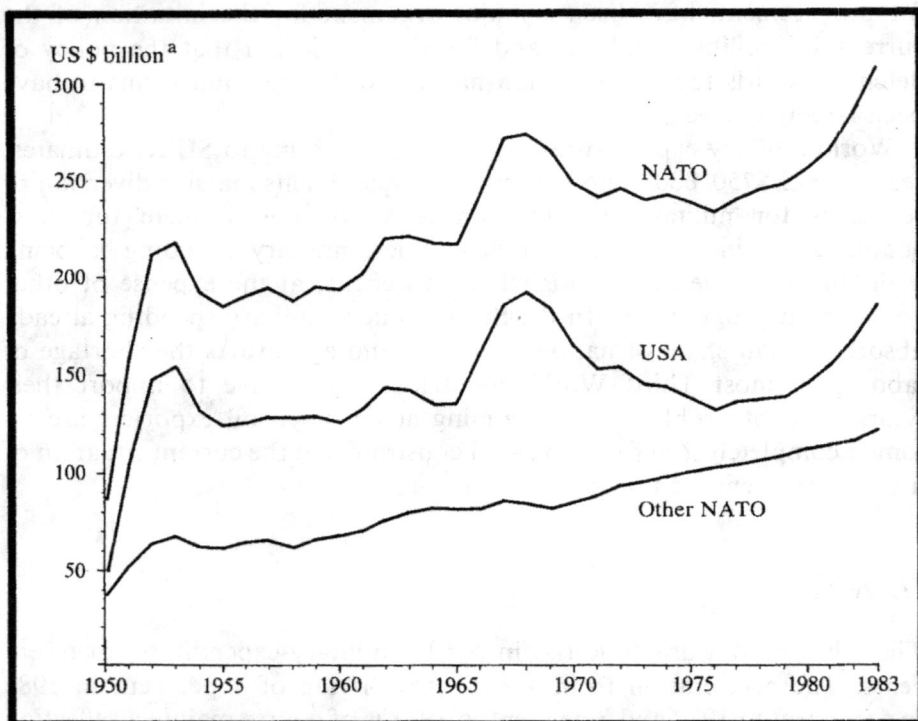

[a] At 1980 prices and exchange-rates.

purchasing power of non-US military spending has not increased as much as the figures in table 3.1 suggest.[2]

The recommendation that all NATO member countries should aim at defence budget increases in the region of 3 per cent per year was first laid out in the Ministerial Guidance approved by NATO defence ministers in 1977. This guidance saw the need for a more comprehensive framework for NATO defence planning, incorporating a longer-term approach than before. The resulting Long Term Defence Programme (LTDP) for the 1980s was adopted by NATO heads of state and government at the 1978 Washington Summit Meeting, at which the 3 per cent target was also endorsed. Robert Komer, adviser for NATO affairs to the US Secretary of Defense during the Carter Administration, traces the origin of the LTDP to a group of Rand and US DoD (Department of Defense) analysts, including himself, in the early 1970s. They felt that NATO's ability to carry out its strategy was increasingly in question. "Moreover, we believed that as the United States disengaged from its long entanglement in South-East Asia, it must remedy its neglect of . . . the defense of Western Europe."[3]

Table 3.1. NATO countries: estimated volume increases in military expenditure

Country	Annual, or average annual percentage increases						Relative size of military spending (USA=100)[a] (1983)
	'Pre-target': From 1972–74 average to 1976–78 average	'Post-target': From 1976–78 average to 1983	1979–80	1980–81	1981–82	1982–83	
USA	−2.0	5.5	3.7	6.9	9.0	11.3	*100*
Canada	3.9	2.8	3.4	1.7	9.8	3.3	*3*
All NATO Europe	2.2	2.5	2.7	0.8	2.3	3.9	*62*
UK	0.3	3.8	8.1	−5.7	5.0	11.2	*16*
NATO Europe (excl. UK) of which	2.8	2.1	1.0	2.9	1.4	1.6	
FR Germany	1.0	1.3	1.3	1.6	−1.3	2.2	*15*
France	3.8	2.6	1.8	2.4	2.1	1.5	*15*
Italy	−0.3	4.9	4.6	2.1	7.0	4.1	*6*
Netherlands	3.4	0.9	−2.7	1.1	−0.4	0.5	*3*
Belgium	5.1	0.5	2.0	0.9	−3.3	−3.6	*2*
Turkey	17.6	0.5	−5.3	23.5	9.3	−2.5	*2*
Greece	14.3	0.8	−13.5	18.3	2.0	0.1	*1*
Denmark	3.2	1.8[b]	1.6	1.1	2.9	..	*1*
Norway	4.1	2.5	1.1	1.1	3.9	1.6	*1*
Portugal	−13.5	1.4	8.5	−0.5	0.1	0.9	*0.5*
Luxembourg	5.8	5.0	16.4	3.4	0.9	2.0	*Negligible*
Total NATO	−0.3	4.2	3.3	4.2	6.3	8.2	

[a] Based on 1983 military spending figures, at 1980 prices and exchange-rates.
[b] From 1976–78 average to 1982.

Source: SIPRI Yearbook 1984, Appendix 3A, table 3A.2.

With the advent of the Carter Administration, efforts were made to strengthen the US contribution to NATO forces. They recognized, however, that an exclusive US force improvement scheme would not be politically feasible: "... our Congress and electorate would insist that any US effort be matched by those of our allies."[4] The purpose of the 3 per cent target was to "produce a certain amount of peer pressure"[5] in anticipation of economic and political constraints to the provision of the additional resources required by the LTDP.

Allied burden sharing has continued to be a very sensitive issue in the United States. The DoD has therefore to submit to Congress each year a *Report on Allied Contributions to the Common Defense*, which surveys a variety of statistical indicators of burden sharing. The most recent report is somewhat more critical of the allies than previously. The conclusion is that the trends up to 1982, "if they continue, threaten to undermine the progress achieved in prior years towards a more equitable distribution of the allied defense burden".[6]

The US allies have responded to these reproaches by pointing to their physical contributions to NATO forces. NATO Europe provides 90 per cent of the ground forces, 80 per cent of the combat aircraft, 80 per cent of the tanks and 90 per cent of the armoured divisions stationed in Europe in peace-time.

General Bernard Rogers, NATO Supreme Allied Commander, Europe, has for some years pressed for an acceleration in NATO military spending to an average annual volume growth of 4 per cent over six years in order for NATO to be able to exploit more advanced military technologies. Advances in targeting and guidance technologies and in conventional munitions offer the capability of striking WTO targets at an early stage and deep into its territory. The reliance on tactical nuclear weapons would thereby be reduced, and thus the nuclear threshold raised. European NATO members have so far hesitated to incorporate these emerging technologies into NATO strategy, mainly for four reasons: the more offensive character of the strategy involved, the fact that most of the required military equipment is produced by US defence industries, doubts about the technical feasibility and effectiveness of these new weapon systems, and the costs involved. West German officials have also complained about the difficulty of simultaneously convincing public opinion of the need to install medium-range nuclear missiles and to raise military expenditure so as to reduce the reliance on nuclear weapons. At their meeting in December 1983, NATO defence ministers, although pressed by the US Defense Secretary to adopt specific weapon systems for future production, decided to continue their study of the use of emerging technology for weapon purposes (see chapter 5).

The final communiqué from this meeting did not reaffirm the usual

NATO commitment to the 3 per cent target. Instead, the ministers "agreed to do their utmost to make available the resources needed", and emphasized the importance of making the most effective use of available resources.[7]

Yet, in a recent interview Rogers claimed that in practice NATO members have already committed themselves to a 4 per cent volume increase in their military expenditure. The only effective instrument available to NATO for persuading member countries to commit themselves to additional force improvements is, according to Rogers, the NATO Force Goals. Adopted by NATO defence ministers every even-numbered year, they become national commitments to force improvements in specific detail and by certain dates. The 4 per cent figure is calculated on the basis of NATO Force Goals for the period 1983–88, which were approved by NATO defence ministers in May 1982.

When commenting on the failure of individual west European NATO countries to reach the 3 per cent target, Rogers points to the US example of trimming social expenditures for the benefit of military spending. Nevertheless, he is not content with current US military spending trends: in view of the world-wide military commitments that the United States has taken upon itself, he finds it unlikely that the United States is going to fulfil the 1983–88 NATO Force Goals it has agreed to, in spite of the high volume increase in the FY (fiscal year) 1983/84 military budget.[8]

The high rate of growth in NATO Europe military expenditures for 1983 is entirely the consequence of the 11 per cent rise for the United Kingdom. It seems, however, as if the economic burden of rapidly rising military budgets has now become politically unacceptable, and in 1983 it announced that the 3 per cent target would be abandoned after FY 1985/86. West German and French military expenditure plans already provide for a less than 3 per cent growth rate. Belgium and Denmark have all along had great difficulties living up to the 3 per cent target. The Belgian government decided in 1983 that Belgium could not afford the $500 million required for the planned purchase of Patriot missile system units, which are to become a vital part of the NATO conventional air defence system in the late 1980s. It also asked for the Belgian share in the NATO common fund for infrastructure to be reduced. The Danish parliament voted in 1982 for the cancellation of Denmark's share in NATO infrastructure costs, but this was opposed by the minority government. Dutch military expenditure growth rates have averaged 0.9 per cent in the post-target period. However, in its 1983 Defence White Paper the Dutch government announced its commitment to annual defence budget increases of 2 per cent in real terms until 1987, and recommended a 3 per cent growth rate thereafter. The Norwegian government has also decided to increase the defence budget substantially—by 20 per cent in real terms over the period 1983–88. The planned increase in procurement expenditure is still higher, since its share of the defence budget is to increase from 20 to 25 per cent over the same period.

In general, however, the European NATO members fear that an increased defence burden would under current economic circumstances pose a security risk in the form of social unrest. Former West German Chancellor Helmut Schmidt went as far as to say: "The economic mess today is a greater danger right now to the coherence and political stability of the alliance than the Soviet threat." [9]

The United States

In 1983 President Reagan persisted in his commitment to large increases in military spending, pushing forward towards the proclaimed goal of a "rearmed America", which has been the centrepiece of his presidency. The FY 1984 (fiscal year 1983/84) military budget marked the sixth consecutive year of real growth in US military spending, an unprecedented development since World War II.

The FY 1985 DoD budget request submitted to the US Congress in February 1984 calls for $305 billion, a 13 per cent real increase over FY 1984 (table 3.2). If approved, this would be the largest annual military budget increase in the Reagan presidency. The total funding request for national defence, which includes atomic energy defence activities in the Department of Energy, is $313.4 billion. The Congress, in passing a FY 1984 DoD budget of $258.2 billion—$265.3 billion in total for national defence—had slowed the pace of the Administration's military build-up. The FY 1985 request marks a determined effort to make up for much of the 1984 reduction and bring the Reagan military programme back close to its planned five-year level of funding.

According to the DoD's long-range forecasts, another big budget increase of 9.2 per cent is planned for FY 1986. Subsequently, however, the annual increases would fall to the level of 3–4 per cent each year. Defense Secretary Weinberger projects that: "if we are allowed to continue on the path we have set, we can look forward to a time, only two fiscal years from now, when defense increases can begin to slow dramatically".[10] Such promises of future restraint may be helpful in getting Congressional support at present but whether the DoD can control spiralling defence costs remains to be seen.

Procurement

The US fiscal year 1985 defence budget includes a 20.5 per cent real increase in investment authority, comprising arms procurement, RDT&E

Table 3.2. US Administration budget estimates for fiscal years 1984–89 (as of 1 February 1984)

Figures are in $ billions.

	1984	1985	1986	1987	1988	1989
Total budget authority						
Total national defence, current prices	265.3	313.4	359.0	389.1	421.6	456.4
Total Department of Defense, current prices	258.2	305.0	349.6	379.2	411.5	446.1
Total Department of Defense, constant (1985) prices	269.9	305.0	333.0	344.7	357.9	371.7
Percentage change	*3.7*	*13.0*	*9.2*	*3.5*	*3.8*	*3.9*
Outlays						
Total national defence, current prices	237.5	272.0	310.6	348.6	379.7	409.1
Total Department of Defense, current prices	231.0	264.4	301.8	339.2	369.8	398.8
Total Department of Defense, constant (1985) prices	241.8	264.4	286.7	306.8	319.5	330.1
Percentage change	*8.8*	*9.3*	*8.4*	*7.0*	*4.1*	*3.3*

Source: FY 1985 Department of Defense Budget, News release from the Office of the Assistant Secretary of Defense (Washington, D.C., February 1, 1984); and *Budget of the United States Government FY 1985* (US Government Printing Office, Washington, D.C., 1984).

(research, development, testing and evaluation) and military construction. If approved, its share of the total defence budget will rise to 48.8 per cent against 45.5 per cent in 1984. Most of the outlays for weapon systems currently authorized will, however, fall on later years. Thus, during fiscal year 1985, only one-quarter of total investment outlays are intended for new programmes.

There is a strong emphasis on the modernization and expansion of nuclear forces in the current US rearmament programme. Of requested DoD budget authority for 1985, 21.5 per cent is devoted to nuclear forces, against 19.0 per cent two years ago. As a share of total national defence authority, costs for nuclear forces are to increase from 21.1 to 23.3 per cent over these three years.[11] The Scowcroft Commission and its supporters in Congress rescued from probable defeat the most controversial part of the Reagan military programme, the MX missile. Procurement funding and quantities of major nuclear weapon systems are summarized in table 1.4.

One of the first decisions of the Reagan Administration upon taking office at the beginning of 1981 was to initiate a major programme to modernize and expand the naval forces. As a result, the size of the US Navy has increased from 479 deployable battle force ships at the end of FY 1980 to 525 ships at the end of FY 1984. The 1985–89 ship-building programme, providing for an average of 28 new deployable ships per year, will, with allowance for the retirement of old ships, bring the size of the naval fleet to 545 ships by the end of FY 1985, the intention being to have built a 600-ship navy by the end of this decade.

Production numbers for other major conventional weapon systems are presented in table 3.3.

Long-term costs

A major question has been raised about the long-term costs of the Reagan military programme. Defense Department analyst Franklin Spinney and others point to the tendency on the part of DoD to underestimate weapon costs as well as the full budget costs of present programmes in future years.

In Congressional hearings during 1983,[12] Spinney testified that, because of basic structural problems which take a long time to remedy, unit costs of weapons do not decline as rapidly as assumed in DoD cost projections. As a result, either the allocations to an unchanged procurement programme have to be increased in later years or the production level be reduced. This is in fact what is happening. Between the defence plan for fiscal years 1983–87 and the first draft of the 1984–88 defence plan—a period of only five months—the cost estimates for 45 weapon systems were increased for two or more of the four common years. The production quantity was also reduced for 29 of these systems as well as for 15 other weapon systems.

Table 3.3. Production of selected major conventional weapon systems in the United States, fiscal years 1983–86

Designation	Description	1983[a]	1984[b]	1985[c]	1986[d]
Aircraft					
F-14 Tomcat	Fighter	24	24	24	24
F-15 Eagle	Fighter	39	36	48	60
F-16 Fighting Falcon	Fighter	120	144	150	216
F/A-18 Hornet	Fighter/strike	84	84	84	102
AV-8B Harrier	Fighter	21	27	32	46
C-5B Galaxy	Transport	1	4	10	16
KC-10A	Tanker	8	8	8	12
AH-64 Apache	Helicopter	48	112	144	144
UH-60 Black Hawk	Helicopter	96	84	78	78
Armoured vehicles					
M-1 Abrams	MBT	855	840	720	720
M-2/3 Bradley	MICV	600	600	710	900
LVT	Amphibious ASSV	453	416	244	–
LAV	APC	134	236	292	–
DIVAD Sergeant York	SP-AAG	96	130	132	144
Missiles and rockets					
AIM-9M Sidewinder	AAM	2 420	2 050	1 000	1 220
AIM-7M Sparrow	AAM/SAM	1 471	1 379	923	1 313
AIM-54A/C Phoenix	AAM	108	265	400	567
AIM-120A AMRAAM	AAM	–	–	174	1 042
AGM-65 (IIR) Maverick	ASM	900	1 980	4 690	8 200
Laser Maverick	ASM	12	263	600	1 500
AGM-88 HARM	ASM	289	722	1 674	2 461
AGM-114A Hellfire	ASM	3 971	4 870	6 464	7 880
BGM-71 TOW	ATM	13 000	20 200	21 822	22 014
MIM-104 Patriot: missiles	SAM	287	440	585	815
: launch units		12	12	15	18
MLRS: rockets		23 640	36 000	50 472	72 000
: launch units		72	76	44	29

[a] Actual.
[b] Planned.
[c] Proposed.
[d] Proposed for authorization.

Source: Secretary of Defense Caspar W. Weinberger, *Annual Report to Congress, Fiscal Year 1985* (US Government Printing Office, Washington, D.C., February 1984).

For the last completed five-year defence plan studied by Spinney, that for 1978–82, 9 per cent fewer tactical fighter aircraft than planned were purchased, in spite of there being no budget cuts that could affect cost growth. Indeed, actual appropriations exceeded the plan by 2 per cent. Spinney maintains that recent defence plans are based on unrealistic learning curve effects, which relate unit cost to increased production and experience. In the 1983–87 defence plan, declining unit costs were planned for 77 per cent of a sample of 111 weapon systems. For 10 per cent of these, the planned cost reduction was greater than 65 per cent, including the

MX missile with an 81 per cent decline in unit cost over this period. Spinney also charges that operation and maintenance cost estimates are too low, since the Defense Department assumes that the use of high technology will lower operating costs. Alice Rivlin, head of the Congressional Budget Office, agrees, stating that the Army "lacks the techniques to project comprehensive estimates of future operating and support costs for a modernized Army".[13] Rivlin has predicted that an influx of advanced new weapons could result in a substantial rise in operating costs, only part of which was being anticipated.

In 1983 the politics of scarcity began to be felt in the Pentagon as competition accelerated over the allocation of future military budgets. Navy Secretary Lehman and Deputy Defense Secretary Thayer quarrelled publicly over the Navy's share of future budgets and the viability of expensive surface warships. As a vast new programme to build defences against ballistic missiles began to take shape in response to President Reagan's call for a reorientation of US nuclear policy, costs of $18–27 billion for fiscal years 1985–89 were reported. Richard DeLauer, Under Secretary of Defense for Research and Engineering, characterized these costs as "staggering".[14] It was unclear where all the money for a new antiballistic missile (ABM) system would come from, on top of all the other programmes already under way.

Several actions were taken by Congress to force the Defense Department to be tougher in its contracting. Congress approved legislation establishing an independent arms testing office and requiring the Defense Department to secure guaranties on future weapons. Efforts by Congress to encourage greater competitiveness in defence procurement face severe limitations. Defense Secretary Weinberger himself has commented: "Unfortunately, competition does not always come easily to the defense marketplace. Once a firm has won a contract for the initial research on a complex weapons system, it has a head start—indeed an almost unbeatable advantage—in competing for later development and production contracts. In other words, there is usually only one bidder in these situations."[15]

A number of conflicts of interest regarding officials in the Defense Department were raised in 1983. The House Committee on Government Operations in a November 1983 report asserted that the DoD's advisory boards were stacked with business executives who promoted their companies' products, and many were selected from "the old-boy network within the military-industrial complex".[16]

Some defence officials were quick to point out that Congress itself plays a major role in pushing up levels of military spending. Former Deputy Defense Secretary Carlucci suggested that Congress was responsible for about $20 billion in higher defence procurement costs because of "irrational" budgeting.[17] Secretary Weinberger proposed that there should be a two-year budget cycle, because too much time was being consumed in bargaining between members of Congress and the Defense Department every year and budget action was always too late.[18]

Important criticism continued to be voiced by the so-called military reformers. Critics such as Senators Gary Hart and Sam Nunn argued that too much emphasis was being placed on high technology weapons of excessive cost and uncertain reliability. Lawrence Korb, Assistant Secretary of Defense for Manpower, Reserve Affairs and Logistics, agreed that the Defense Department was "a house divided against ourselves", with admirals and generals preoccupied with force structure and weapon modernization. Korb states: "Since 1980, when this administration came into office, funds for modernization have almost doubled while funds for readiness and sustainability have gone up only 33 per cent".[19]

Military objectives

The Reagan Administration continues to strive towards its major military objectives:

1. Modernization of US strategic nuclear forces, with new submarines and submarine-based missiles, bombers, land-based ballistic missiles and a massive cruise missile programme.

2. Pursuit of expanded nuclear options at both the strategic and theatre levels, including improved command, control and communications capabilities, to provide a capability to fight and, perhaps, "prevail" in a prolonged nuclear war.

3. Acquisition of a 600-ship navy, with the objective of being able to take on the Soviet Navy and defeat it in areas adjacent to the Soviet Union.

4. Increased emphasis on US technological superiority through more spending on a wide variety of research and development programmes, including possible means of defence against ballistic missiles and greater use of space for military purposes.

5. Expanded capability for conducting warfare in Third World areas, particularly in the Middle East, the Persian Gulf and Central America, and an ability to fight in two or more wars simultaneously.

6. Continued improvements in conventional forces for war in Europe, in conjunction with US military allies, anticipating the possibility of a prolonged conventional war with the Soviet Union.

7. Increased compensation and prestige for military personnel, making a military career more attractive for the all-volunteer force.

The Carter Administration initiated many of the programmes the Reagan Administration is pursuing. The extreme zeal and scope of President Reagan's military effort, however, are distinctively his own.

It is widely alleged that the Reagan Administration is pursuing military objectives that far outstrip available capabilities. General David Jones, former Chairman of the Joint Chiefs of Staff, pointed out "the mismatch between strategy and forces to carry it out". This discrepancy, he said, "is greater now than it was before because we are trying to do everything".[20] This perception was heightened by the simultaneous US military involvement in Grenada and Lebanon.

The basic premise of Reagan's defence programme is that the Soviet Union presents a very dangerous military threat to the United States and its allies and that something close to an emergency had been created through alleged neglect of defence in the decade before Reagan was elected in 1980. The big increases in military spending that are to be sustained over a period of 5–10 years, the huge investment in new nuclear weapon systems and the expansion of the US Navy all flow from assessments of the US–Soviet military balance that stress Soviet strengths and US weaknesses.

An underlying pessimism about the capacity of the United States and its allies to defend themselves seems to condition the views of top Reagan officials. This was most explicitly stated by Richard Perle, the Assistant Secretary of Defense for International Security Policy: "Democracies will not sacrifice to protect their security in the absence of a sense of danger. And every time we create the impression that we and the Soviets are cooperating and moderating the competition, we diminish that sense of apprehension".[21]

In 1980 US public opinion by and large shared Reagan's fears. By 1983, however, more Americans believed that the USA and the USSR were approximately equal in military strength. The change in US public opinion following the Soviet shooting down of a South Korean airliner in September 1983, together with the generally favourable US public response to the invasion of Grenada, rekindled the Reagan Administration's commitment to a tough policy toward the Soviet Union and revived hopes that the mandate for military budgets had not yet been lost.

Congress and the 1983/84 defence budget

It appeared for a time in 1983 that the US defence build-up was losing support. The aggressive war-fighting rhetoric of the Reagan Administration's first two years had provided impetus to the creation of a nation-wide movement for a nuclear freeze. There was a growing apprehension that the Administration might be initiating more military projects than the country would be able or willing to pay for later in the decade. Many members of Congress, including some Republican supporters of President Reagan, argued for the need to moderate the military build-up to help reduce the enormous federal budget deficit, especially because big reductions had already been absorbed by many non-military federal programmes.

In Congress, the debate over military spending was framed primarily in terms of what the percentage increase should be between the FY 1983 and

1984 budgets. The budget process requires that overall ceilings on military funding be set. The Administration sought a 10 per cent real increase, while a variety of smaller increases were advocated in Congress. About 4–5 per cent eventually resulted from the lengthy Congressional budget process towards the end of 1983: an approved FY 1984 budget for national defence that rose about half as much as the Reagan Administration initially requested.

Judged purely in these terms, it would seem that the Administration had suffered a setback. But debates over percentages tend to distract attention from the central reality that the huge military build-up is continuing. The discussion was not so much concerned with cutting the military budget as with slowing the rate of increase. Congressional committees tinkered with the military budget, stretching out or delaying a programme here, cancelling or trimming a programme there. But only binary chemical weapons failed to receive support. All the major weapon programmes received substantial funding. Navy Secretary Lehman argued that it was too late for Congress to halt the drive for a 600-ship navy: "We've already accomplished it because we front-loaded the budget".[22] The huge increases in funding for procurement of weapons have tended to incorporate large future budgets and restrict the ability of Congress to change budget priorities.[23]

In November 1983 Secretary Weinberger summed up the results of Congress' actions on the FY 1984 military budget:

Some 300 items were reduced in small amounts, but the general overall result is that we have endorsement, approval and appropriations for all of the President's major programs and weapons systems except the chemical warfare weapons that were requested. With the cuts that were made, primarily the effect of that will be that we will have all the weapons systems the President feels is essential but we will take a little longer to get them and they will cost quite a bit more because of the reductions that were made in the rate of acquisition and in the most economic quantity that we had requested in our budget.[24]

Since the forecast rates of inflation and fuel costs have been lowered and the MX programme altered, which helped cushion the impact of Congress cuts in the DoD budget, reductions are less severe than they appear. Nevertheless, Secretary Weinberger has requested a huge increase in his FY 1985 budget to try to make up for Congressional reductions and restore the Administration's full five-year defence build-up programme.

It is likely that Congress will continue to trim the edges of the military budget. Both Democrats and Republicans have reacted to the rapid increase requested for the fiscal year 1985 military budget, and the high budget deficits projected up to 1987. However, because there is still widespread suspicion about the Soviet Union and concern about the adequacy of US military forces in the light of the country's extensive overseas military involvements, it may be expected that the Reagan military build-up will continue.

III. Costs versus resources

In an increasing number of countries, the debate over resource allocation for military purposes is intensifying. On the one hand, low rates of growth and attempts by governments to limit budget deficits by cutting back expenditure exert pressure on defence budgets and accentuate the resource competition between the military and civil sectors. On the other hand, costs of goods and services purchased by the military are increasing, constituting an upward pressure on defence budgets which will probably increase during the 1980s.

The major source of cost growth in military expenditure items is the modernization of weapon systems. The incorporation of rapidly increasing levels of technological progress in weapons, especially in combination with decreasing production series, leads to higher fixed costs per unit, notably the costs for RDT&E. The ratio between military procurement and military RDT&E expenditures is now about 2 : 1 in both the United States and the United Kingdom.[25] As a result of these developments, the procurement requests of, for example, the US Air Force have increased between fiscal years 1974 and 1984 from an average of $6 million to $22 million per fighter aircraft. After adjusting for the general rate of inflation, this amounts to a cost increase in real terms of about 6 per cent per year, largely attributable to product improvements. Another example of the same phenomenon is the estimate that British procurement costs for the Tornado multi-role combat aircraft in the mid-1980s will absorb annual expenditures corresponding to 52 per cent of total 1979/80 outlays for air systems, implying that the air force has "to sacrifice other air systems, whilst the remaining services will have to accept older equipment so lengthening the queue for replacement weapons".[26] In FR Germany, the high and rising costs of the Tornado have already led to the cancellation and postponement of other major weapon programmes.[27] By 1975, the cost trends for military hardware items led a senior Pentagon official to make the forecast that "if the trends which have prevailed so consistently over the last half-century were to continue for a few more decades, we will reach a point in the year 2036 where the Defense Department will literally be able to afford only one aircraft".[28] This statement, for which the phrase the Final Law of Economic Disarmament has been coined, although very simplistic, captures the problem well. Even if quality may be substituted for quantity in some areas, not all quality increases are accompanied by decreased quantities, future costs are frequently underestimated and, even more important, the effectiveness of rising technological sophistication is increasingly being questioned even within military establishments.

With increased complexity and sophistication of weapons, the requirements for their operations and maintenance also increase. According to estimates made by the US Congressional Budget Office, the fielding of the M-1 Abrams battle tank will increase the annual costs of operating and supporting a tank battalion by 41 per cent compared to the requirements for a battalion equipped with M-60-A1 tanks. The modernization of mechanized infantry battalions through the replacement of the M-113 armoured personnel carrier with the Bradley Fighting Vehicle Systems is estimated to raise annual operating and support costs by 59 per cent.[29]

Further, more complex weapons also require more skilled manpower, resulting in increased costs for military personnel as well, both in training and remuneration. A recent collection of country case studies on this subject concludes that escalating personnel costs, which are likely to continue throughout the 1980s, will make it impossible for countries to maintain readily forces of the size that were hitherto possible.[30]

Decision makers faced with this cost-versus-resource dilemma may try to solve it by increasing the allocations for procurement at the expense of other sections of the military budget. This appears to be what has occurred in a number of NATO countries (table 3.4). The share of total military expenditure devoted to major purchases of military equipment has generally been rising in these countries during the past 10 years, reversing the previous trend. Over the period 1974–83, this share has trebled in Canada and increased by at least one-half in Belgium, FR Germany, the Netherlands, Norway and the United Kingdom. For the United States, the trend is less marked, but the plans are for major increases in the procurement share over the next five years, in spite of extraordinary increases in total military expenditure.[31] There is, however, a limit to this kind of solution to the problem, since it eventually leads to a decrease in the readiness and effectiveness of the forces.

In the longer term it can be expected, therefore, that current procurement policies and cost trends will result in a redistribution of resources in favour of the military sector. Throughout the 1970s, most of the countries listed in table 3.5 have increased the volume of military expenditure, the major exceptions being Australia and the United States. Still, with the exception of Spain, the shares of total central government expenditures devoted to the military sector have generally been declining during at least the first half of the 1970s, since welfare programmes have been given priority within rapidly expanding total budgets.

As can be seen from table 3.5, in most countries the share of military expenditure in total government expenditure has stopped falling, and in other countries it has been declining much more slowly. Only in the United

Table 3.4. Expenditure for major purchases of military equipment[a] as a share of total military expenditure, fiscal years[b] 1974–83

Figures are percentages.

Country	1974 or 1974/75	1975 or 1975/76	1976 or 1976/77	1977 or 1977/78	1978 or 1978/79	1979 or 1979/80	1980 or 1980/81	1981 or 1981/82	1982 or 1982/83	1983 or 1983/84
Belgium	8.8	9.0	11.0	11.9	13.9	13.1	14.4	14.0	13.6	14.9
Canada	5.9	6.3	8.0	8.5	10.0	13.8	15.4	15.9	17.4	18.8
Denmark	19.3	19.0	19.4	21.8	16.4	16.3	18.1	17.5	16.8	17.3
France[c]	44.7	42.6	41.1	39.2	40.2	43.0	44.5	46.0	47.8	46.9
FR Germany	11.9	11.8	13.2	12.5	13.0	13.7	14.8	17.3	17.3	17.6
Italy	15.2	13.9	13.1	15.3	16.2	15.1	17.5	17.3	13.2	18.5
Netherlands	13.2	15.7	15.5	21.0	18.3	20.2	18.0	18.8	20.4	22.0
Norway	11.6	11.6	11.4[d]	14.2[d]	18.3	19.5	19.3	19.0	19.5	18.3
UK	17.2	19.3	20.6	22.0	23.0	23.2	25.2	26.5	25.4	28.2
USA	18.1[e]	17.5[e]	17.4	17.5	20.0	19.5	20.3	21.3	23.9	26.1

[a] These figures "must be viewed with some reservation as they only cover 'major purchases of equipment', and it is often difficult to draw the line accurately between the purchase of equipment, and expenditure on buildings and installations. In most cases, total spending on equipment would be considerably higher than indicated in the table." (*NATO Review*, No. 1, February 1979).

[b] Calendar year for all countries except Canada and the United Kingdom (fiscal year: April–March); Denmark (fiscal years 1974/75–1977/78: April–March; fiscal year 1978: April–December; fiscal year 1979 onwards: January–December); Turkey (fiscal years 1974/75–1981/82: March–February; fiscal year 1982: March–December; fiscal year 1983 onwards: January–December); and the United States (fiscal years 1974/75–1975/76: July–June; fiscal year 1976/77 onwards: October–September).

[c] There are no comparable NATO figures for France. The figures used here are for capital expenditure (Titre V). 1974–80 *Budgét Définitif*; 1981–82 *La Loi de Programmation*; 1983 *Budgét Initial*. Figures for *La Loi de Programmation* and *Budgét Initial* are normally higher than *Budgét Définitif*.

[d] Excluding missiles.

[e] Including ammunition and explosives.

Sources: Successive NATO press releases on "Financial and Economic Data Relating to NATO Defence", also reproduced yearly in *NATO Review*. French sources: *Assemblée Nationale* No. 3150, Défense Tome I, 11 October 1977; No. 1979, Défense Tome I, 9 October 1980; *Sénat*, No. 95, Tome III, Annexe 42, 22 November 1982.

Table 3.5. Military expenditure as a share of central government expenditure[a] in OECD countries,[b] 1970–83

Figures are percentages.

	1970	1971	1972	1973	1974	1975	1976	1977	1978	1979	1980	1981	1982	1983
Australia	20.6	19.4	18.8	17.4	15.0	12.3	11.4	11.2	10.9	11.0	11.5	11.9	11.9	10.7
Austria	5.6	5.1	5.1	5.0	5.1	5.2	5.1	5.1	5.2	5.2	5.2	5.1	5.1	4.9
Belgium[c]	13.7	13.3	12.8	12.4	12.0	11.6	11.5	11.1	11.0	10.7	10.5	10.2	9.3	9.4
Canada	13.5	12.3	11.1	10.8	9.9	8.8	9.2	9.4	9.5	9.1	9.0	8.7	8.9	8.6
Denmark[d]	8.4	8.4	8.2	7.3	7.7	7.7	7.3	7.4	7.3	7.2	7.3	7.1	7.0	: :
Finland	6.9	7.3	7.5	7.5	6.8	6.6	6.6	6.1	6.2	6.4	6.8	6.7	6.8	6.7
France	20.4	20.1	19.9	19.8	19.4	18.2	18.7	18.8	18.6	18.5	18.7	18.1	17.3	18.1
FR Germany	27.5	27.2	27.3	27.1	27.8	24.1	23.9	23.2	22.6	22.4	22.5	22.3	22.0	22.4
Italy	13.7	13.6	14.3	12.5	12.4	10.8	9.8	9.6	7.4	7.7	7.4	6.9	6.2	6.3
Japan	: :	8.5	8.3	8.0	7.6	7.4	7.0	6.7	6.1	6.0	5.9	5.9	5.9	6.1
Netherlands	13.4	12.7	12.4	11.8	11.6	10.9	9.8	10.6	9.4	9.5	9.2	9.3	9.0	9.0
Norway[e]	10.8	10.1	9.4	9.1	8.7	8.9	8.2	8.0	7.2	7.1	6.7	6.7	7.0	6.3
Spain	12.3	11.8	12.7	13.4	13.7	13.8	14.2	13.3	11.7	11.9	11.5	11.3	11.0	10.0
Sweden	14.8	14.3	14.1	13.6	12.2	11.5	10.8	10.3	10.0	9.9	9.5	9.3	8.7	8.3
Switzerland[c]	32.3	31.4	30.0	27.6	26.1	25.9	26.1	25.0	24.1	24.6	23.8	25.0	25.3	25.3
UK	19.0	19.3	19.4	18.2	16.7	15.3	15.2	15.3	14.9	15.0	15.6	14.3	15.0	16.5
USA	38.1	33.9	31.8	29.7	28.7	25.5	23.6	24.0	23.7	24.0	23.9	24.7	25.7	27.2

[a] Central government expenditures are defined to include current and capital expenditure of central government, and to exclude social security funds. The exclusion of social security funds makes the figures conform better to national budget data for most countries.
[b] Excluding Ireland, New Zealand and Yugoslavia.
[c] Current disbursements only.
[d] National public accounts definition.
[e] Including social security funds.

Sources:

Military expenditure data:
SIPRI military expenditure registers, *SIPRI Yearbook 1984*, appendix 3A. The latest figures are budget estimates.

Central government expenditure data:
1970–81: OECD data as given in *OECD National Accounts 1964–81* (Paris, 1982), and in *OECD Financial Statistics*, 1983–I and II. The exceptions are Denmark, all years, and the 1981 figures for Belgium and Spain, for which national statistical yearbooks and budget documents have been used.
1982–83: Figures have been derived on the basis of the growth rates in central government expenditures according to a public accounts definition. The sources used include basically national statistical yearbooks and budget documents.

States and the United Kingdom has there been a significant rise in the share during the past two years. Expenditure plans in the United States confirm the marked reversal towards a rise in the proportion of total expenditures going to the military.

Moreover, according to government spending plans, the military sector is scheduled to absorb an increasing proportion of central government expenditures in several countries (figure 3.2). Again, the most extreme example is the United States. The approved budget for fiscal year 1984 provides for a rise in the share of DoD outlays in the total federal budget from an actual 25.1 per cent in FY 1982, on a public accounts basis, to 27.1 per cent in FY 1984, and a further rise is projected to 33.5 per cent in FY 1988.[32]

FR Germany

The expenditure plans for FR Germany also provide for a rise in the military expenditure proportion—by one percentage point over the period 1982–87.[33] Yearly nominal increases of 3.8 per cent are planned for the military, while the allocation for education and R&D is to increase by only one-half per cent per year, and reductions are planned for, among others, social security and public communications expenditures.

The 1984 budget includes a nominal increase over the previous year of 3.7 per cent for defence, while total federal expenditure is to rise at only half that rate. Allocations for military investment show a disproportionate rise of 7.1 per cent. At the end of 1983 two major arms projects were agreed upon. In November, the West German and French defence ministers signed an agreement to develop and manufacture an anti-tank helicopter. FR Germany plans to procure 212 of these, known as the PAH-2. In December an agreement was signed with the United States for the procurement of an air defence system to protect US and West German bases in FR Germany. The system will include 36 Patriot and 87 Roland missile systems, the former produced in the United States and the latter jointly by FR Germany and France. Parliamentary decisions on these two projects are due in the spring of 1984. Future plans also include the purchase of 200 units of the Multiple Launch Rocket System (MLRS), to be delivered during 1987–94. The total cost for FR Germany of these three weapon systems alone is currently estimated to be more than 12 billion DM ($8 billion). The new fighter aircraft planned for the 1990s involves far greater sums than that, and decisions are pending also for a new battle tank for the next decade. When this new expenditure is added to the as yet largely unpaid bills for previously approved programmes, annual financial requirements can be expected to accelerate in volume terms beyond the current 12.58 billion DM procurement budget.

Figure 3.2. Military expenditure as a share of central government expenditure in six Western industrial countries, 1970–87

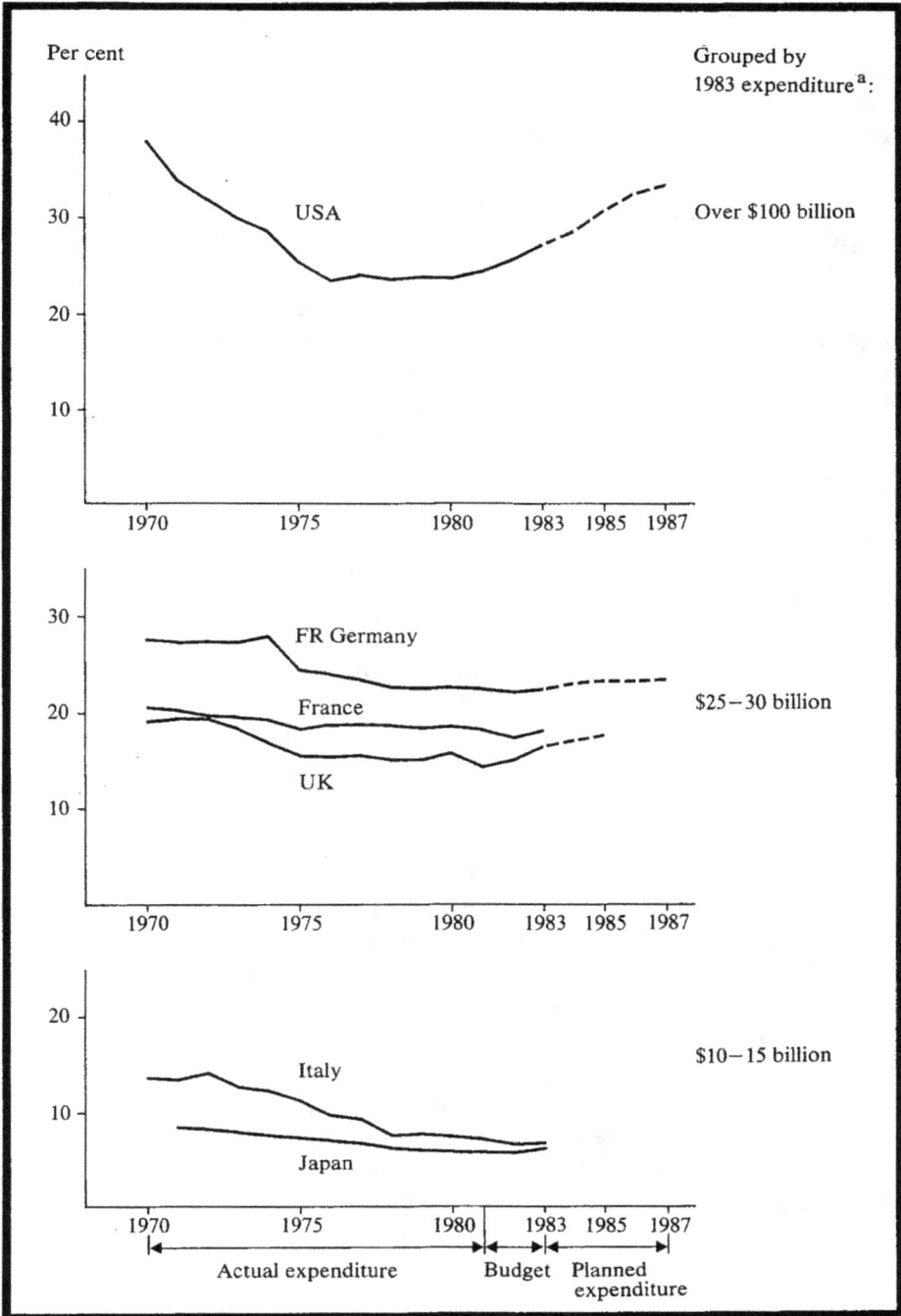

The United Kingdom

Economic growth has been slower in the United Kingdom since the end of World War II than in any other major industrial country. Studies show that military spending has taken place not at the expense of current private consumption nor government spending on the social sectors but at the expense of investment in productive capacity.[34]

Since 1970, the share of military expenditure going to the purchase of equipment (defined more broadly than in table 3.4) has grown from 33 per cent to an estimated 46 per cent in 1982, while personnel costs have fallen from 47 per cent to 38 per cent. In general, equipment costs grow 6–10 per cent faster than general inflation and it has been calculated that current programmes could grow by a further 2–4 per cent per year in real terms unless cuts are made.[35] The government, taking note of this runaway situation, has recently announced that future increases in defence spending will be based on the general rise in prices in the economy rather than on the inflation rate specific to the military sector.

The 3 per cent goal will be dropped after FY 1985/86 and defence equipment expenditure subject to a cost-chasing exercise. Yet savings are to be achieved by technical adjustments "within acceptable limits" without cuts in major programmes or change in strategy. At the same time, for example, the purchase of 8–12 Type 23 frigates costing £100 million each is planned, principally for ASW (anti-submarine warfare) duties in the north Atlantic, but not unconnected with Britain's activities in the south Atlantic. These are a particularly heavy drain on Britain's resources, due to the logistic problems involved. Additional costs of £1 860 million have been agreed upon for the Falklands/Malvinas over the next three years,[36] though it is felt that the full costs of the re-equipment programme and the new airport have not been taken into account.

According to current plans the military budget is to grow at the expense of government spending in the welfare sector, since current political thought permits neither major tax increases nor increases in budget deficits. Expenditure plans show an increase in the military expenditure share (on a public accounts basis) from an actual 16.4 per cent in FY 1981/82 to a planned 18.0 per cent in FY 1983/84. Although no separate figures are presented for planned central government expenditures for the two years thereafter, these can be roughly deduced,[37] giving a further rise of about 0.5 per cent by FY 1985/86. Between the fiscal years 1981 and 1985 rising shares are planned also for law, order and protective services and for social security. Declining shares are scheduled for education, housing and other environmental services, industry, energy and trade and, to a lesser extent, for transport.

France

After a period of relative strength, French economic growth has stagnated in 1983 and the OECD (Organization for Economic Co-operation and Development) forecasts no real growth in 1984. Declining investment, balance-of-payments difficulties and inflation have also contributed to the government's economic problems. A temporary freeze on government expenditure in the autumn of 1982 resulted in delays and cancellations of 7.6 per cent of defence payment credits and 23 per cent of programme authorizations, and in February 1983, 20 per cent of the 1983 authorizations were delayed for nine months. Despite these obvious financial difficulties, the five-year defence plan published in April allows for a 2 per cent annual growth in defence spending in real terms over the period 1984–88. The overall economic five-year plan announced at the same time does not provide for any specific growth target.

The defence programme has been given special treatment in that the budgeted amounts and delivery dates of major purchases were passed as law, which is seen as guaranteeing that resources will be made available for its fulfilment. Within the programme, totalling 830 billion francs over these five years, 'absolute priority' has been given to procurement, which is to take a slightly growing share—from 49 to 51 per cent—of the total. Thirty per cent of the procurement budget will be spent on nuclear weapons and, while manpower is to be cut by 5 per cent over five years, remaining units will be re-equipped and a new 50 000-man Rapid Action Force (FAAR) created.

The share of central government spending going to the military reached a low point in 1982 and is planned to stay at about the same ratio until 1984.[38] Thereafter amounts are not specified for particular years. Already it seems likely that additional resources will be needed to finance the ambitious procurement programme, since budget estimates were made on the basis of optimistically low inflation forecasts. Thus, the defence plan is to be reconsidered in the autumn of 1985, and this is generally seen by observers as an opportunity to adjust budgets upwards in line with cost realities. The financing of equipment programmes is based on a forecast of 6.2 per cent inflation in 1984 and 5 per cent in each of the following four years, although inflation is currently 9 per cent. Pressure has therefore already been placed on the government to stick to the details of the programme regardless of the cost, and the Minister of Defence announced that despite economic difficulties "the sacrifice will not fall on defence".[39]

The 1984 military budget does not deviate from the five-year plan in nominal terms and has been allowed to grow slightly faster than the overall budget, while taxes and social security charges have risen. It is highly unlikely, however, that any real growth of military spending can be achieved without a budget supplement.

Japan

Japan is yet another example of a country in which a dichotomy has arisen between overall economic and defence planning. In accordance with a decision taken in November 1976, defence spending is not to exceed 1 per cent of GNP. More specifically, defence expenditure decisions are to be taken in the light of the growth of national income and of the government's budgetary situation.[40] While Japanese national income is growing faster than that of its competitors in the old industrial countries, current growth at about 3 per cent a year is much slower than during the expansionary period of the 1960s and 1970s. Defence plans, however, call for expenditure growth of between 6.3 and 8 per cent annually in real terms in the fiscal years 1983–87.

Mounting budget deficits led to the introduction of an austere budget for FY 1983/84 when total spending was projected to increase by only 1.4 per cent, the smallest rise for 28 years. Cuts were made in education, pensions and agricultural support, but military spending was allowed to increase by 6.5 per cent. Even this, however, was not enough to meet equipment targets, and a Defense Agency request for procurement under long-term contracts for new front-line equipment was cut by about 30 per cent.[41] Although military expenditure was allowed to rise despite budget constraints, the US Secretary of Defense commented that it was insufficient to achieve the stated goals and that an even greater defence build-up was needed. The Japanese Ministry of Finance presented a budget proposal for FY 1984 under which military expenditure would increase by approximately 5 per cent while total government spending increased by only 0.5 per cent. Following the intervention of Prime Minister Nakasone, the Defense Agency's request for a 6.55 per cent increase was agreed to by the Cabinet early in 1984.[42]

Other Europe

Austria is an exceptional case, where military expenditures have taken a virtually constant share of total government expenditures every year since 1970. Although the new Austrian chancellor has announced the introduction of a tighter budget policy, he is also pledged to continue the welfare policy of his predecessor, which points to no future change in trend. The replacement of Austria's SAAB 105 light jet aircraft with a new combat aircraft has been under discussion for some time. In 1981 the Austrian National Defence Council recommended the purchase of 24 Dassault–Bréguet Mirage 50 aircraft at a total cost corresponding to more than half of the Austrian defence budget at that time. Procurement has, however, been postponed for financial reasons, and the purchase is being reconsidered.

In *Sweden* the long-term halt in the share of government expenditures devoted to the military has not been interrupted. By 1983 a marked gap had, however, developed between approved military activities and the resources planned for these. The 1982 Defence Decision covering the period 1983–87 included a constant military budget in real terms over these five years, with guaranties of price compensation by use of a military price index specifically designed for this purpose. The Defence Decision provided for a continued modernization of the armed forces although at a somewhat reduced rate and at the expense of 5 800 defence employees over a 10-year period. A major project is the initiation of indigenous development and production of the JAS-39 Gripen second-generation multi-role combat aircraft for the Air Force. The government has decided to purchase 140 of these aircraft by the end of the century at a total cost (at 1981 prices) exceeding the current defence budget.

In 1983 the economic level for military defence was slightly reduced in relation to the 1982 Defence Decision in line with the overall restricted government budget, which did not provide cost compensation for the devaluation of the Swedish crown. This, in combination with increased costs arising from a higher dollar rate, devaluation and tax increases, has resulted in a debate about the economic crisis of the Swedish defence establishment.

In his 1984–89 plan for military defence,[43] the Supreme Commander of the Swedish armed forces concludes that the military's purchasing power has been so substantially reduced over the past year that the intentions of the 1982 Defence Decision in many respects cannot be achieved. In order to revert to the objectives set out in the 1982 Defence Decision, the Supreme Commander estimates that sums of the order of 5 billion Swedish crowns are required for the next three financial years in addition to the 58 billion crowns planned, over and above full price compensation. For each of the two years thereafter, a further 1 billion crowns would be required.

The government has promised a supplementary allocation for anti-submarine warfare which, according to the military, is much below what is required, but has also announced its intention to limit price compensation to 4 per cent—the expected rate of general inflation; this is strongly opposed by the military. Since major decisions are now required to reconcile planned military activities with planned resource allocations, the defence budget proposal was omitted from the annual general draft budget presented in January 1984. The government has since then tried to negotiate a deal with the parliamentary opposition on how to raise more money for the military, including measures such as increased petrol taxes and spending cut-backs for local authorities.

Conclusion

It has been argued for some time now that the provision of welfare at current levels in the Western industrial world is being eroded by economic stagnation. A further constraint on civil expenditure programmes is the escalating requirements of the military sector, especially the runaway costs connected with sophisticated military technology. This section has dealt only with the proportion of central government expenditure required for military purposes; the share of total resources going to military ends has not been discussed. There are signs that increasing proportions of government funds will be devoted to military purposes in the near future in a number of countries, leaving fewer monetary resources for welfare programmes within budgets.

The two related questions of the degree of military preparedness people wish to maintain and the sacrifice needed in terms of costs must be addressed by the electorates in each country. Since military demands are in many respects insatiable, arms procurement plans require an open debate. Major weapon programmes have long lead times and large sums of money are involved, making it difficult to stop them once they have been started. Neither governments nor electorates have therefore time to be complacent.

IV. The WTO

The total figure for WTO military spending is heavily dominated by the Soviet Union. The combined military expenditures of its east European allies amount to less than one-tenth of the total. The rate of increase for these countries levelled off between 1976 and 1981 to an average of 1.9 per cent per year. The estimate for 1982 shows a 4.7 per cent real growth, and in 1983 the increase is even greater. Part of the acceleration in recent years may, however, be explained by an increasing discrepancy between the official price index series, which SIPRI uses for deflation purposes, and actual price developments.

Among the Soviet allies, the German Democratic Republic has both the highest and the most rapidly increasing military budget. Since 1974 its military expenditure has increased at an average annual rate of over 6 per cent, and over the past four years it has approached 7 per cent. Hungary has announced a record military budget for 1983. With a real increase of almost 50 per cent over 1982, its share of the total state budget has increased from 4 to 6 per cent.

Poland and Romania have increased their military spending by less than 2 per cent per year over the past 10 years, one reason for this comparatively slow growth probably being economic constraints. Polish military spending actually declined over the period 1977–81. In spite of political turbulence and very rapid price increases in 1982, military spending was, however, raised by a full 13 per cent in real terms. The military budget announced for 1983 shows a nominal rise of 10 per cent, which will amount to a real decrease unless supplemental allocations have been made during the course of the year. Romania took the rather unusual step in 1983 of pledging to hold its military expenditure until 1985 at the 1982 level.[44] The pledge was accompanied by a call to all member countries of the two power blocs, particularly the Soviet Union and the United States, to halt the arms race.

The Soviet Union

The Soviet Union persists in reporting low defence budget figures, showing a slightly declining trend over the past decade to 17 054 million roubles in 1983.[45] No further information is provided. Since neither the levels nor the trend in the reported figures can possibly cover the sums required to finance the combined Soviet military effort as documented in Western sources, little attention is paid to this figure. Therefore, any assessment of Soviet military expenditure, its content and effects has by and large to rely on information published in Western sources, most of which originates from intelligence services. This is not without risks, since the examples of misestimation are plentiful.[46]

Soviet military expenditure estimates are published annually by the US Central Intelligence Agency, by the Defense Intelligence Agency (DIA) of the US Department of Defense, and by NATO. The estimates made by the CIA are derived mainly by use of the building-block method. About 1 000 distinct physical components of Soviet military activities are identified, counted and costed in dollar as well as in rouble terms.[47] The data on numbers of physical units and unit costs are based on intelligence information and are classified. Thus, it is only the methodology used which is open to debate. The dollar estimates are by and large rough measures of what it would cost to reproduce the combined Soviet military activities in the United States, for example at the pay scales of US volunteer military personnel and at US defence industry manufacturing efficiencies. These estimates suffer from such methodological deficiencies as to make them unsuitable for purposes of international comparison.[48] This is by now so widely acknowledged that it has led a senior NATO official to warn against their use as an argument for military expenditure increases in NATO member countries: "It is time to restore the confidence of Western public opinion in the estimates made by the intelligence services, but this cannot be accomplished if such disputable methods are continued as comparing Soviet expenditures in dollar terms with those of the USA and NATO. Public opinion will rarely be persuaded thereby to pay more for defence. Indeed, even the opposite effect might be achieved." [49] In line with this, NATO publishes only rouble estimates of Soviet military expenditures. It is more appropriate to use these estimates for assessing the growth rate in Soviet resource consumption for military purposes and the burden imposed by the military sector on the Soviet economy.

In March 1983, the CIA announced a major downward revision in its Soviet military expenditure estimates. Prior to this revision, the annual CIA reports had consistently concluded that the long-term volume trend in Soviet military expenditures on a dollar basis is 3 per cent, while on a rouble basis the growth rate has averaged 4–5 per cent per year. The difference in growth rates between dollar and rouble estimates has been explained by "the greater weight that the rouble valuation gives to faster growing elements, and the tendency of Soviet procurements to shift over time toward higher-technology weapons in which the US has a comparative advantage". [50] According to CIA estimates for the period 1967–77, the relatively fast-growing Soviet military investment costs (at about 4 per cent per year) represented over one-half of total Soviet rouble defence costs but only 30 per cent of dollar costs. On the other hand, the relatively slow-growing military manpower costs accounted for only one-sixth of total rouble costs, but 35 per cent of total dollar costs. [51]

According to the revised CIA estimates, [52] the long-term growth in total Soviet defence costs in rouble terms has slowed to 2 per cent per year since 1976 from a 4–5 per cent trend during the period 1966–76. This is due to the downward revision of CIA estimates for Soviet procurement of military equipment to an almost flat trend since 1976, which was only partially offset by the tendency for newer, more sophisticated arms to cost more. The exact trend in revised rouble procurement costs has, however, never been explicitly stated anywhere. Other resource categories have continued to grow at steady rates; 3–4 per cent for operations and maintenance, and slightly less than 2 per cent for personnel costs. The revised dollar estimates show a 2 per cent growth rate in costs for total Soviet military activities, and a flat trend for procurement costs since 1976.

DIA officials immediately disputed the CIA interpretation of Soviet military equipment trends. In spite of slower than expected arms production rates, previously estimated expenditure rates were not overstated, they claimed, since the dollar costs per weapon were higher owing to technological advances in Soviet weapons and inefficiency in production.[53] In the DIA's annual report to Congress some months later, however, a graph was presented in which the dollar estimates of Soviet military expenditures were shown to have shifted from a 4 per cent growth path over the period 1970–76 to a 2 per cent trend through to 1981. The only comment made on this marked change in trend was that "since 1970 the total dollar costs of Soviet defense programs has risen in real terms at an average annual rate of about 3 per cent, marking continuous growth in the overall level of Soviet military activity".[54] Thus, although the CIA and the DIA compile their physical estimates of military expenditure components independently of each other, they arrive at the same trends when applying the CIA dollar cost methodology to their physical numbers.

The DIA, however, considers its rouble estimates much more relevant than its dollar estimates for analysing Soviet priorities. In rouble terms, the DIA estimates that Soviet military expenditures have increased at a rate of 6.5 per cent per year from 1970 to 1981. This new and higher than previously reported rate of growth is expressed in current prices, contrary to the normal practice of calculating all growth rates in volume terms. It is based on the assumption that military spending has increased at the same rate as the total Soviet state budget, and on "other evidence".[55] However, no other evidence has been presented by the DIA to show that this is a realistic assumption.

On the DIA estimates, Soviet military expenditures increased over the period 1970–81 from 50 to 100 billion roubles in current prices. According to the DIA there was no slow-down in the nominal rate of growth in total military spending, in spite of an estimated deceleration in procurement rates from 9–11 per cent in the first half of the 1970s to 6–9 per cent in the latter half.[56] Further, it is their estimate that the military burden on the Soviet economy has increased over the period, with military expenditure as a share of GNP increasing from 12–14 per cent to 14–18 per cent in 1981. This is contrary to the CIA estimate of military expenditures as having taken a constant share of Soviet GNP since 1970.

The new and contradictory intelligence estimates are discussed and compared in a recent US Congressional study, which in part relies on classified intelligence material. The conclusion is that the DIA's rouble estimates for Soviet military spending and GNP "have limited utility for policymakers because they are not adjusted for inflation, are based on a definition of Soviet defense that is different from the definition of US defense, and contain wide margins of error. The DIA considers its methodology classified, making it difficult for outsiders to evaluate its measures."[57]

The revised military expenditure estimates for the Soviet Union have major policy implications for its adversaries. It is true that Soviet military spending even according to the new estimates is high and comfortably

Table 3.6. US Defense Intelligence Agency estimates of Soviet production of certain military items, 1978–82

Military item	1978	1979	1980	1981	1982
Ground forces matériel					
Tanks	3 000	3 500	2 100	2 000	2 500
Other armoured fighting vehicles	5 500	5 700	6 300	5 200	4 500
Towed field artillery	1 400	1 500	1 400	1 600	1 700
Self-propelled field artillery	700	500	300	400	500
Multiple rocket launchers	550	600	700	700	700
Self-propelled AA artillery	300	300	300	300	200
Towed AA artillery	100	–	–	–	–
Aircraft					
Bombers	30	30	30	30	30
Fighters/fighter-bombers	1 250	1 300	1 300	1 350	1 100
Transports	400	400	350	350	350
Trainers	50	25	25	25	25
ASW aircraft	10	10	20	10	10
Helicopters	650	750	750	750	750
Missiles					
ICBMs	225	225	250	200	175
IRBMs	100	100	100	100	100
SRBMs	250	300	300	300	300
SLCMs	600	700	750	750	800
SLBMs	250	200	200	175	175
ASMs	900	900	1 000	1 000	1 000
SAMs	53 000	53 000	53 000	53 000	53 000
ATGMs	35 000	40 000	45 000	60 000	62 500
Naval ships					
Submarines	13	12	13	11	8
Major combatants	11	11	11	9	9
Minor combatants	50	55	65	45	55
Naval support ships	5	7	8	5	4

Source: The Allocation of Resources in the Soviet Union and China—1983, Statement by Major General Schuyler Bissell before the Joint Economic Committee of the US Congress, 28 June 1983.

accommodates considerable additions to Soviet forces, but as regards Soviet priorities and intentions there is a difference in the conclusions to be drawn from pre- and post-revision estimates. When formulating the tenth five-year plan in 1975, the Soviet leadership, faced with declining economic growth rates, chose to reduce sharply the growth rate in civil investment. Since then, Western analysts have been wrestling with the question: why did the Soviet Union not restrain its military spending in 1975? This question has been the more intriguing since 1975 was a particularly good time for reducing the military expenditure growth rate.

The 1975 decision to sacrifice growth for defense came after the onset of détente, after SALT I and the Vladivostok agreement had recognized Soviet stategic parity with the

United States, after the U.S. had suffered defeat in Vietnam, after substantial Soviet theater buildups in Europe and the Far East had improved the military balance, after a decade of rapid increases in Soviet defense expenditures and several years of declining United States spending, in real terms, for defense. The decision was roughly coincident with the Helsinki agreement that virtually ratified Soviet World War Two gains in Eastern Europe. Then, if ever, was a time when economic constraints might safely have been given their due weight against the claims of defense. Yet an opposite choice was made, to maintain the growth rate of defense spending while sharply cutting the growth rate of investment. In effect, investment funds were diverted to defense.[58]

The revised Soviet military expenditure estimates do not support conclusions which are based on pre-revision estimates, such as that "the prolonged Soviet military build-up is relatively insensitive not only to changes in the international climate and in U.S. military policies, but also to changes in Soviet economic circumstances".[59]

Soviet arms production figures have been reported annually by the DIA since 1981. Figures for production are of course not identical to those for procurement. The former include military equipment produced for export and exclude annual Soviet imports of about 600–800 armoured vehicles from the east European countries. However, DIA data published before the revision for the period 1977–81 indicate that aggregate growth rates for arms procurement differ little from production rates, although the levels are significantly different, especially for vehicles, artillery, fighter and trainer aircraft, and minor surface combatants.[60]

The 1983 version of the DIA arms production data is reproduced in table 3.6. The number of weapons produced by the Soviet Union is shown to be very high. Indeed, for most weapon categories, the Soviet production levels by far surpass those of the combined NATO countries. Growth rates for production are, however, generally low. Over the period 1978–82 production rates have remained constant or have declined for 18 of the 25 weapon categories listed.

Various possible explanations have been given for the long-term deceleration in Soviet military procurement numbers and costs since 1976. According to the CIA, it is due to "a combination of factors including technological problems, industrial bottlenecks, and policy decisions".[61] Since the slow-down coincides with reduced growth rates also for Soviet GNP, total industrial production and the machinery and metal-working industry output, it has been suggested that "it is likely—but cannot be proved—that the defense slowdown is the result of economic constraints".[62]

Since the mid-1970s, the US Department of Defense has voiced its concern that the rapid Soviet investments in military R&D would erode the US lead in military technology. The studies of military technology trends and comparative levels are few and do not cover recent years. Again, the only source of information is official US assessments, the basis of which is unknown. The emerging picture is, as one recent publication puts

Table 3.7. US DoD assessment of relative US/Soviet technological levels in deployed military systems[a]

Deployed system	1980 USA superior	1980 USA–USSR equal	1980 USSR superior	1982 USA superior	1982 USA–USSR equal	1982 USSR superior
Strategic						
ICBM		×			×	
SSBN/SLBM	× →					
SSBN					·×	
SLBM				× →		
Bomber	× →			×		
SAM			×			×
BMD			×			×
Anti-satellite			×			×
Cruise missile				×		
Tactical land forces						
SAM (including naval)		×			×	
Tank			← ×		×	
Artillery	× →				×	
Infantry combat vehicle			×			×
Anti-tank guided missile		×			×	
Attack helicopter	× →				×	
Chemical warfare			×			×
Theatre ballistic missile		×			×	
Air forces						
Fighter/attack aircraft	×			× →		
Air-to-air missile	×			×		
PGM	×			× →		
Airlift	×			×		
Naval forces						
Nuclear-powered submarine		×			×	
Anti-submarine warfare	× →			×		
Sea-based air	× →			×		
Surface combatant		×			×	
Cruise missile		×			× →	
Mine warfare			×			×
Amphibious assault	× →			×		
C³I						
Communications	× →				×	
Command & control		×			×	
Electronic counter-measures		×			×	
Surveillance and reconnaissance	× →			× →		
Early warning	× →			× →		

it, that the United States is shown to enjoy a general technological lead in deployed military systems (table 3.7), although the lead is smaller than in basic technology areas. "This points to the success of the Soviet acquisition process in creating effective weapons on the basis of a generally lower technological level in industry." [63]

Starting with the 1976–80 development plan, the Soviet Union has embarked on a new strategy for economic growth which is based on high rates of technological progress instead of, as traditionally, on massive labour and capital investment. This has been necessitated by the recent sharp fall-off in labour supply due to low birth rates, and by the continuous decline in capital/output ratios. The expected results have, however, not been attained because of institutional obstacles in the Soviet economic structure.[64] Growth rates in both aggregate output and labour productivity have been decelerating during recent years. It remains to be seen whether economic reforms which have been intensely debated in the Soviet press during the past year will be implemented and effective. If not, the high priority given to the military sector in the Soviet Union will impose an increasing economic burden—which is already substantial—with the defence industry employing an increasing share of scarce labour resources.

V. China

China is the only major power committed to contain defence spending, to utilize military industrial plants for civilian purposes and to give priority to the modernization of industry, agriculture and science. Military spending has clearly been the subject of restraint since 1979, the year of the Viet Nam invasion, when the policy of the four modernizations was announced. In 1983 the official military budget fell in real terms and as a percentage of government spending (table 3.8). This, however, is not the whole picture. Costs for major equipment purchases and military R&D are embedded in other parts of the budget, the Chinese philosophy being that it is necessary to 'reside' resources in various sectors of the economy so that a transition from peace-time to wartime production can be made smoothly should the

---

[a] These are comparisons of system technology level only, and are not necessarily a measure of military effectiveness. The comparisons are not dependent on scenario, tactics, quantity, training or other operational factors. Systems farther than one year from IOC (Initial Operational Capability) are not considered.

The arrows denote that the relative technology level is changing significantly in the direction indicated.

Source: Holloway, D., *The Soviet Union and the Arms Race* (Yale University Press, New Haven, 1983), pp. 138–39. The original sources of these tables are the annual posture statements to the US Congress of the US Under Secretary of Defense, Research and Engineering.

need arise.[65] The use of spare capacity in the defence industries to produce capital and consumption goods for the civilian sector has been emphasized this year, particularly the saving in foreign exchange which this has involved.[66] Clearly, Chinese authorities are finding it necessary to make more consumer goods available to the public and are prepared to sacrifice growth in heavy industry for the sake of adapting products to 'market demands'.[67] At the same time they are trying to modernize their armed forces using domestic resources, since, as Defence Minister Zhang Aiping stated in the spring of 1983, it is neither realistic nor possible to "buy defence modernisation from abroad".[68]

A solution to these conflicting goals can be found in the defence policy statements which emphasize the importance of nuclear deterrence, a re-evaluation of the position that any enemy could be defeated by the sheer weight of Chinese numbers. Funds are therefore to be concentrated on the domestic production of guided missiles, nuclear fuel and bombs and on a streamlined, more professional armed service.

Observers comment that, since China already has nuclear know-how, compared to bringing its forces up to scratch with conventional weapons of modern sophistication a nuclear programme may be cheaper. The economic consequences of this will depend on China's determination to stick to its priorities of raising living standards and creating a modern agricultural and industrial nation.

Table 3.8. China's military expenditure as a share of total government spending, 1977–83

Figures are in billions of yuan.

	1977	1978	1979	1980	1981	1982	1983
Government spending	84.4	111.1	127.4	121.3	109.0	115.3	126.2
Military spending (official budget only)	14.9	16.8	22.3	19.4	16.9	17.9	17.9
Share of military spending (%)	17.7	15.1	17.5	16.0	15.5	15.5	14.2

Sources: For government spending: *International Financial Statistics* (International Monetary Fund, Washington, D.C., November 1983). For military spending; SIPRI, *World Armaments and Disarmament, SIPRI Yearbook 1983* (Taylor & Francis, London, 1983), p. 158. The 1983 figures for both government spending and military spending are from *Fifth Session of the Fifth National People's Congress (November–December 1982)* (Foreign Language Press, Beijing, 1983); and *The First Session of the Sixth National People's Congress (June 1983)* (Foreign Language Press, Beijing, 1983).

Notes and references

[1] This figure has been estimated by applying the US inflation rate since 1980 to the constant price world total. Had the total for 1983 been estimated using 1983 dollar exchange-rates, the figure would have been significantly lower. One major reason for this difference is the strength of the dollar in 1983. Measured against all other major currencies, the dollar has risen in value by about 20 per cent between 1980 and 1983.

[2] The NATO data are liable to subsequent revisions, especially for the most recent years. Thus, compared to the original estimates, the 1982 real growth rates have been revised from 6.9 to 6.2 per cent for total NATO, while the growth rate for NATO Europe is unchanged, in spite of substantial revisions for most individual countries in this group.

[3] Komer, R., 'The origins and objectives', *NATO Review*, June 1978, p. 10.

[4] Komer (note 3), p. 11.

[5] Brown, H., in *Department of Defense Appropriations for 1980*, Hearings before a Subcommittee on Appropriations, House of Representatives, Part 1, February 1979 (US Government Printing Office, Washington, D.C., 1979), p. 539.

[6] *Report on Allied Contributions to the Common Defense*, US Department of Defense, March 1983.

[7] *NATO Review*, Vol. 31, No. 6, 1983.

[8] *Armed Forces Journal International*, September 1983, p. 74.

[9] *International Herald Tribune*, 11 January 1984.

[10] Weinberger, C. W., *Annual Report to Congress—Fiscal Year 1985* (US Government Printing Office, Washington, D.C., 1984), p. 8.

[11] *The Defense Monitor*, Vol. 12, No. 7, 1983, tables on p. 3 as updated by D. T. Johnson, Center for Defense Information, Washington, D.C.

[12] 'Cost Estimating for Weapons Systems', in *Department of Defense Appropriations for 1984*, Pt 2, Hearings before a Subcommittee of the Committee on Appropriations, House of Representatives (US Government Printing Office, Washington, D.C., 1983), pp. 665–808.

[13] Halloran, R., 'National security decisions to be focus of broad inquiry', *New York Times*, 22 June 1983.

[14] Hiatt, F., ' "Staggering" costs predicted', *Washington Post*, 11 November 1983.

[15] Weinberger, C., Letter to *New York Times*, 9 December 1983.

[16] House Committee on Government Operations, *Defense Science Boards: A Question of Integrity*, 28 November 1983, p. 5.

[17] Archibald, G., ' "Irrational" budget process is said to boost defense costs by $20 billion', *Washington Times*, 14 June 1983.

[18] Halloran, R., 'Weinberger and Senate arms panel politely trade charges over budget', *New York Times*, 29 July 1983.

[19] 'Korb says services fail to show loyalty to Sec Def', *Army Times*, 29 August 1983.

[20] Knickerbocker, B., 'Reagan defense buildup prompts strategy debate', *Christian Science Monitor*, 28 July 1983.

[21] Gutman, R., 'The nay-sayer of arms control', *Newsday*, 18 February 1983.

[22] Dewar, H., 'Pentagon diet appears to be a slim hope', *Washington Post*, 30 April 1983.

[23] SIPRI, *World Armaments and Disarmament, SIPRI Yearbook 1983* (Taylor & Francis, London, 1983), p. 142.

[24] Department of Defense transcript of press conference, 22 November 1983.

[25] Ganzler, J., *The Defense Industry* (MIT Press, Cambridge, Mass., 1980), p. 101; Nott, J., 'Economic constraints and British defence', *Survival*, March/April 1982.

[26] Hartley, K., 'Defence with less money? The British experience', in Harries-Jenkins, G. (ed.), *Armed Forces and the Welfare Societies: Challenges in the 1980s* (Macmillan, London, 1982), p. 42.

[27] See, for example, SIPRI, *World Armaments and Disarmament, SIPRI Yearbook 1982* (Taylor & Francis, London, 1982), pp. 115–16.

[28] Augustine, N.R., 'One plane, one tank, one ship: trend for the future?' *Defense Management Journal*, Vol. 11, No. 2, April 1975.

[29] *Army Ground Combat Modernization for the 1980s: Potential Costs and Effects for NATO* (United States Congressional Budget Office, US Government Printing Office, Washington, D.C., November 1982).

[30] Harries-Jenkins (note 26).

[31] SIPRI (note 23), p. 141.

[32] *Special Analysis. Budget of the United States Government FY 1984* (US Government Printing Office, Washington, D.C., 1983).

[33] *Finanzbericht 1984*, Bundesministerium der Finanzen (Bonn, 29 July 1983).

[34] Smith, R. P., 'Military expenditures and investment in OECD countries, 1954–73', *Journal of Comparative Economics*, No. 4, 1980; de Grasse, R. *et al.*, *The Cost and Consequences of Reagan's Military Build-up* (Council on Economic Priorities, New York, 1982), quoted in Chalmers, M., *The Cost of Britain's Defence*, Peace Studies Papers No. 10 (University of Bradford, May 1983).

[35] Chalmers (note 34), p. 61.

[36] House of Commons, Third Report of the Defence Committee, Sessions 1982–83, "The Future Defence of the Falkland Islands", HC-154 (HMSO, London, 1983).

[37] *The Government's Expenditure Plans 1983–84 to 1985–86* (HMSO, Cmnd 8789-I, London, February 1983).

[38] Assemblée Nationale, France, *Rapport Général sur le Project de Loi de Finances pour 1984*, No. 1735, Annexe No. 44: Défense (6 October 1983).

[39] *Financial Times*, 22 April 1983; *Le Monde*, 22 April 1983; *Air et Cosmos*, 30 April 1983.

[40] *Defense of Japan 1982* (Defense Agency, Japan), English translation (The Japan Times, Ltd.), p. 185.

[41] *Asian Security 1983* (Research Institute for Peace and Security, Tokyo, 1983), p. 233.

[42] *Japan Times Weekly*, 11 February 1983.

[43] *Programplan för det militära försvaret 84–89* ["Programme for the Military Defence of Sweden 1984–89"], Report of the Supreme Commander to the Government (Stockholm, September 1983).

[44] *LUMEA* (Romanian Foreign Policy Weekly), No. 3, 14 January 1983, p. 12.

[45] 'Law of the Union of the Soviet Socialist Republics on the State Budget of the USSR for 1983', in *Daily Review*, 25 November 1982.

[46] See, for example, Prados, J., *The Soviet Estimate, US Intelligence Analysis and Russian Military Strength* (Dial Press, New York, 1982).

[47] An informative and easily accessible description of this methodology is given in the annual publication by Sivard, R. L., *World Military and Social Expenditures* (World Priorities, Leesburg, Va.).

[48] See, for example, SIPRI, *World Armaments and Disarmament, SIPRI Yearbook 1979* (Taylor & Francis, London, 1979), pp. 27 ff.; Holzman, F. D., 'Soviet military spending: assessing the numbers game', *International Security*, Spring 1982, pp. 78–101.

[49] Rupp, R., 'Beurteilung der Sowjetischen Militärausgaben', *Soldat und Technik*, No. 2, 1982 [SIPRI translation].

[50] Burton, D. F., 'Estimating Soviet defense spending', *Problems of Communism*, No. 3–4, 1983, p. 88.

[51] For rouble shares, see *Estimated Soviet Defense Spending: Trends and Prospects*, SR78-10121, CIA, June 1979. For dollar shares, see *A Dollar Cost Comparison of Soviet and US Defense Activities, 1967–77*, SR-10002, CIA. January 1978.

[52] 'USSR: economic trends and policy developments', Office of Soviet Analysis, Central Intelligence Agency, 14 September 1983, in *The Allocation of Resources in the Soviet Union and China—1983*, Hearings before the Joint Economic Committee of the US Congress, 20 September 1983.

[53] *International Herald Tribune*, 4 March 1983.

[54] *The Allocation of Resources in the Soviet Union and China—1983*, Statement by Major General Schuyler Bissell before the Joint Economic Committee of the US Congress, 28 June 1983, pp. 25–26.

[55] *The Allocation of Resources in the Soviet Union and China—1983* (note 54), p. 19. See also pp. 23–24.

[56] 'Soviet Defense Trends', A Staff Study prepared for the Joint Economic Committee of the US Congress, September 1983, pp. 2–3.

[57] 'Soviet Defense Trends' (note 56), p. 3.

[58] Rush, M., 'Guns over growth in Soviet security policy', in *Soviet Military Economic Relations*, Proceedings of a Workshop on July 7 and 8, 1982, Joint Economic Committee of the United States Congress (US Government Printing Office, Washington, D.C., 1983), p. 234.

[59] Rush (note 58), p. 235.

[60] See tables in *Allocation of Resources in the Soviet Union and China—1982*, Part 8, Hearings before the Joint Economic Committee, US Congress (US Government Printing Office, Washington, D.C., 1982), pp. 36 and 73–75.

[61] CIA (note 52), p. 10.

[62] 'Soviet Defense Trends' (note 56), p. 26.

[63] Holloway, D., *The Soviet Union and the Arms Race* (Yale University Press, New Haven, Conn., 1983), p. 140.

[64] Berliner, S., 'The prospects for technological progress', in Bornstein, M. (ed.), *The Soviet Economy* (Westview Press, Co., 1981).

[65] *Financial Times*, 11 December 1982.

[66] *Xinhua*, 14 April 1983; *Sichuan Provincial Service*, 17 April 1983; *Far Eastern Economic Review*, 25 August 1983.

[67] Report of the 1983 Plan for National Economic and Social Development, presented by Yao

Yilin at the First Session of the Sixth National People's Congress, 7 June 1983, reprinted in English in *Chinese Documents*, First Session of the Sixth National People's Congress, June 1983 (Foreign Language Press, Beijing, 1983), p. 77.
[68] *Far Eastern Economic Review*, 7 April 1983.

Appendix 3A

World military expenditure, 1974–83

For the sources and methods for the world military expenditure data, see *SIPRI Yearbook 1984*, appendix 3B. For the conventions used in the table and for footnotes, see page 89.

Table 3A.1. World military expenditure summary, in constant price figures

Figures are in US $ mn, at 1980 prices and exchange-rates. Totals may not add up due to rounding.

	1974	1975	1976	1977	1978	1979	1980	1981	1982	1983
USA	143 656	139 277	131 712	137 126	137 938	138 796	143 981	153 884	167 673	186 544
Other NATO^a	97 606	99 582	101 524	103 214	107 037	109 355	112 297	113 234	116 153	(120 627)
Total NATO	241 262	238 859	233 236	240 340	244 975	248 151	256 278	267 118	283 826	(307 171)
USSR	[120 700]	[122 600]	[124 200]	[126 100]	[128 000]	[129 600]	[131 500]	[133 700]	[135 500]	[137 600]
Other WTO	10 166	10 942	11 418	11 735	12 073	12 228	(12 400)	(12 550)	(13 135)	[13 530]
Total WTO	[130 866]	[133 542]	[135 618]	[137 835]	[140 073]	[141 828]	[143 900]	[146 250]	[148 635]	[151 130]
Other Europe	12 903	13 423	14 047	14 029	14 232	14 979	15 470	15 348	15 291	(15 338)
Middle East	28 481	35 076	38 670	37 256	37 017	38 893	[40 695]	(45 990)	[52 350]	[50 000]
South Asia	4 569	5 006	5 681	5 497	5 739	6 220	6 460	6 895	7 620	7 865
Far East (excl. China)	[17 970]	[19 930]	[21 750]	[23 220]	[25 630]	[26 610]	[27 600]	[28 790]	[31 100]	[32 950]
China^b	[35 000]	[36 800]	[37 600]	[36 200]	[40 500]	[52 700]	[42 600]	[36 300]	[37 700]	[35 800]
Oceania	3 976	3 845	3 831	3 848	3 913	4 029	4 270	4 488	4 623	4 868
Africa (excl. Egypt)	9 489	11 416	12 618	12 971	13 198	[13 526]	(13 555)	[13 590]	[13 800]	[14 100]
Central America	1 351	[1 502]	[1 700]	2 173	2 312	2 468	2 484	2 625	2 815	(2 825)
South America	7 998	8 911	9 444	10 170	9 980	9 941	10 230	10 584	[15 745]	(14 745)
World total	**493 865**	**508 310**	**514 195**	**523 539**	**537 569**	**559 345**	**563 542**	**577 978**	**613 500**	**636 790**
Industrial market economies^c	258 406	255 354	249 849	257 175	262 836	267 659	276 931	287 357	304 573	328 944
Non-market economies^c	168 252	173 151	176 341	177 654	184 557	198 868	190 991	187 335	191 486	192 661
Major oil-exporting countries^c	25 282	32 990	36 962	35 508	37 102	37 807	40 221	45 235	51 510	48 745
Rest of the world^c	40 817	45 583	49 698	51 774	51 495	53 375	53 701	56 274	64 011	64 408
With 1981 *per capita* GNP:										
<US $410	6 878	7 225	7 756	7 379	8 004	8 458	8 646	9 132	9 964	10 207
US $410–1 699	11 437	13 792	14 859	15 778	14 064	14 835	13 963	14 781	15 777	16 641
>US $1 700	22 502	24 566	27 083	28 617	29 427	30 082	31 092	32 361	38 270	37 560

Conventions

: :   Information not available or not applicable
( )   Uncertain data
[ ]   Estimates with a high degree of uncertainty

Notes

[a] Spain is not included in NATO but in Other Europe, since military expenditure data according to the NATO definition are not yet available for Spain.

[b] The Chinese series is given in constant prices from 1975.

[c] The economic groupings used here are as follows.

Industrial market economies: Australia, Austria, Belgium, Canada, Denmark, Finland, France, FR Germany, Ireland, Italy, Japan, Luxembourg, Netherlands, New Zealand, Norway, Spain, Sweden, Switzerland, UK and USA.

Non-market economies: Albania, Bulgaria, China, Cuba, Czechoslovakia, German DR, Hungary, North Korea, Mongolia, Poland, Romania and USSR.

4. The trade in major conventional weapons

THOMAS OHLSON and MICHAEL BRZOSKA

Superscript numbers refer to the list of notes and references at the end of the chapter.

I. Introduction

Critics of the international trade in weapons often argue that instead of buying peace and security, arms transfers aggravate economic and social insecurity in the Third World by draining precious foreign exchange, natural resources and human skills from basic needs. The arms trade statistics for the period 1979–83 seem to indicate that this view has made some impact in recent years. The annual values for the past five years show a flattening out—and even some decline—since 1980. However, compared with the previous five-year period, the total volume of transfers of major conventional weapons, measured in constant US dollars, is still about 30 per cent greater.

The new trend is not, however, the result of international detente or drastic revisions in national security policies. The explanation is instead to be found in the serious economic problems currently experienced in the world, particularly in the Third World. Such problems as deep debt or declining oil revenues are the main reasons for the current decrease in the demand for conventional weapons. One of the main trends in the arms trade since World War II is the gradual shift from near-monopoly to increasing competition in arms supply. The first phase, during the 1950s and most of the 1960s, can be described as hegemonic and oligopolistic. The second phase is the commercial oligopolistic period of the 1970s, while the present 'polypolistic' phase is characterized by a growing number of suppliers of weapons of all kinds, and a shift towards a buyer's market. From 1970, economic determinants of arms supply have gained impetus relative to political determinants, and Third World arms producers and newcomers from the west European arms export periphery, such as Spain, have entered the market.

As shown in section III, these developments—in combination with the present world-wide economic crisis—have increased competition among the suppliers. A growing number of arms producers try to sustain an indigenous arms industry while at the same time they face cut-backs in domestic procurement for budgetary reasons, and exports are seen as a solution.

Some of the reasons for, and consequences of, these new developments in the arms trade are described in section V. Section VI reviews some implications for arms transfer control. There is also a discussion in section IV of arms resupply in the Iraq–Iran war.

II. The flow of arms: general trends

Over the period 1979–83 the volume of major weapons delivered has ceased to grow. (All tables and figures in this chapter are based on the SIPRI values of major weapons *actually delivered* in the given year or years; for the valuation method used, see *SIPRI Yearbook 1984*, appendix 7D.) The slow decline after 1980 is statistically valid, even making allowance for further upward revisions as more transfers are identified. The main reason for this decline is budget constraints following from the economic recession.

Of special interest in the arms trade statistics are the positions of the Soviet Union and the United States in the rank order of suppliers. As usual, there is no simple answer to the question of who is the largest arms supplier in the world. Some of the points to be made from comparing Soviet and US arms transfers are the following:

1. The aggregate figures for the five-year period 1979–83 show that the Soviet Union and the United States account for just over a third each of *total* arms exports: 37 per cent for the USSR and 35 per cent for the USA. The Soviet Union is the largest supplier to the Third World, while the United States leads in supply to the industrialized countries.

2. The annual values and shares for the past five years (table 4.1, figure 4.1) show that the United States has been in the lead in total arms exports since 1981, and that its exports to the Third World are increasing. The Soviet lead in the five-year totals is accounted for by that country's large export figures for 1979. The explanation for the general upward trend in US arms exports is the expansive arms export policy pursued by the Reagan Administration.

3. A large share of the total arms exports of both countries is directed to the Third World: 69 per cent for the USSR and 50 per cent for the USA. The USA, however, has about twice as many recipients in the Third World and it has granted about five times as many production licences. This shows that countries that receive weapons from the Soviet Union are getting them in very large numbers. Syria is currently the obvious case in point. The USA's smaller proportion going to the Third World is explained by the large number of weapons produced under US licence by west European and Japanese arms manufacturers.

Table 4.1. The largest major-weapon exporting countries: the values and respective shares for 1979–83

Figures are SIPRI trend indicator values, as expressed in US $ million, at constant (1975) prices; shares in percentages. Figures may not add up to totals due to rounding.

Country	1979	1980	1981	1982	1983	1979–83	Per cent of total exports to Third World, 1979–83
USSR	6 921	6 486	4 962	4 736	4 070	27 174	
	46.1	42.4	33.8	32.7	30.3	37.2	69.1
USA	3 901	5 512	5 519	5 704	5 264	25 900	
	26.0	36.0	37.6	39.3	39.1	35.5	50.3
France	1 633	1 194	1 292	1 227	1 192	6 539	
	10.9	7.8	8.8	8.5	8.9	9.0	79.3
UK	446	515	601	743	527	2 831	
	3.0	3.4	4.1	5.1	3.9	3.9	77.3
Italy	483	377	526	579	458	2 424	
	3.2	2.5	3.6	4.0	3.4	3.3	93.3
FR Germany	468	295	403	284	750	2 201	
	3.1	1.9	2.7	2.0	5.6	3.0	55.4
Third World	349	271	396	438	332	1 785	
	2.3	1.8	2.7	3.0	2.5	2.4	97.3
Others	810	660	989	792	856	4 106	
	5.4	4.3	6.7	5.5	6.4	5.6	65.4
Total	15 011	15 310	14 688	14 503	13 449	72 960	

Figure 4.1. The Soviet and US shares of world exports of major weapons: total exports and exports to the Third World, 1979–83

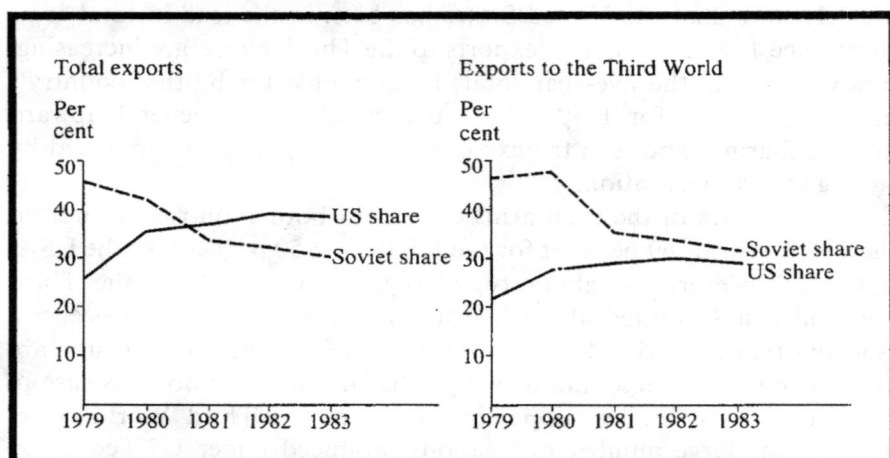

Figure 4.2. Percentage shares of imports of major weapons by the Third World: by region, 1964–83

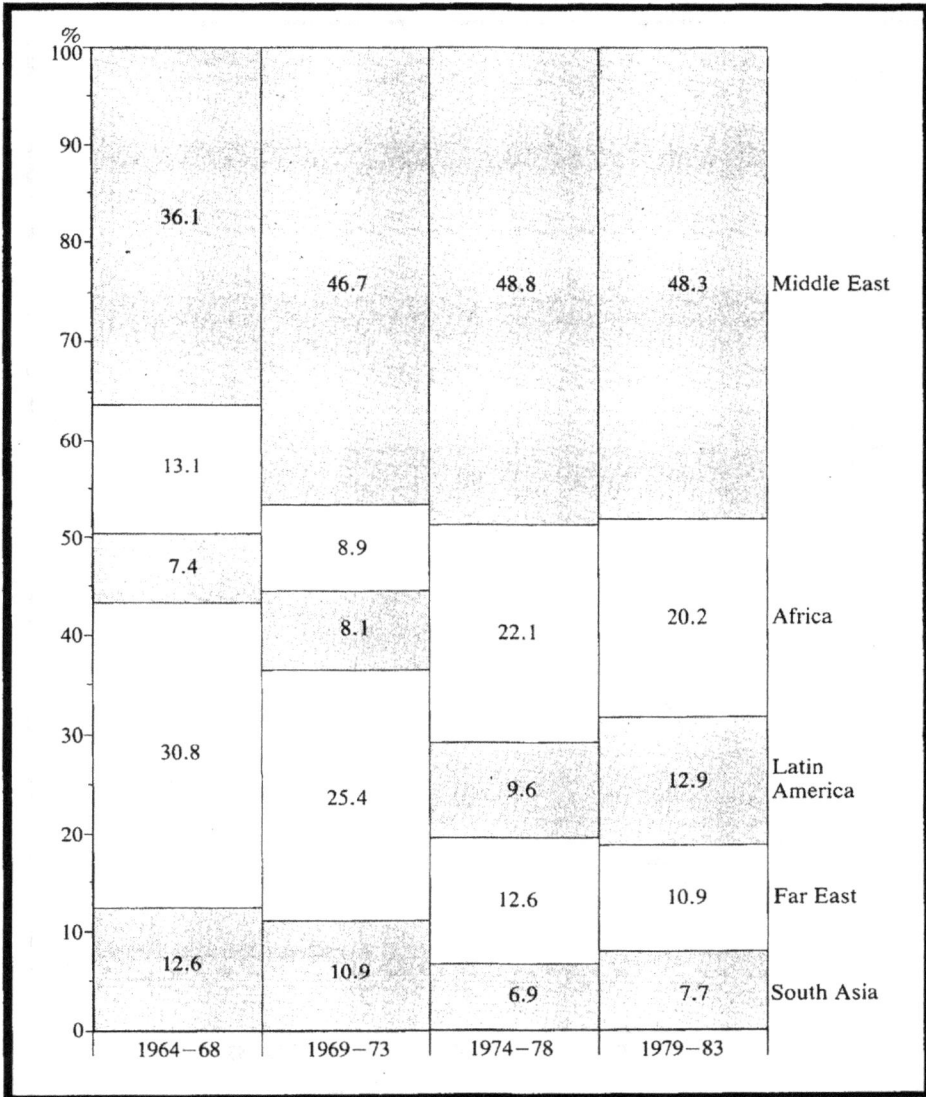

% 100				
90				
80	36.1			
		46.7	48.8	48.3	Middle East
70				
60	13.1			
50	7.4	8.9		
40		8.1	22.1	20.2	Africa
30	30.8			
		25.4	9.6	12.9	Latin America
20				
			12.6	10.9	Far East
10	12.6	10.9		
			6.9	7.7	South Asia
0	1964–68	1969–73	1974–78	1979–83	

4. The long-term trends in arms exports to the Third World are shown in figure 4.3. The Soviet Union has—in terms of consecutive five-year totals and except for the period 1974–78—been the largest arms exporter to the Third World for the past 20 years.

Several other notable facts show up in the statistics.

1. About 65 per cent of the total arms flow during 1979–83 consists of imports by the Third World. The rate of growth of this share, however, is

Figure 4.3. Percentage shares of exports of major weapons to the Third World regions listed in figure 4.2: by supplier, 1964–83

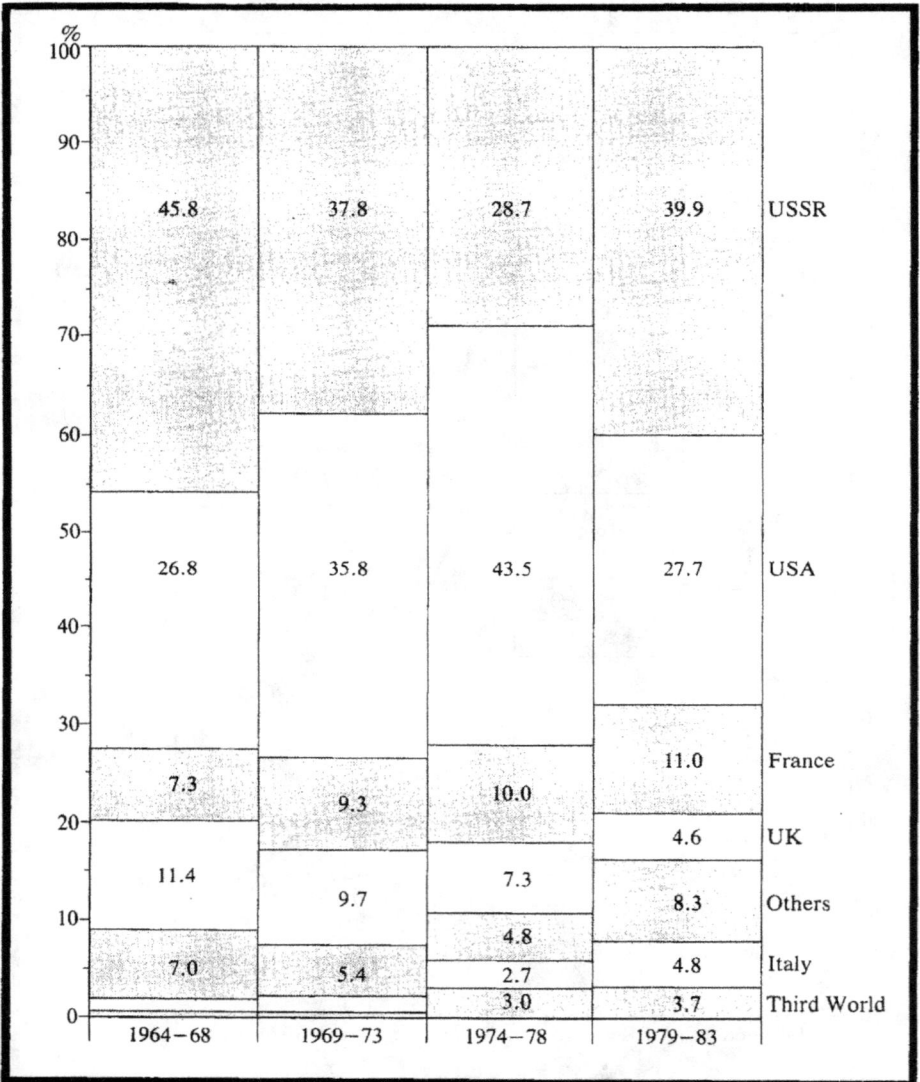

	1964–68	1969–73	1974–78	1979–83	
USSR	45.8	37.8	28.7	39.9	
USA	26.8	35.8	43.5	27.7	
France	7.3	9.3	10.0	11.0	
UK				4.6	
Others	11.4	9.7	7.3	8.3	
			4.8		
Italy	7.0	5.4	2.7	4.8	
Third World			3.0	3.7	

slowing down. From 1964–68 to 1969–73, the volume almost doubled; and it more than doubled in the next period, 1974–78. But from then to the most recent period, 1979–83, the increase was only 20 per cent.

2. The Middle East still accounts for almost 50 per cent of all Third World arms imports. The Latin American share is rising, while African arms imports are decreasing slightly (figure 4.2).

3. The five highest-ranking Third World arms importing countries—Syria, Libya, Iraq, Egypt and Saudi Arabia—alone account for about

94

Table 4.2. Rank order of the 20 largest Third World major-weapon importing countries, 1979–83

Percentages are based on SIPRI trend indicator values, as expressed in US $ million, at constant (1975) prices.

Importing country	Percentage of total Third World imports	Importing country	Percentage of total Third World imports
1. Syria	*11.8*	11. Algeria	*2.2*
2. Libya	*9.2*	12. Morocco	*2.2*
3. Iraq	*8.9*	13. Viet Nam	*2.0*
4. Egypt	*7.7*	14. Korea, South	*1.8*
5. Saudi Arabia	*7.0*	15. Peru	*1.8*
6. India	*5.5*	16. Taiwan	*1.8*
7. Israel	*4.7*	17. Indonesia	*1.7*
8. Cuba	*2.8*	18. Jordan	*1.5*
9. Argentina	*2.8*	19. Pakistan	*1.3*
10. Yemen, South	*2.2*	20. Kuwait	*1.2*
		Others	*19.9*
		Total	*100.0*
		Total value	**47 097**

45 per cent of all Third World arms imports (table 4.2).

4. FR Germany increased its arms exports drastically in 1983, mostly due to warship deliveries to Latin America. Approximately 18 per cent of West German arms exports during 1979–83 was accounted for by weapons produced under licence from FR Germany—no other supplier exceeds 10 per cent.

5. The Third World countries taken together are slowly increasing their share of total arms exports, and they now account for 3.7 per cent of Third World imports.

6. Spain has increased its arms exports considerably over the past five years. Previously negligible as an arms exporter, Spain accounted for 3.8 per cent of arms exports to the Third World in 1983.

III. The suppliers

The Soviet Union

Soviet arms exports are the most important, if not the only powerful, instrument of Soviet policy in the Third World. But the issues of how and why the arms trade is used are hotly debated issues. Those issues can only be inferred from known facts because of the dearth of information from the Soviet Union. Furthermore, there is disagreement about what facts are known.

US information on Soviet arms trade

In the report on Soviet arms exports in *SIPRI Yearbook 1983* it was claimed that Soviet arms exports are guided by a mixture of policy aims, among which the commercial has become more prominent.[1]

In the United States, many subscribe to what might be labelled 'the master plan' view. In the words of a writer in the *Armed Forces Journal International*:

Unlike the West, the USSR does not export major amounts of arms to a wide range of buyers. The USSR heavily concentrates its exports and advisory efforts on a few key countries. While the end result often seems to further Third World extremism or to allow Third World nations to exploit the divisions between East and West, it is clear that the USSR is trying to create client states that will either serve Soviet interests or serve the purpose of exacerbating regional conflicts and rivalries which will damage the West.[2]

If indeed this has been the aim of Soviet policy in the Third World, the results have been poor. In some cases, the buyers have even behaved contrary to Soviet interests; in others, Soviet interests have shifted. To take four examples—the first four countries in the Third World with which the Soviet Union had 20-year treaties: Egypt (treaty signed in 1971) turned to the USA as its main supplier; India (1971) diversified its arms supplies in the late 1970s and is a strong proponent of non-alignment; Iraq (1972) did not receive weapons in the first months of its war with Iran and now is only reluctantly supplied; and Somalia (1972) turned to the West when the Soviet Union did not support its war efforts against Ethiopia. On the other hand, Soviet relations with Afghanistan, Angola, the Congo, Ethiopia, Mozambique, South Yemen, Syria and Viet Nam— countries with which 20-year treaties of friendship were signed between 1976 and 1981—are better, though not entirely smooth.

This view of an aggressive Soviet arms export policy is supported by figures the US government presents. In general, two types of figure are given: numbers of weapon systems and US dollar values for exports to individual countries or regions. In both types of data the Soviet Union emerges as the foremost supplier to the Third World.

These data have drawbacks. The prices put by the USA on Soviet weapon systems are not published. They seem to be derived from estimates of the 'use value' of weapon systems. The absolute numbers of weapon systems are not a very good measure: they do not take account of the diverse quality, age, level of sophistication, and so on of the weapons transferred.

There is also a problem with the reliability of these figures. An example is given in table 4.3.

Data from various US government sources are compared in columns 1 and 2, as well as column 6 (which is constructed from columns 4 and 5)

Table 4.3. US estimates of Soviet deliveries of major weapons, 1977–82

Weapon	1977–82 (1)	1977–81 (2)	1982? (3)= (1)−(2)	1978–82 (4)	1977 (5)	1977–82? (6)= (4)+(5)	1977–81 (7)=(2)	1982? (8)= (6)−(7)	5-year average 1978–82 (9)= (4)÷5
Tanks/SPGs	7 065	7 050	15	6 530	1 430	7 960	7 050	910	1 306
APCs and ACs	8 660	8 640	20	8 070	1 855	9 925	8 640	1 285	1 614
Artillery (100-mm and over)	9 590	8 450	1 140	7 800	2 590	10 390	8 450	1 940	1 560
Major surface combatants	32	32	0	32	4	36	32	4	6
Minor surface combatants	126	128	−2	127	16	143	128	15	25
Submarines	6	6	0	7	0	7	6	1	1
Supersonic combat aircraft	2 235	2 230	5	2 150	440	2 590	2 230	360	430
Subsonic combat aircraft	290	290	0	216	100	316	290	26	43
Helicopters	910	915	−5	1 030	70	1 100	915	185	206
Other military aircraft	345	345	0	340	45	385	345	40	68
Surface-to-air missiles	11 680	11 670	10	6 530	6 015	12 545	11 670	875	1 306

Sources:
Column 1: US Department of Defense, *Soviet Military Power*, 2nd ed. (US Government Printing Office, Washington, D.C., 1983), p. 13.
Column 2: Statement of Lt. General A. Williams, Director, Defense Intelligence Agency, before the Subcommittee on International Trade, Finance and Security Economics of the Joint Economic Committee, US Congress, Washington, D.C., June 29, 1982, p. 20.
Column 4: Statement of Major General Schuyler Bissell, Deputy Director, Defense Intelligence Agency, before the Subcommittee on International Trade, Finance and Security Economics of the Joint Economic Committee, US Congress, Washington, D.C., June 28, 1983, p. 15.
Column 5: US Department of State, *Conventional Arms Transfers to the Third World, 1972–81*, Special Report No. 102, August 1982, p. 13.

and column 7 (identical to column 2). Both resulting columns 3 and 8 should give figures for 1982. There are large discrepancies between these two columns, column 3 showing up as especially unreliable. The numbers in columns 3 and 8 are in general below the figures for the 5-year average 1978–82. The exception is artillery pieces with calibres of 100 mm or more.

There may be several explanations. One is that the numbers in the sources cited cannot and are not intended to be taken precisely. A second explanation is that the estimates for Soviet deliveries in 1977–81 have recently been revised downwards. This would be contrary to usual practice, since more transfers are normally identified over time. A third explanation is that the Soviet deliveries indeed declined in 1982, although it is improbable that they declined to the extent suggested by column 3 of table 4.3.

Soviet arms export policy

The SIPRI estimates of Soviet arms exports indicate a slight downward trend since 1980, both for total exports and for exports to Third World regions, albeit from a very high level (see *SIPRI Yearbook 1984*). Since 1979 there has also been a reduction in the number of new arms transfer agreements (see figure 4.4).[3] This is in line with the delivery data since there is a time lag between order and delivery dates. Figure 4.4 also shows another development: the number of agreements covering the transfer of new weapons has diminished while the number of orders for second-hand weapons has remained stable. Soviet deliveries do not always consist of new equipment; substantial numbers of ships, aircraft and armoured vehicles supplied are old. This of course adds to the problems of interpreting US data on numbers delivered; both old and new equipment are added together.

Both US and SIPRI statistics indicate certain changes in Soviet arms export policy after 1979. Indications come not only from numbers for orders and deliveries but also from cases of countries that were traditional Soviet clients but which the Soviet Union became reluctant to supply. The Soviet Union has shown some restraint in the Iraq–Iran war. Angola and Mozambique are not able to defend their borders or even large parts of their territories against South African raids. Libya's attempt to influence events in Chad was not wholeheartedly supported by Soviet deliveries (though this probably was not necessary given the very large amounts of Soviet weapons already in Libyan hands).

It is unclear why Soviet arms exports declined during 1980–83. One general reason is the economic crisis in most recipient countries. The Soviet Union also has economic problems that might have contributed to a less generous attitude towards military assistance through subsidized arms supplies. One observer of Soviet arms export policy has noted:

Figure 4.4. Soviet arms trade agreements: the distribution of new, refurbished and second-hand weapons, 1976–82

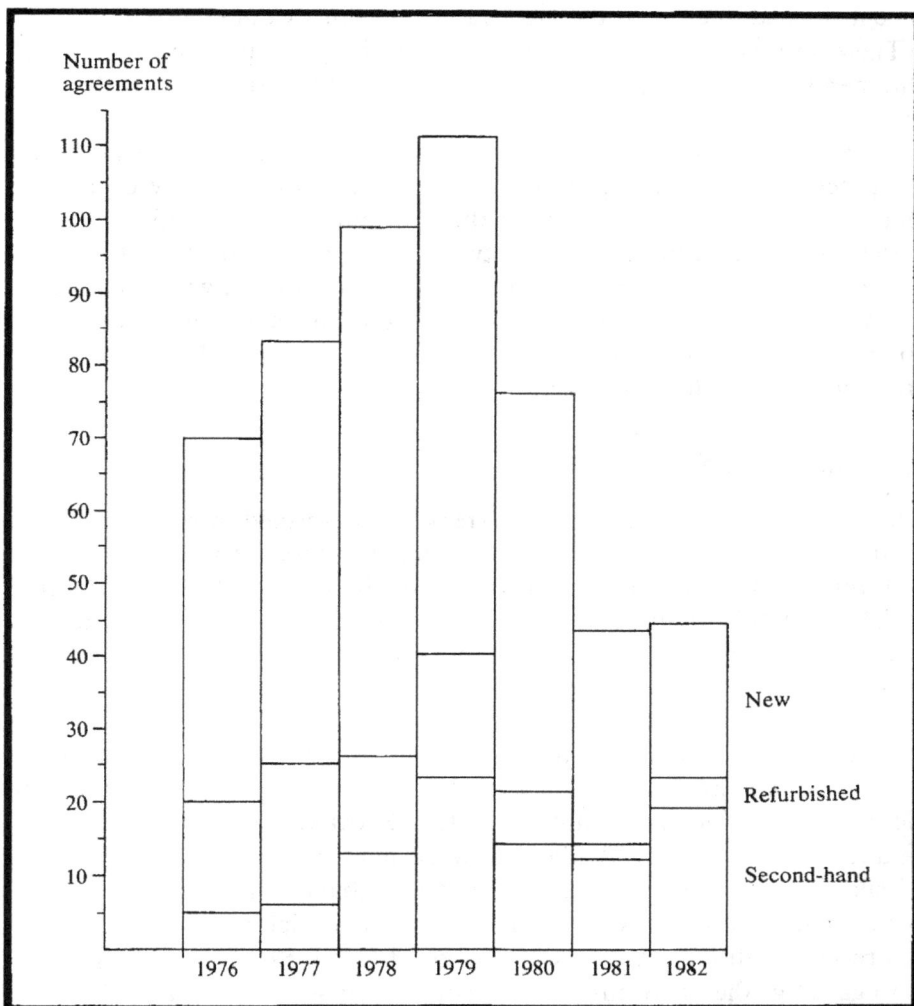

"It has also grown clear in recent years that Moscow's resolute arms aid policy has resulted in unsuspected follow-up costs." He goes on to conclude: "So it is hardly surprising that the Soviet leaders have decided to stop for breath for a while to consolidate what has already been achieved."[4]

Several political circumstances also enter into the assessment. The invasion of Afghanistan gave the Soviet Union a militaristic image throughout the Third World. The Soviet Union may also be afraid of direct clashes with a more aggressive USA. Finally, the USSR might have thought in terms of 'linkage' between restraint on their side in the Third

World and success in negotiations on arms control. If this were true, then changes in Soviet arms transfer policy could have been expected once it seemed likely that the Geneva negotiations would fail.

There are signs that the Soviet attitude has begun to change again. Shipments to Libya have resumed. Syria has received the SS-21 surface-to-surface missile, a powerful weapon even with a conventional warhead. The Soviet Union has also upgraded Syrian air defence and ground forces equipment. The Syrian losses in 1982 in the Lebanon war have been more than made good by the delivery of the SA-5 missile, T-72 tank and SS-21 missile. It is also reported that between 5 000 and 7 000 Soviet military advisers were sent to Syria to man many of these modern weapon systems.

Another case in point is India. In 1983 the Soviet Union succeeded in obtaining Indian consent to a major offer of Soviet tanks, aircraft and production technology (see section IV).

The United States

US arms transfer policy has been extensively described in previous SIPRI Yearbooks.[5] The policy declares that arms transfers are a key instrument of foreign policy: potential arms sales are judged by their contribution to US security. Compared to 1981, public concern about arms sales has decreased: other issues were predominant during 1983. Hence, applications of the arms transfer policy, in the form of deliveries and new contracts, quietly proceeded.

Deliveries of F-16 aircraft to Pakistan and Venezuela started during the year, and several new contracts were signed: FR Germany and the Netherlands decided to acquire the Patriot SAM system, Israel is receiving an additional 75 F-16s, Thailand ordered fighter aircraft, helicopters and missile-armed corvettes, Saudi Arabia and Lebanon ordered large quantities of main battle tanks and other armoured vehicles, and South Korea will receive additional batches of Improved Hawk SAMs.

Regarding the Taiwan–China issue (discussed in *SIPRI Yearbook 1983*),[6] in 1983 the United States delivered 66 refurbished F-104G Starfighter aircraft and offered Taiwan $530 million worth of missiles, armoured vehicles, tank conversion kits and spare parts. China's reaction to these agreements was surprisingly mild: Chinese Prime Minister Zhao Ziyang said in early January 1984 that China would not demand a halt to US arms transfers to Taiwan, even though he considered the recent US–Taiwanese agreements a violation of the 1982 US–Chinese communiqué which requires the United States to reduce the quantity and quality of weapons sold to Taiwan.[7] These deliveries are the main obstacle to improved relations between the USA and China, but China seems willing to put this issue aside. This should, in part, be seen in the light of the agreements made during Defense Secretary Weinberger's visit to China in September 1983, covering the transfer of US military and dual-use technology to China. US technology is vital to China's industrial modernization programme.

Another notable development is increasing US willingness to supply sophisticated surveillance and battle management aircraft. These aircraft represent a significant addition to the military capabilities of the recipient, as demonstrated by the Israeli E-2C Hawkeyes used in 1982 in the Lebanon war. The Hawkeyes have also been ordered by Egypt and Singapore, and other Third World countries are currently negotiating for purchases. Five E-3A Sentry AWACS aircraft were sold to Saudi Arabia in 1981. E-3As have also been deployed by the USA to survey wars, for example in Sudan (the Chad civil war with Libyan involvement) and in Saudi Arabia (the Iraq–Iran war). Some of the information gained was in both cases shared with the host country.

Consequently, arms transfers remain a key foreign policy instrument. However, others—notably military aid and the direct use of US military force—are becoming increasingly important. Military aid[8] is granted to countries considered of vital strategic or political importance to the USA, and which lack the funds to pay for what they want. The FY 1984 Foreign Military Sales (FMS) request was for $5.4 billion, of which $1 billion in forgiven credits to Egypt and Israel. This compares to total FMS financing of $2.8 billion for 1981 and $4.0 billion for 1982. Israel and Egypt will account for approximately 50 per cent of total US military assistance during 1983–84.[9] One specific reason for granting military aid is to obtain base rights in exchange—for example, in Kenya, Morocco, Oman, the Philippines and Somalia. Another reason is to support countries with a hostile Soviet-armed neighbour—for example Chad, Egypt and Sudan.

In 1983 the United States used military force in Grenada and Lebanon. The threat of similar actions is felt throughout Central America. US advisers were present in Chad during the summer of 1983. This new attitude was underlined by Secretary Weinberger in February 1983: "Our plans and programs must, therefore, focus on strengthening our ability to respond effectively, with military force if necessary, in several strategically important areas, and in circumstances ranging from small-scale incidents to major military operations".[10]

France

French arms exports were analysed in *SIPRI Yearbook 1983*.[11] It was argued that sales of arms and military technology are critical for the French economy and that the export dependency of the French arms industry is steadily increasing. The percentage of arms sales in relation to French defence procurement and arms exports taken together increased from 14.8 per cent in 1970 to 38.1 per cent in 1980 and to 42.5 per cent in 1982.[12] For many of the key companies, such as SNIAS–Aérospatiale, Dassault–Bréguet and Thomson–CSF, it is well above 50 per cent. France now relies more than ever on arms exports in order to sustain employment and output, lower the price of equipment for its own forces, reduce the budget deficit and help to pay for large oil imports.

During its three years in power the Socialist government has not—in spite of election rhetoric—taken any steps to reduce arms exports. On the contrary, it has found it necessary to try to expand them. The political justification for this economic pragmatism is the view that arms clients should have the possibility of choosing suppliers who do not demand political or other commitments in exchange for arms sales, as the United States and the Soviet Union do. The only countries currently embargoed from French arms sales are Chile and South Africa. Other countries to which France is currently reluctant to supply weapons are Iran, Libya and Nicaragua.

The value of French arms export contracts, as reported and measured by the French government in current francs, amounted to 33.8 billion francs in 1981. This figure rose to 41.6 billion francs in 1982, largely due to the sale of Mirage 2000 fighters to Egypt and India and large orders for a variety of weapons from Iraq. The estimated figure for 1983 is about 32 billion francs,[13] with sales of the Mirage 2000 to Peru and the United Arab Emirates, and Kuwaiti orders for AS-332 Super Puma helicopters armed with AM-39 Exocet anti-ship missiles and for a sophisticated radar air defence system. Egypt added several follow-on contracts to its earlier orders for Mirage and Alpha Jet aircraft, and continued its purchases of French arms production technology—in December a production licence for the Super Puma helicopter was acquired.

The drop in order value in 1983 has seriously worried the French government and the almost exclusively state-owned arms industry. Marc Cauchie, director of export sales for the French government's General Armaments Agency, described the decreasing global demand for weapons as a "worldwide crisis".[14]

The French government is therefore looking for new and improved ways to promote arms exports: offices will be set up to handle arms sales to specific regions or countries; naval equipment—now accounting for approximately 10 per cent of French arms exports—will be subject to special marketing efforts; a diversification of recipients will be sought—currently the vast majority of arms sales are to the Middle East; and the French arms industry will be urged to seek long-term commitments through technology transfer programmes rather than outright weapon sales.

The magnitude of the arms trade in the future will largely depend on global economic developments. France seems to be in a favourable position relative to its competitor suppliers for a number of reasons. First, it has, and will continue to have, most of its arms clients in the Middle East. Saudi Arabia, Iraq, Egypt and the smaller Gulf states are among its principal customers. It can be assumed that the fall in oil revenues will not reduce their defence spending drastically. Feelings of insecurity, now fuelled also by the Iraq–Iran war and the Syrian–Israeli confrontation in Lebanon, will keep demand high. Second, the French arms industry offers a wide range of equipment, both sophisticated high-technology weapons and cheaper and more rugged weapons for poorer clients. Third, with troops in Chad and Lebanon, and large quantities of weapons on the Iraqi side against Iran, and in the recent Falklands/Malvinas conflict, France is currently very active on the international scene. This results in a long list of battle-proven weapons, and it contributes to France's reputation as a reliable arms supplier. Fourth, among the industrialized arms-producing countries, France is undoubtedly among those most ready to furnish its clients with arms production technology. Finally, many Third World countries opt for reduced dependence on the two major powers and instead try to seek other sources for their weapons.

A case in point is the Saudi decision in January 1984 to place an order with France worth 35–40 billion francs.[15] This contract covers the development and delivery of ground radars and Shahine missile batteries for a low-level air defence and is the largest weapon contract from a foreign buyer ever received by France. It alone surpasses the total order value for French arms during 1983. The contract can be seen as a follow-on to the so-called Sawari deal from 1980, which covered naval equipment, and it is an example of the attempts of the recipients to acquire weapons from several suppliers. This French air defence system will operate jointly with the AWACS aircraft and their related ground radar stations. The latter equipment, which will provide high-altitude reconnaissance, is part of the so-called AWACS deal between the USA and Saudi Arabia, finalized in 1981.

The United Kingdom

After a low point in 1980, many British arms producers were able to increase their arms exports to the Third World in both 1981 and 1982. Deliveries dropped again in 1983, but this seems to be due to the timing of the fulfilment of orders and not a result of decreasing demand for British arms. 1983 was a very successful year for the British industry, with many substantial orders for Jaguar and Hawk aircraft, Sea King helicopters, Chieftain and Vickers Mk-3 tanks, missiles and ships. British arms exports will most probably rise substantially in the future. The official figures already show this trend: they more than doubled between 1979 and 1982.[16]

Britain had for some time after World War II been the second largest major weapon exporter until it was surpassed by the Soviet Union in 1955 and by France in 1975. Since then, the level of British sales has been equalled by Italian exports of major weapons.

There were basically four reasons for this loss of importance: (a) the general reduction in Britain's importance in world politics, including decolonization; (b) the shrinking of Britain's military industrial base due partly to cuts in the growth of military expenditures; (c) a concentration on products for the British armed forces, with little R&D for export products; and (d) restrictions on arms transfers, especially in the explosive growth phase of the arms market in the 1970s, when for instance an embargo was invoked against arms sales to Chile, a traditional British customer. The situation has changed under the Conservative government. Almost immediately after coming to power it adopted a new approach, outlined in Prime Minister Thatcher's speech at the opening of the Farnborough Air Show in 1980. Today the Minister of State for Defence Procurement, Geoffrey Pattie, described as the "supersalesman"[17] of British arms, sees his brief as encompassing defence sales as well as procurement. Within the government an enlarged Defence Sales Organization (DSO) helps to channel requests from foreign governments to companies, to advertise British products in magazines, exhibitions and the annual British Defence Equipment Catalogue, and to acquire export permits. The primary body to deal with export licencing is the Defence Secretariat 13 in the British Ministry of Defence (MoD). It has two basic interests: to safeguard sensitive technology and to promote exports.[18] A complicated weighting system of both products and countries has been introduced to ensure that the first aim is reached, so that attention can be devoted to the second.[19] Of the approximately 6 000–7 000 licence applications received per year, fewer than 3 per cent are formally refused, while it was previously as much as 7 per cent.

The type of weapons offered has also changed. First, the British arms industry has regained a strong technological position. It has a lead among European companies in military electronics, as well as in fields of special metallurgy, aircraft and aircraft engine design and production. A number of weapon systems have even been sold to the United States, a very protected market, among them Rapier missiles and Hawk trainer aircraft.

Second, and more important for Third World buyers, weapons are now more tailored to the demands of potential customers. Minister Pattie has said that one of his jobs is persuading the armed services to think in terms of foreign sales.[20] There are stripped-down versions of some weapon systems, such as the Hawk and Jaguar aircraft, and products exclusively for export, such as the Vickers Mk–3 MBT.

Finally, a most convincing argument in relevant circles is that British arms are 'battle-proven'. The Falklands/Malvinas campaign has been a powerful sales promoter; even before that, increased British military activity had an effect. One of the best British customers is Oman which has bought Jaguar aircraft, ships, missiles and now also the Chieftain tank. The UK actively supported Oman in the guerrilla war of the 1970s.

The policy of increased arms exports is not without costs. The loss of British lives, partly due to the use of British-built arms by Argentina in the Falklands/Malvinas war, was much discussed. The British government put pressure on other governments not to sell arms to Argentina; at the same time it honoured contracts of British sub-contractors for parts of exactly the same systems, for instance electronics for the French-built Exocet missile and engines for the German-built Meko frigate.[21]

On political grounds, the cases of Chile, Indonesia and South Africa are relevant. A second County Class missile destroyer will be supplied to Chile and possibly also Jaguar aircraft, in spite of internal opposition in Chile and opposition also from the United States.[22] Indonesia received Hawk ground attack aircraft, although it was pointed out that they might be used for attacks against opponent forces in East Timor.[23] Fixed radars were exported to South Africa. The government denied that this was a violation of the UN arms embargo. Outside observers suggested that the radars will have a military role. In a handbook on weapon systems, the Marconi S247 radar is only described vaguely, since "information relating to these radars is still largely subject to security restriction".[24]

Finally, the extent of the economic contribution of British arms exports is doubtful. At least in the past, the heavy financial burden of military research and development expenditure was not reduced through arms exports.[25] It is not proven that military R&D, which is increasingly geared towards arms exports, yields much civilian spin-off. Even in the electronics industry, where one might assume that such spin-off is important, it is in fact very limited.[26]

In conclusion, however, it is basically the economic motive that is driving Britain's 'supersalesman' and others in the arms industry to increase their promotion efforts. About 3 per cent of British exports in 1983 were arms exports. It is supplemented, in the UK as well as in other countries, by an interest in keeping a broad industrial arms production base. In Britain this will probably lead to increased pressure to export in the near future, when the decision to buy Trident submarines eats into the procurement budget for conventional weapons, thereby reducing home orders for these weapon systems.

Italy

Italian arms producers feel the general contraction of the arms market perhaps more than other suppliers of weapons. Italian arms production is heavily dependent on exports, which go predominantly to the Third World (see table 4.1). The rapid growth of Italian arms exports seems to have come to a halt. There have been only a few new orders in 1983, among them MB-339A jet trainers by Nigeria, S-211 aircraft by Singapore, Aspide anti-aircraft missiles by Egypt and Thailand, and ship orders by Nigeria and Venezuela—none of the size of the Iraqi order for Lupo and Wadi Class ships in 1980.

This presents a serious problem for the arms industry. A large production capacity was built up in the 1970s and early 1980s. The figure for employment in the military industry (excluding sub-contractors) has more than doubled in this period and now stands at over 80 000.[27] The growth rate was higher than for any other sector of Italian manufacturing in the 1970s.[28] Export dependence of the arms industry has increased to over 70 per cent, from 40 per cent in the early 1970s.[29] Arms exports are an important foreign exchange earner, accounting for about 8 per cent of all exports of engineering goods in 1982.[30]

Weapon transfers are also an important source of R&D funds for the Italian arms industry. Compared to other NATO countries, the amount of military R&D funds provided by the government is very small. But company money, in many cases coming from the investment funds of the state-owned holdings owning most major arms-producing companies, has been provided instead. These quasi-private R&D expenditures mainly have to be recovered through exports.

Data on the economic aspects of Italian arms production and exports are tentative, as the Italian government is reluctant to disclose information. The data it does release tend to overstate the importance of arms exports. For instance, in the Italian White Book on Defence of 1977 (the only one published so far) a figure of 2 300 million lire is given for "business conducted" in 1975 in the section on arms exports.[31] Independent estimates put actual Italian arms exports for that year at around one-sixth of that sum.[32]

Several proposals for more openness and stricter control of arms sales have recently been put forward in the National Assembly. So far, the majority of legislators seems to be content with present export policy, often described as a 'non-policy'. It is based on a ministerial decree, which has not been disclosed to the members of the Assembly.[33]

The drop in orders is not a consequence of any change in the Italian government's approach to arms transfer control. The Iraq–Iran war has been "a god-send for the Italian defense industry".[34] Italian companies

106

have supplied Iraq with a large array of small arms and ammunition and Iran with ordnance as well. So other explanations must be sought. One factor is the phase of the production cycle in which many Italian arms companies currently find themselves. New products are in the development stage, such as the joint Aeritalia/Aermacchi/Embraer (Brazil) project for a new light attack aircraft called AMX and Agusta's A-129 Mangusta attack helicopter. Another point relates to the dependence on foreign technology that has characterized Italian arms production in the past. US companies granted a large number of licences for the production of aeroplanes, jet engines, armoured vehicles and components to Italian companies. FR Germany granted a licence to produce the Leopard 1 tank and its derivatives. Italian companies now regard the capability to produce weapons designed indigenously as technologically preferable. With increased competition, it is no longer easy for Italian arms companies to obtain licences for weapons that they want to export. The potential licencers are also interested in export earnings.

The move towards 'italianization' of production was in part a reaction to past experiences. The United States has on several occasions tried to pressure the Italian government not to allow the sale of arms, for instance in the cases of G-222 transport aircraft to Libya, CH-47C Boeing helicopters to Iran and Lupo Class frigates to Iraq. The instrument used was a veto on parts produced in the USA. The West German government also intervened when Oto Melara tried to export a licence-produced version of the Leopard 1, called the 'Lion'. The Italian manufacturers circumvented these pressures in most cases, for instance, when they installed Rolls Royce instead of General Electric engines on the G-222, or when they redesigned the Lion to the very similar looking OF-40. Still, prospective buyers could not rely on Italian suppliers as they did in the past. The result of the move towards 'italianization' has also been that potential customers are no longer certain that they will get proven, reliable technology; and the original designers of 'first-rank' technology are themselves willing to supply.

At the other end of the spectrum, concerning the 'cheap and rugged' weapon systems, Italian arms producers are feeling increased competition from the Third World and countries of the European arms export periphery. Countries like Brazil have taken Italy's place as a newcomer, but with proven designs. Arms producers in the UK, France and other countries are also trying to produce simplified versions of their more expensive products. The specific position of Italian arms production between the core and the periphery of world-wide arms production currently does not seem to attract the commercial success that the industry needs.

FR Germany

West German arms export policy, described at some length in *SIPRI Yearbook 1983*, has continued to be the focal point of political party and general public interest.[35] Discussions have focused on two issues: (*a*) the 'guidelines' on export policy for war materials and weapon-related materials; and (*b*) the sale of arms to Saudi Arabia.

Several politicians from the ruling coalition have tried to persuade the conservative/liberal (CDU/FDP) government to change the 1982 guidelines devised by the social democratic/liberal coalition government. These critics want to give a more political role to arms exports. They share this view with the arms industry, which has been asking for a relaxation of export regulations since the early 1970s. But there are currently no signs that the government intends to change the guidelines. Strong forces within the CDU as well as the FDP are working against expanding arms exports to the Third World. The Minister of State in the Foreign Office, Alois Mertes, a proponent of a restrictive policy, wrote that all West German governments have seen arms exports in the light of securing peace. This has always been done "through restricting arms exports and active pressure for a fair and controlled reduction of world-wide arms exports".[36]

However, West German arms exports have risen steadily throughout the 1970s and the early 1980s. One of the main reasons is that the guidelines do not regulate all weapon transfers. Thus Iraq could receive Bo-105 helicopters (assembled in Spain) and tank transporters, while Iran could order the TAM, a German-designed tank built in Argentina but powered by an engine delivered from FR Germany.

The guidelines also state that West German participation in arms co-production projects is more important than export control. This, in fact, has been the policy since 1971. In the SIPRI arms trade statistics, exports are counted as the exports of the final country from which the weapon is exported. If exports are valued according to the project share of the countries participating in co-production, the arms export values of FR Germany increase (see table 4.4). Most of the weapons for which FR Germany is a co-production partner are not exported directly from FR Germany. Compared with the UK or France, FR Germany still has more restrictive export regulations; but they do not apply to most co-produced weapon systems (see *SIPRI Yearbook 1984*, chapter 5). In 1983, new co-production agreements were signed: for the PAH-2 anti-tank helicopter programme in conjunction with France and the programme to build a fighter aircraft together with France, Italy, Spain and the UK.

The political issues surrounding arms transfer decisions were discussed intensely in connection with the possible sale of armoured vehicles to Saudi Arabia. The Saudi government has for more than a decade expressed

Table 4.4. West German exports of major weapons: with and without sales of co-produced items, 1979-83

Figures are in US $ million, at constant (1975) prices.

	1979	1980	1981	1982	1983
To all regions					
Direct exports only	468	295	403	284	750
Co-produced items only[a]	51	58	59	39	47
Export including co-production	519	353	462	323	797
To Third World regions					
Direct exports only	229	137	262	122	470
Co-produced items only[a]	22	40	51	32	40
Export including co-production	251	177	313	154	510

[a] Co-produced items are valued according to the West German project share.

interest in buying West German tanks. Chancellor Kohl told the Saudi government during his visit in October 1983 that FR Germany would not supply the Leopard 2 tank but was prepared to discuss the sale of other arms. This was a reference to the Roland and Gepard AAVs as well as the Marder MICV, which the government has classified as defensive weapons. The sale to Saudi Arabia would be a change in West German arms export policy, as FR Germany has so far not directly supplied these vehicles to armed forces in the Third World. Requests from several countries have been turned down. Negotiations for armoured vehicles for Saudi Arabia have led to strong pressure from the Israeli government. A trade-off with Israel (one suggestion has been to supply the Israeli armed forces with the Rheinmetall 120-mm smooth-bore gun) might seem tempting to the West German government but seems not to have been negotiated when Chancellor Kohl visited Israel in January 1984. The Israeli government instead repeated its strong opposition to the Saudi sale, stressing Germany's historical obligations. Kohl stated upon his return that the decision would be made in Bonn, taking Israeli, Saudi and West German interests into account.

In 1983 the West German arms industry finalized three large export contracts with industrialized countries: the sale of six Type 210 submarines (with options on two more) to Norway, four Meko 200 frigates to Turkey and 420 Leopard 2 tanks to Switzerland. These deals are important as the production of Leopard 2s, Tornado MRCAs and Bremen Class frigates—the major projects for the West German armed forces—is slowly being scaled down. The real test of whether the new government will maintain or give up the few restrictions that are still in effect has yet to come. Pressure from the arms industry will build up as capacity utilization decreases.[37]

IV. Some recipient perspectives

The Iraq–Iran war and the arms trade

The Iraq–Iran war, now in its fourth year, has developed into a military and diplomatic stalemate: a war of attrition in which neither adversary appears to have the military strength to defeat the other or the will to negotiate a peaceful settlement of the conflict. Recent developments, however, have increased the likelihood of a technological and/or geo-

Figure 4.5. The Persian/Arabian Gulf region

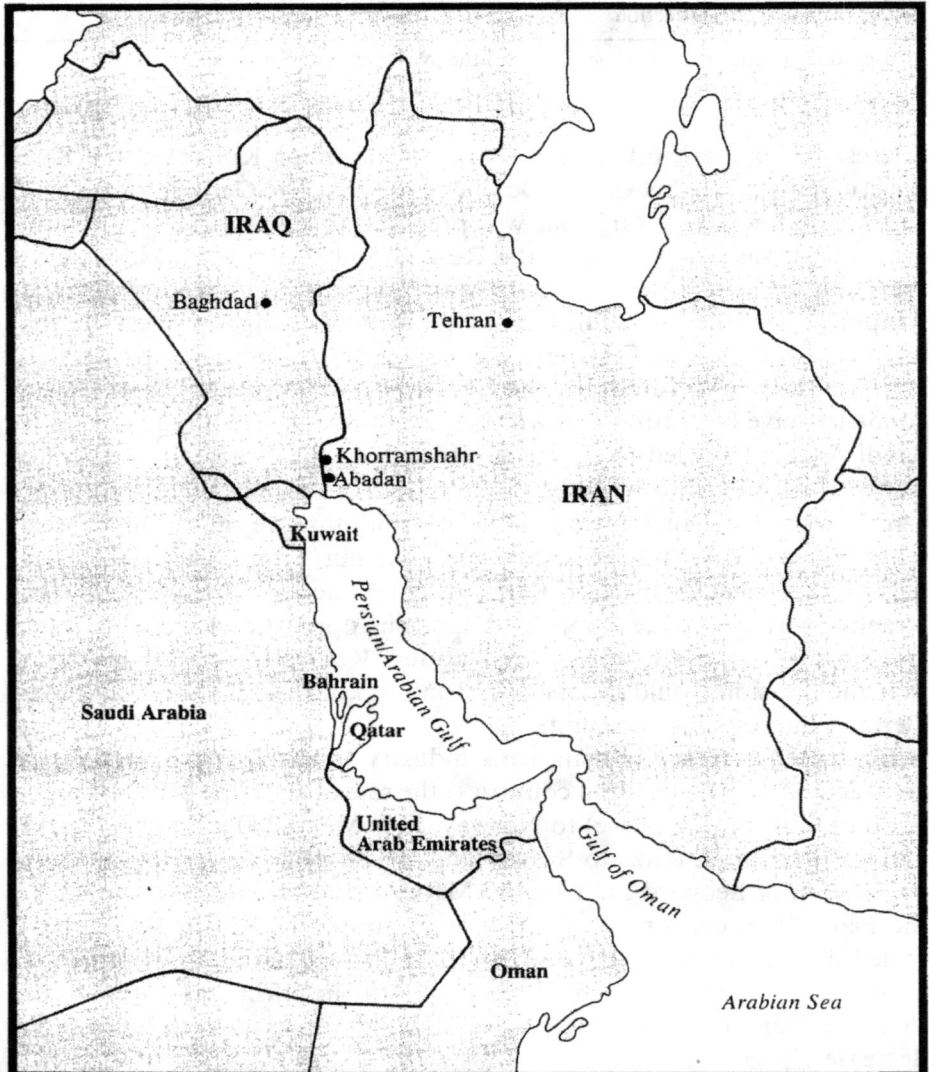

graphical escalation of the conflict—thus making the war a global concern. Arms resupplies continue to reach the adversaries in sufficient quantities for the war to continue.

The factors underlying the Iraqi decision to invade Iran in September 1980 were manifold. Among a complex web of historical, ideological and legal aspects, the issue claimed by Iraq to be most important concerned the border between the two countries along the Shatt-al-Arab River, and some nearby territories. This river is a vital strategic and economic artery for both countries: it provides Iran with its only waterway access to the oil ports of Khorramshahr and Abadan, and it is Iraq's main lifeline to the sea (see figure 4,5). Behind these Iraqi claims there was a broader aim: to destabilize and overthrow the fundamentalist Islamic government in Iran and to take the place of Iran as the predominant military power in the Gulf area. This would also mute the growing domestic unrest in Iraq, which is caused in part by Iran's Islamic revolution.

The Iraqi invasion was obviously based on a misperception of Iran's military capability and will to defend itself. The Iraqi leadership envisaged a quick victory against an enemy weakened by internal turmoil, purges of the officer corps, and arms resupply and maintenance problems. This turned out not to be true. Instead, the protracted and bloody war, with more than 300 000 soldiers and civilians killed, has put severe strains on the economies of the two countries. Both countries have spent a large proportion of their national income on weapons, ammunition and spare parts. Iraq is in the worse situation: it has used up its financial reserves, civilian development programmes have been abandoned, and the country has been forced to drastically reduce its oil exports. Due to war damage and pipeline cut-offs, Iraq was in late 1983 able to export only about one-fifth of the amount of oil exported before the war. Iran's economy is in a better state. It exported in 1983 about three times as much oil per day as Iraq. The Gulf war has become an economic war in which both sides try to disrupt the main source of revenue of the other—the flow of oil.

Although they undoubtedly view Iran as a potentially more dangerous state than Iraq, the reactions of the Gulf states have been cautious—at least in terms of public commitment. None of them, including Saudi Arabia, has the capability to defend itself, should any of them become actively involved in the war. On the other hand, these countries share several common security concerns, for example, the fear of domestic unrest caused by a spreading Islamic revolution, the fear of the hegemonic aspirations of Iraq and Iran, and fear of intervention by the major powers. The formation of the Gulf Cooperation Council (GCC)[38] in 1981 provided a formula to reconcile these security needs. The Gulf states, primarily Saudi Arabia and Kuwait, have provided well over US $20 billion[39] to sustain Iraq's war effort and to prevent an Iraqi defeat—money that protects them from both Iran and Iraq. The political leaderships in the GCC countries are seemingly content with having the two regional powers fighting each other rather than expanding their influence into the smaller states of the Gulf.

The United States and the Soviet Union have both declared their neutrality in the war, they both envisage unpredictable advantages—or losses—from the war, and they have both, directly or indirectly, supplied both belligerents with weapons during the course of the war (see table 4.5). Although a resumption of diplomatic relations with Iraq is expected during 1984, the United States has, by the end of 1983, no diplomatic relations with—and little leverage over—either party. The Soviet Union has diplomatic relations with both Iraq and Iran, a friendship treaty with Iraq and Syria, and strong military ties with Libya. Libya and Syria are also among the main weapon suppliers to Iran. The USSR is thus in a complex situation, with Iraq, Iran and their allies making their claims on support a test of Soviet credibility.

There are several points to be made regarding US and Soviet positions in the Iraq–Iran war. On the one hand, the fact that the war continues reflects their limited abilities to stop the war through diplomacy. On the other hand, they do not perceive the war, in its present and still limited form, as a serious threat to their interests in the area. On the contrary, the Soviet Union is directly supplying Iraq, and it is in the interest of both major powers that their allies deliver weapons to both Iraq and Iran. After the war, Iraq and Iran will have to rebuild their civilian and military structures. The continued limited war thus creates the conditions for Iraq's and Iran's future reliance on the major powers. The nature of this reliance, however, remains highly obscure. The USA and the USSR do not, therefore, wish to limit their future options by committing themselves too deeply at the present stage.

Arms resupply during the war

The weapon flows to Iraq and Iran are illustrated in table 4.5.[40] Only confirmed deliveries of major weapons, or other forms of support, have been included. Arms resupply during war in general is more complex, covert and difficult to verify than in peace-time; the table undoubtedly under-estimates the complexity of the real situation.

The number of arms suppliers increased dramatically after the outbreak of the war: in the case of Iraq, from 3 to 18; and for Iran, from 5 to 17. Second, the supply patterns have changed. Third, unlikely groupings of countries emerge as suppliers, or supporters, of the same party. Iran, for example, has received weapons from such politically disparate countries as Israel, Libya, North and South Korea, South Africa, Syria and Taiwan. Furthermore, both countries rely to a significant extent on private arms dealers and circuitous delivery routes via third countries for their supply of small arms, spare parts and munitions.

Iraq has for several years tried to extend the sources of its weapons and move away from dependence on the Soviet Union. The main Western benefactor of this policy is France, although the USSR is still by far the largest single arms supplier. France has sold to Iraq approximately $5 billion[41] worth of arms since the start of the war, mostly on credit terms but also in exchange for oil. During 1982–83, Iraq accounted for 40 per cent of total French arms exports.[42] In 1983, France leased to Iraq five Super Etendard fighters armed with Exocet anti-ship missiles. This shows France's fear of an Iraqi defeat; it also increases Iraq's capacity to attack oil tankers and other targets in the Gulf. Other French deliveries include Mirage fighters, missile-armed helicopters and Roland surface-to-air missiles. Egypt, Italy and Spain are also among the main suppliers of arms to Iraq. Egypt has retransferred weapons from a multitude of original suppliers. Egypt's arms exports to Iraq during 1982 reportedly totalled $1 billion.[43]

Iran's main suppliers of major weapons are Libya, Syria and North Korea. It is reported that 40 per cent of Iran's arms imports during 1982, or $800 million, came from North Korea.[44] Support has also been given by Israel, South Africa and Taiwan, often referred to as pariahs in the international system. With foreign assistance, Iran is also in the process of enhancing its significant, indigenous capacity to produce weapons and munitions. Otherwise, Iran is heavily dependent on the private, international market for supplies. The most absurd example is probably the case of the private arms dealer who purchased captured Iranian equipment —M-47 tanks, howitzers and mortars—from Iraq, and then resold it to Iran.[45]

Effect on regional arms procurement

Many of the current procurement programmes of the GCC countries were initiated before the war started, fuelled by other regional developments, for example the Iranian revolution and emerging Shi'ite fundamentalist movements in the largely Sunni Muslim-dominated GCC states, Iraq's growth as a major regional power and the Soviet invasion of Afghanistan. The present threats arising from the Iraq–Iran war have resulted in further military acquisition programmes in the neighbouring oil-producing Arab states. Since late 1980, all of the six GCC members have purchased major warships or missile-armed fast attack craft, sophisticated jet fighters, helicopters, main battle tanks or other modern armoured vehicles, and a wide range of anti-air, anti-ship and anti-tank missiles.

The main threat currently seen by the GCC states is an Iraqi attack on tankers passing through the Gulf, and the likely ensuing Iranian attempts

Table 4.5. Arms resupply and other support to Iraq and Iran, 1980–83

Country[a]	Iraq Major weapons before war	Major weapons during war	Other support during war	Iran Major weapons before war	Major weapons during war	Other support during war
USA		× [b]		×	× [c]	× [c]
USSR	×	×	×	×	× [d]	× [d]
China		×		×		
Belgium			× [e]			
France	×	×	×	×	× [f]	
FR Germany		× [g]	× [g]			
Greece					× [e]	× [e]
Italy		×	×	×	×	
Portugal			× [e]			
Spain		×	×			
United Kingdom			× [e]	×		× [e]
Czechoslovakia	×	×				
German DR	×	×			×	
Hungary	×					
Poland	×	×				
Yugoslavia	×					
Austria		× [h]				
Switzerland	×				×	
Egypt	×	× [e,i]				
Israel				×	×	
Jordan	×	× [e,i]				
Kuwait			× [j]			
Saudi Arabia			× [j]			
Syria					×	×
United Arab Emirates			× [j]			
Yemen, South						×
Pakistan			×			
Korea, North	×	×			×	×
Korea, South					× [k]	×
Philippines			× [j]			
Taiwan						×
Viet Nam						×
Algeria					×	×
Libya					×	×
Morocco			×			
Ethiopia			× [e]			
South Africa					×	
Sudan			× [i]			
Argentina				×	× [e,i]	
Brazil	×	×	×		× [j]	

[a] Sometimes without official sanction or knowledge.
[b] 60 Hughes helicopters; Learjet 35A reconnaissance aircraft; Hercules transports.
[c] Not officially sanctioned; private dealers and individual companies; often via Israel.
[d] Via Libya, North Korea, Syria and WTO countries.
[e] Small arms, ammunition, or spares.
[f] Last three of 12 Kaman Class FACs ordered 1974.

to mine, or otherwise block, the Straits of Hormuz. In effect, all security threats in the area are threats to the oil flow. This makes them not only a regional but also a global concern. From the outset of the war, the United States and the Soviet Union have striven to keep the conflict from spreading beyond Iraq and Iran. The USA has pledged to protect free shipping through the Gulf.[46] US policy in the region is focused on protecting Western access to Gulf oil by supporting friendly regimes and building up US military installations in the Gulf.

Foreign intervention is unwanted, and the Gulf states are trying to prevent such a development, primarily through substantial arms imports. Another effort is the possible setting up of a joint GCC rapid deployment force: extensive manoeuvres have already taken place under the GCC umbrella. Another method is more co-ordinated arms procurement, as exemplified by the recent Saudi Arabian decision to acquire a complete low-level air defence radar network from France, including improved Shahine/Crotale surface-to-air missiles; and the simultaneous Kuwaiti order for a similar French air defence radar system.

Conclusions

The main conclusions to be drawn from the facts concerning the arms trade in the Iraq–Iran war are the following:

1. The weapon flows are in many ways different from those before the war. There is a dramatic increase in the number of suppliers, the patterns of supply are different from those before the war, and there are supplier groupings and interests which are not easily explained along standard political lines.

2. The procurement methods of wartime supply are different. Secret trade routes and arms merchants play a more significant role than in peace-time. The private, international arms market is booming. Many governments also profit markedly from the war.

3. The United States and the Soviet Union are maintaining a low profile—support is primarily given indirectly to both parties, often through their allies.

4. Except possibly for France, very few of the states involved in the arms resupply show signs of wanting to see an end to the war.

5. A massive rearmament process is likely to emerge in Iraq and Iran once the war ends, particularly in the field of high-technology weaponry. This will affect arms procurement policies throughout the region.

---

g Bo-105 helicopters direct and from Spain; Roland-2 SAMs from Euromissile; tank transporters.
h GHN-45 155-mm howitzers via Jordan.
i Training, military advisers or troops.
j Financial support.
k US-made AAMs for F-4 Phantom fighters.
l Armoured vehicles via Libya.

6. The prospects for arms trade restraint in the area seem bleak. The flows of arms resupply illustrate the fierce competition between supplier states. There are many semi-official and private suppliers willing to furnish the belligerent states of this conflict with weapons and other forms of support.

India and Pakistan

One of the exceptions to the general decline in arms transfers in the early 1980s is in the trade with India.

In 1983 India reportedly ordered Sea King helicopters and Sea Eagle missiles from the UK, RBS-70 missiles from Sweden, and BMP-1 MICVs, T-74 tanks, and MiG-29 and MiG-25 Foxhound aircraft from the Soviet Union. It also negotiated for the transfer of artillery weapons from the USA, although no deal was signed since the US government was unwilling to deliver the technology for licensed production. India then discussed the purchase of 155-mm artillery pieces with several west European countries.

More significant than such direct transfers are the licensing agreements which India concluded in 1983: for the Soviet MiG-27 (production of 200 is planned), the West German Do-228 transport aircraft and the follow-on production of Jaguar aircraft. The MiG-29 and the T-74 may also be licence-produced in India. The production plans of the Indian arms industry already include future licensed production or assembly of Milan anti-tank missiles, Type 209 submarines and Mirage 2000 aircraft. In addition, other projects are being pursued with foreign assistance, such as the Light Combat Aircraft for which West German, British and French companies have made proposals, and the MBT-80 Chetak tank, powered by a West German engine. Some of these projects might be cancelled, but there will be an increase in the capacity of the arms industry, which is among the largest in the world, employing about 250 000 people.[47]

As a consequence of increased arms production and increased pressure to export, a new arms export policy was adopted by India in 1983. The aim is to promote the export of small arms, military vehicles, electronics and helicopters, but not such weapon systems as tanks or fighter aircraft. In 1983 eight Chetak helicopters were sent to the USSR. If this Indian-produced derivative of the French Alouette helicopter performs well in competition with Soviet-built military helicopters, a large order may follow.

India's procurement and production plans are often viewed in the light of development issues. India is still among the 20 poorest nations in the world: more than half of the population lives below the subsistence minimum as defined by international development aid organizations. However, its industrial sector is rather large, larger for instance than Belgium's. The regular Indian response to this type of criticism is threefold: first, that, compared with the industrialized countries, India is

World military expenditure.
The massive diversion of resources for military consumption is a growing problem for most countries. In the longer term it can be expected that current procurement policies and cost trends will result in a redistribution of resources in favour of the military sector.

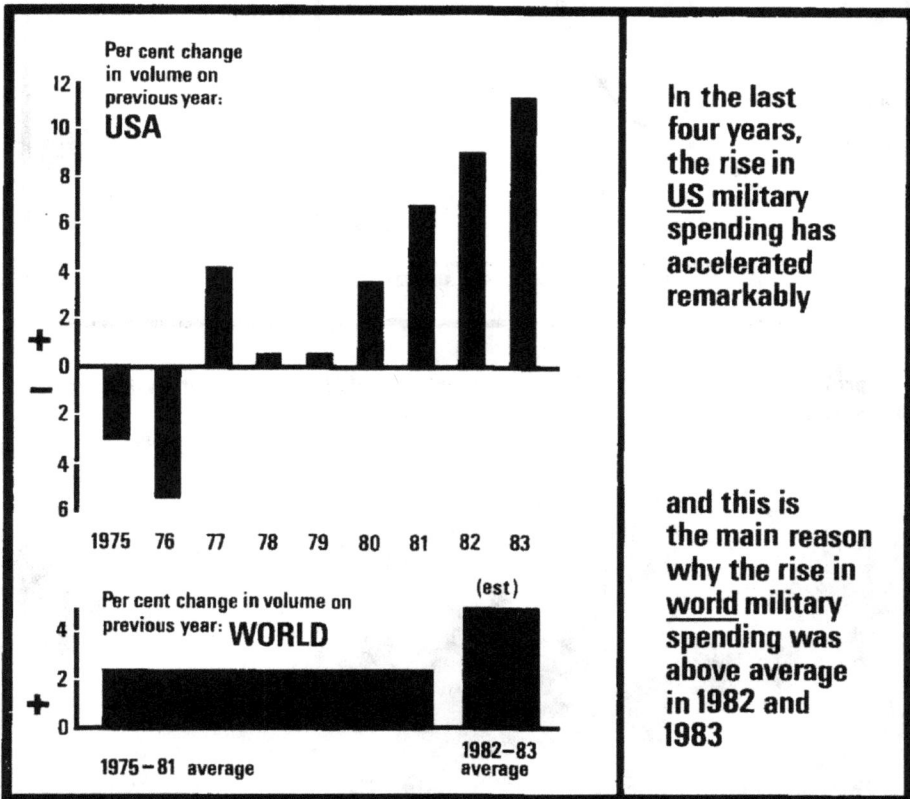

Per cent change in volume on previous year: **USA**

12
10
8
6
4
+ 2
– 0
2
4
6

1975 76 77 78 79 80 81 82 83

Per cent change in volume on previous year: **WORLD**

4
+ 2
0

1975 – 81 average

(est)

1982 – 83 average

In the last four years, the rise in US military spending has accelerated remarkably

and this is the main reason why the rise in world military spending was above average in 1982 and 1983

The world trade in conventional weapons.

More arms do not make mankind safer, just poorer. The transfer of arms makes the world less stable, conflicts become more frequent and the disposition to solve them peacefully decreases.

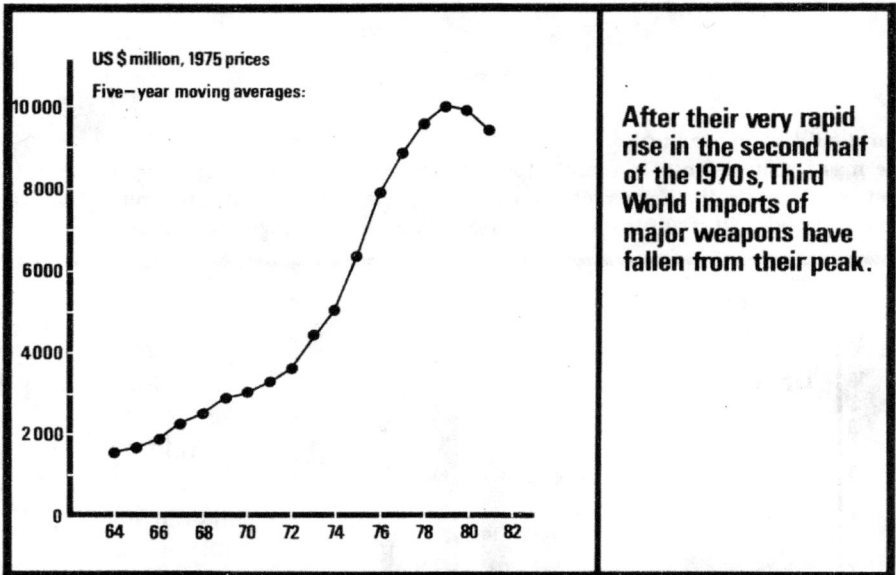

US $ million, 1975 prices

Five-year moving averages:

After their very rapid rise in the second half of the 1970s, Third World imports of major weapons have fallen from their peak.

The proliferation to the Third World of highly sophisticated conventional weapons, like this Soviet Mig-25 fighter-interceptor, continues.

Source: *Soviet Military Power*, 2nd ed. (US Government Printing Office, Washington, D.C.), 1983, p. 29.

Transfer of major conventional weapons—such as this Soviet T-74 battle tank—is a powerful foreign policy instrument for the major suppliers. Many arms industries are increasingly dependent on arms exports.

Source: Soviet Military Power, 2nd ed. (US Government Printing Office, Washington, D.C.), 1983, p. 39.

This picture shows a French Super Etendard naval fighter armed with an AM-39 Exocet anti-ship missile. Five of these aircraft were delivered to Iraq in 1983.

Nuclear weapon tests.

With each nuclear blast, prospects for curbing the nuclear arms race diminish, while the dangers of nuclear weapon proliferation increase. Testing continues to be indispensable for the nuclear weapon powers to carry into effect their nuclear armament programmes.

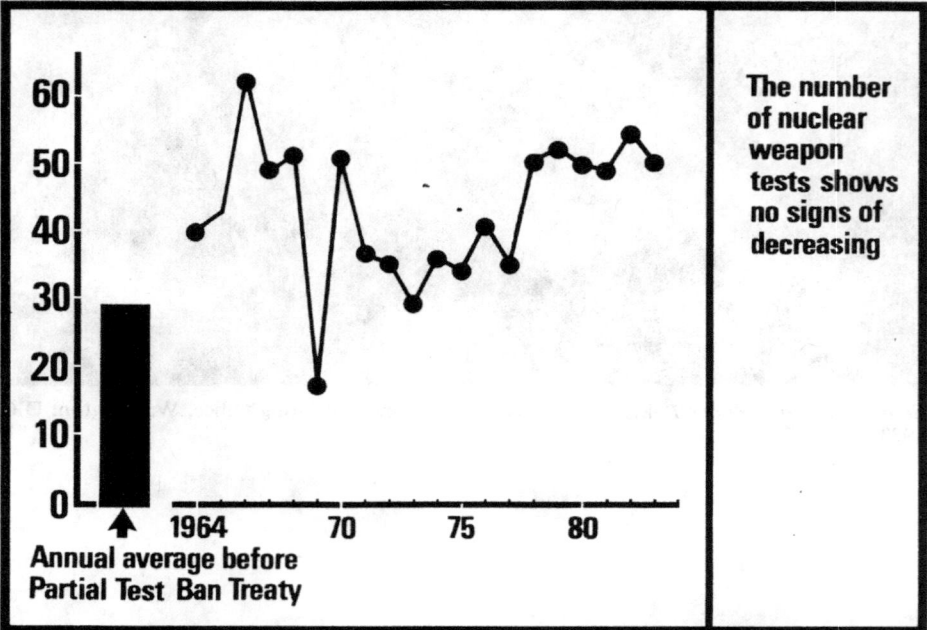

The number of nuclear weapon tests shows no signs of decreasing

Annual average before Partial Test Ban Treaty

The US and Soviet strategic nuclear weapon capability.
The nuclear balance is not delicate. There is no military need for parity. There is no rational military use which could be made of some margin of superiority.

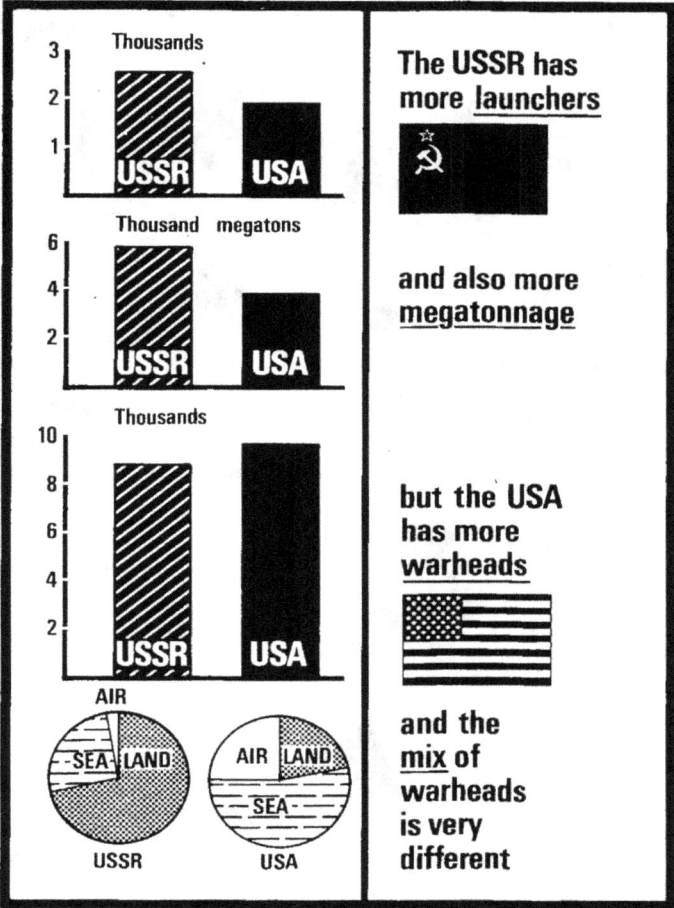

The USSR has more <u>launchers</u>

and also more <u>megatonnage</u>

but the USA has more <u>warheads</u>

and the <u>mix</u> of warheads is very different

Insofar as their objective was to prevent the deployment in western Europe of Pershing II and cruise missiles, the west European peace movements failed. However, insofar as their objective was to persuade people to their point of view, the movements have had considerable success.

Nine Pershing II missiles were declared operational in FR Germany in early 1984. The Soviet Union sees this missile as a particularly dangerous weapon because it is considered accurate enough, and has a long enough range, to destroy Soviet command centres.

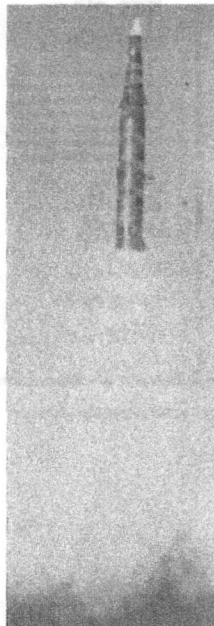

Loading a 135-mm nerve gas shell onto a conveyor belt at the Chemical Agent Munitions Disposal System at Tooele, Utah. The subsequent process will neutralize the nerve gas in the shell.

Photograph courtesy of Tim Kelly, *Salt Lake City Tribune.*

During 1983 there were frequent allegations of the use of chemical weapons in the Iraq–
Iran war.

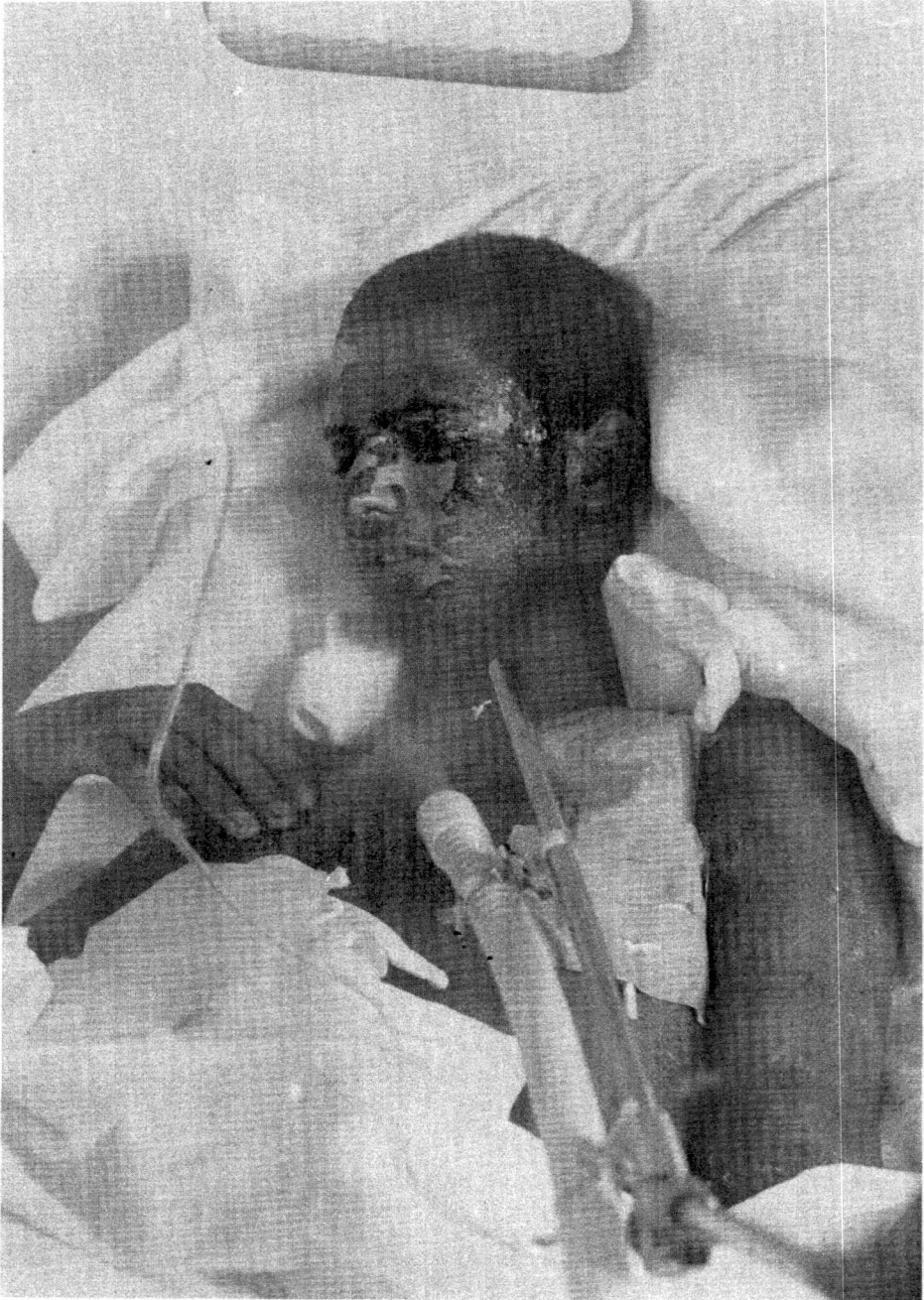

relatively unarmed; second, that the economic burden for India is below the Third World average if military expenditure is measured as a share of gross national product; and, finally, that India has threats to its security which it must counter. The biggest such threat is seen in Pakistani military force.

The Pakistani armed forces were in 1983 not able to order as many weapons as they wished to have, owing to financial problems. New orders include US-built G-134 Mohawk surveillance aircraft. Deliveries of F-16 aircraft from the United States and Q-5 Fantan-A aircraft as well as tanks from China substantially increased Pakistani military power.

There are at least four interrelated reasons for this continuing armament process on the Indian subcontinent. One is the availability of finance to the Indian government. Owing to its inward-looking development policy, India has not been as hard-hit by the world recession as other countries. A second point is the superpower interests in the region, especially after the Soviet invasion of Afghanistan. This was one factor in the rapprochment between Pakistan and the USA, including a commitment of $3 200 million of aid (financing the supply of helicopters, artillery and armoured vehicles) as well as the transfer of 40 F-16 fighter aircraft. Third, there are signs that India is more interested in becoming a major regional power. Finally, an important factor seems to be the Pakistan–India clash, involving the two countries in an action–reaction pattern of arms procurement.

An example is the acquisition of front-line fighter aircraft by the two countries. Until the late 1970s, there was a clear and simple pattern: wars led to the acquisition of new aircraft models in order to replace lost aircraft. The pattern was changed dramatically when India started to introduce the MiG-21bis, the Jaguar, the MiG-23 and the MiG-25. Pakistan acquired the F-16, at present the most modern aircraft in the region, which in turn was used by the Indian armed forces as a reason to order even more modern models (table 4.6). The recent Indian orders of Soviet aircraft are at least partly due to the Soviet invasion of Afghanistan, as this was the decisive factor motivating the US government to offer F-16 aircraft to Pakistan.

Whether or not the Indian and Pakistani perceptions of threat are real, they in any case strengthen the case for those in both countries interested in acquiring modern weapon systems, possibly far beyond what could be justified in the light of the security needs of both countries. It also clears the field for foreign arms salesmen eager to sell their products. They are, of course, currently more attracted to the economically better-off India.

In 1983 *HMS Invincible*, called by the *Times* the "most glamorous of the Falkland war veterans",[48] visited India on its tour around the world to show British arms. Less spectacular but more successful were the Soviet

Table 4.6. India and Pakistan: fighter aircraft introduced since 1963

India Designation (supplier)	Year	Pakistan Designation (supplier)
MiG-21 (USSR)	1963	
	1964	
	1965[a]	
	1966	F-6 (PR China)
	1967	
Su-7 (USSR)	1968	Mirage III (France)
	1969	
	1970	
	1971[a]	
MiG-21MF (USSR/India)	1972	Mirage V (France)
	1973	
	1974	
	1975	
	1976	
MiG-21bis (USSR)	1977	
	1978	
Jaguar (UK/France)	1979	
MiG-23 (USSR)	1980	
MiG-25 (USSR)	1981	
	1982	F-16 (USA)
	1983	Q-5 Fantan-A (PR China)
	After 1983	
MiG-27 (USSR/India)		
MiG-29 (USSR)?		
MiG-25 Foxhound (USSR)?		
Mirage 2000 (France)		

[a] Wars in 1965 and 1971.

efforts to sell in the past two years. The Soviet share in Indian arms procurement has dropped sharply since the late 1970s. Their interest in the Indian market does not seem to be different from that of other sellers, namely a basically commercial one. The balance of trade between India and the Soviet Union is increasingly in favour of India. Due to the secrecy both countries attach to arms deals, it is not known to what extent the Indian diversification of arms suppliers has added to this. But certainly the Soviet Union is very interested in a closer tie with Indian arms procurement again.

V. The determinants of supply and demand

Any attempts to restrain the international trade in conventional weapons will have to be based on, among other things, an insight into the factors that propel the trade in arms. Consequently, it is important to list these factors.

Supply factors

The incentives to export weapons are multiple. They can be grouped into two basic categories: political and economic factors. They are at work on different levels: the international, the national and the sub-national (industrial) levels.

Starting at the global or international level, the political factors are determined by the world-wide East–West conflict. One instrument in this hegemonic struggle is arms transfers. Obviously, the factors on the international level are primarily applicable to the major powers, the USA and the USSR. But other suppliers, such as France or Sweden, can use global rationales by pointing out that their weapons come free of political, military or economic strings. In the hegemonic conflict arms transfers are intimately intertwined with attempts to exert political leverage. Arms sales are seen as a means to establish or maintain influence in a region or a country, or to prevent other countries from becoming influential. Buying a modern weapon system is normally a long-term commitment from both parties: with the direct acquisition follows supply of spare parts, technical assistance, maintenance, training and education throughout the lifespan of the weapon. Economically, the aim is to ensure the stability of civilian markets and the inflow of necessary raw materials.

From a national point of view, there are such factors as the influence on the military elites of the recipients; burden sharing; standardization; and access to transit rights, facilities and spares. Furthermore, the longer production runs resulting from arms exports are claimed to be beneficial for a number of reasons: they lower national arms procurement expenditures through lower unit prices and help recoup some of the R&D costs; they ensure a stable employment level; and they provide an industrial capacity to increase production for national defence, should such need arise. In times of pressures to economize on domestic procurement expenditures, such arguments become very powerful. Also, arms exports generate insight into military R&D and production in other countries. Finally, there is the suggestion that arms exports, at least in the short term, help to improve the balance of payments, and that arms transfers open doors for civilian exports; conversely, restrictions on arms exports, it is argued, will cause other hidden losses to the economy.

On the sub-national or industrial level, the pressures to export arms are of a purely economic nature. First of all, in the West there are often specific, structural differences between the defence industry and the ideal free market enterprise. For example, *prices of weapons do not normally fall with reduced demand*; instead they tend to rise. Added demand from abroad holds the price rises down and the firm remains competitive. Another difference is that *supply does not always adjust to demand* because of the need for excess capacity in case of war. Arms exports help to finance this excess capacity. Second, arms exports are a highly profitable business for the arms industries: even if the weapons are sold on favourable credit terms for the recipient, the export earnings are normally guaranteed by the supplier's government. Third, in many defence industries arms exports account for a substantial part of total turnover, and with relatively large barriers to entry and exit this comprises yet another strong and built-in pressure to export. A substantial number of companies entered the arms business in the 1970s when demand boomed and they found it difficult to move back to civilian production in times of general slack in civilian markets.

Despite this, economic constraints in the recipient countries have so far caused a slow-down of the international arms trade in the 1980s. This has led arms manufacturers to intensify their marketing effort, illustrated for instance by the increasing number of arms fairs and exhibitions (see table 4.7). There is also a tendency for arms industries to dissociate themselves from their respective governments. From an arms control perspective there is an important point to be made: the various determinants listed above are not always pulling in the same direction. There is an inherent tendency towards a collision of interests between the political and economic determinants. This has most often occurred in countries with restrictive arms export policies—such as Sweden and FR Germany—taking the form of a clash between the government and the industry; but it also happened in the USA when President Carter's policy aimed at restraining US arms exports.

Demand factors

The pressures to import arms can be identified on levels similar to those for the pressures to export. On a regional or sub-regional level, there is the almost automatic pressure arising from circular arms procurement patterns, as exemplified by the case of India and Pakistan (see section IV). The key phrase is 'enhancement of national security'. It is a very ill-defined proposition, used to legitimize both the preparation to counter-attack and the acquisition of large weapon arsenals for internal repression.

Other factors on the national level are prestige reasons, and the proposition that the import of modern weapons and weapon technology is beneficial from the point of view of industrialization and development. There are also actors at the sub-national level—the military elite is the most important one: often it has vested interests and exerts a major influence

120

Table 4.7. Major international exhibitions of military equipment

First year	Name	Location (country)	Frequency[a]	Type of exhibit[b]	Organizer[c]	Exhibitors[d]
1983	Natsedes	China	?	N	E/S	I
1983	Expol	France	?	P	E	I
1982	World Defense Expo	USA	1	C	E	I
1981	Cairo Military Exhibition	Egypt	3	V	E	I
1980	Asian Aerospace	Singapore	3	A	E	I
1980	Defendory	Greece	2	V	E/S	I
1980	Feria Internacional del Aire	Chile	2	A	S	I
1979	Defence Components Exhibition	UK	2	C	E/S	N
1978	International Naval Technology Expo	Netherlands	2	N	E	I
1976	British Army Equipment Exhibition	UK	2	G	S	N
1976	Electronics for National Security[e]	Belgium	2	EC	E	I
1976	Mostra Navale	Italy	2	N	S	N
1971	Royal Naval Equipment Exhibition	UK	2	N	S	N
1968	Satory	France	2	G	S	N
1968	Bourget Navale	France	2	N	S	N
1946	US Armed Forces Communications and Electronics Association	USA	1	EC	S	I
1945	Association of the US Army	USA	1	G	S	I
1932	Farnborough International Air Show	UK	2	A	S	I
1909	Salon Aérospatiale du Bourget	France	2	A	S	I

[a] Number of exhibitions per year.
[b] Exhibition of   A = Aircraft (civil/military)
         P = Internal security/Police equipment
         C = Components
         V = Various types
         G = Ground forces equipment
         N = Naval equipment
         EC = Electronics/Communication equipment
[c] Organizer is either S: State/national organization or E: Exhibition company.
[d] Exhibitors are either N: National or I: International.
[e] Former name and location: Military Defense Electronics Exposition/International Defense Electronics Exposition, FR Germany.

on arms procurement decisions. Inter-service rivalry is a related factor which often leads to excessive arms imports.

The obvious restraining factor on the demand side is cost. When measured against the national security needs of a country plagued by economic problems, the cost of modern and sophisticated weapon systems may be deemed too high, particularly if the weapons do not seem appropriate for the relevant conflict scenarios.

VI. Arms transfer control

International efforts to limit the global arms trade have come to a virtual halt. None of the various suggestions and initiatives of the past decade has led to any action.

Major initiatives of the 1970s were the unilateral restrictions adopted by the Carter Administration in 1977 and the bilateral Conventional Arms Transfer Talks by US and Soviet delegations in 1977 and 1978. Important suggestions came forward within the UN: one was the revival of the idea of publishing international arms trade and possibly also arms production statistics; another was the final document of the first Special Session on Disarmament in 1978, which called for consultations between the major arms suppliers and recipients on the subject of arms transfers. The Brandt Commission—a body of international development experts—proposed a tax on arms transfers. On the side of the recipient countries, there is the 1974 Declaration of Ayacucho by which eight South American countries agreed to try to create a situation in which a ban on the procurement of sophisticated offensive weapons would occur.

The need for control of the trade in conventional weapons has become even more urgent now than in the past. Some of the basic rationales for arms transfer limitations are now more relevant.

1. The transfer of arms is often a political act, and with the present tensions between the USA and the USSR there is a danger that a conflict between their respective arms clients could escalate into a major power confrontation.

2. The arms market is today a buyer's market due to the global over-capacity of arms production, and the proliferation of arms production capabilities. Hence, the world becomes less stable than before, conflicts become more frequent, and the disposition to solve them peacefully decreases.

3. The imports of arms and military technology in general are an economic burden for all countries, but especially for those with limited foreign exchange earnings. The current extreme indebtedness of many countries in the Third World is aggravated by arms imports.

Prospects for the future

New attempts at control of arms transfers will have to be based on experience gained from the failures. Control has to lie in the interests of the participating parties. There are various proposals for action, such as: supplier versus recipient control; unilateral, bilateral, regional/global multilateral measures; quantitative or qualitative restrictions, and so on. Among the proposals, most attention should be given to those that: (a) combine diverging interests; (b) help to change or re-evaluate interests; or (c) provide countervailing interests.

For those suppliers that use arms exports as a foreign policy instrument, the danger of horizontal escalation is such a countervailing interest. It has led to tacit self-restraint in the past—in the field of nuclear technology, but also in the field of conventional armaments. In North and South Korea, for example, the Soviet Union refrained from supplying mobile air defence systems while the USA did not supply any advanced aircraft until 1981, when the Reagan Administration decided to sell F-16 aircraft to South Korea.[49] Currently, the perception of such a common interest does not seem to be very strong despite the recent conflicts, and the experiences learned from them, in the Middle East.

The economic determinants of arms exports, now so prominent for a large and growing number of suppliers, are at least partly outweighed by the so-called opportunity costs of arms; resources can only be used once, either for arms or civilian use. Furthermore, the long-term development potential—and thus the prospects for world trade in general—grow if civilian goods rather than arms are traded. As the economic benefits now accrue differently than they would if more civilian goods were exchanged, a compensation scheme would have to be devised. If this were achieved, a multilateral limitation involving suppliers with economic motives could be in the interest of all of them.

In the light of the detrimental effects of arms exports, this would seem to be an attractive development for all parties involved, especially the recipient countries. However, a very serious objection to such arms transfer limitations is raised by a number of recipient states. They are afraid that their security interests are not fully appreciated. This claim is based on the assumption that security can be bought through arms—a crucial and highly controversial assumption. The Brandt Commission, for instance, stated: "More arms do not make mankind safer, just poorer".[50] It seems vital for Third World countries—and, indeed, for all countries— to re-examine the issues of militarization and security needs in the light of the costs and consequences. One important aspect here is that Third World conflicts—real or perceived—are regionally based, even if they are often enmeshed in and fuelled by the competition between the major powers. Therefore, there is much room for initiatives toward arms limitations from the recipient's side. This should be paralleled by continued similar efforts on the part of the supplying countries.

One important confidence-building measure for any such discussion is open reporting on trade in and production of conventional arms. Secrecy promotes suspicion. More openness would also stimulate public debate of arms transfers, both in supplier and recipient states. Public debate, in turn, stimulates reconsideration and re-evaluation of the interests and determinants of the arms trade and the ways to control it.

Finally, any action to reduce the overcapacity in arms production will reduce the economic pressures to export arms—pressures which are an important determinant of the current level of the arms trade, independent of the security needs of the recipients or suppliers. There is increasing activity by trade unionists working in the arms industry to move away from arms production for exports.[51] The arguments in favour of planning conversion from arms production to civilian production, put forward by the UN expert committee on disarmament and development,[52] are further strengthened when seen in connection with arms exports.

Notes and references

[1] SIPRI, *World Armaments and Disarmament, SIPRI Yearbook 1983* (Taylor & Francis, London, 1983), pp. 361–69.

[2] Cordesman, A., 'The Soviet arms trade: patterns for the 1980s', *Armed Forces Journal International*, August 1983, p. 34.

[3] The order statistics presented here only indicate major trends. They suffer from the same shortcomings as the US data on numbers delivered, including the fact that orders of different magnitude are treated equally.

[4] Krause, J., 'Soviet military aid to the Third World', *Aussenpolitik*, Vol. 34, No. 4, 1983.

[5] SIPRI (note 1), pp. 273–75; and SIPRI, *World Armaments and Disarmament, SIPRI Yearbook 1982* (Taylor & Francis, London, 1982), pp. 177–82.

[6] SIPRI (note 1), pp. 274–75.

[7] *Washington Times*, 4 January 1984.

[8] US military assistance programmes include: Foreign Military Sales (FMS), the Economic Support Fund (ESF), the Military Assistance Program (MAP), International Military Education and Training (IMET) and Peace-Keeping Operations (PKO).

[9] *Foreign Assistance and Related Programs Appropriations for 1984*, Hearings before a Subcommittee of the Committee on Appropriations, House of Representatives, 98th Congress, first session, Part 1 (US Government Printing Office, Washington, D.C., 1983), pp. 1327–36.

[10] Weinberger, C. W., *Annual Report to the Congress—Fiscal Year 1985* (US Government Printing Office, Washington, D.C., February 1984), p. 203.

[11] Kolodziej, E. A., 'French arms trade: the economic determinants', in SIPRI (note 1), pp. 371–90.

[12] *Armed Forces Journal*, June 1983, p. 42.

[13] *Le Monde*, 19 January 1984, p. 1.

[14] *International Herald Tribune*, 10 January 1984.

[15] *Aviation Week & Space Technology*, 23 January 1984, p. 16.

[16] UK Ministry of Defence, *Statement on the Defence Estimates 1983*, 2 (Her Majesty's Stationery Office, London, 1983), p. 14.

[17] 'Britain's supersalesman hits the road', *Defense Attache*, No. 2, 1983, p. 11.

[18] Pearson, F., 'The question of control in British defense sales policy', *International Affairs*, Vol. 28, No. 2, 1983, pp. 213–16.

[19] Edmonds, M., 'The British government and arms sales', *ADIU Report*, Vol. 4, No. 6, 1982, pp. 10–12.

[20] See note 17.

[21] *Times*, 10 March 1983.

[22] *Times*, 21 November 1983.

[23] Campaign against the arms trade, *Newsletter* 63, 23 November 1983, p. 3.

[24] Pretty, R. T. (ed.), *Jane's Weapon Systems 1982/83* (Macdonald & Co., London, 1983), p. 490.

[25] Taylor, T., 'Research note: British arms exports and R&D costs', *Survival*, No. 22, 1980, p. 259.

[26] Report to the electronics EDC by Sir Ieuan Maddock and observations by the Ministry of Defence, '*Civil Exploitation of Defense Technology*', London, February 1983.

[27] Battistelli, F., *Armi: Nuovo modello di sviluppo? L'industria militare in Italia* (Einaudi, Turin, 1980), pp. 208–209; and *Financial Times*, 11 November 1983.

[28] Rossi, S. A., *Italy*, in M. Leitenberg and N. Ball (eds), *The Structure of the Defense Industry* (Croom Helm, London, 1983), pp. 230–38.

[29] Battistelli (note 27), pp. 281–85; and *Frankfurter Allgemeine Zeitung*, 7 April 1983.

[30] Rossi (note 28), p. 244.

[31] Ministerio delle difesa Italiana, *Libro bianco della difesa* (Ministerio della Difesa, Rome, 1977), p. 305.

[32] Battistelli (note 27), p. 282; Rossi (note 28), p. 244.

[33] Archivio Disarmo, *Legislazione e controllo politico, la legge sul commercio di materiale bellico* (Archivio Disarmo, Rome, 1982).

[34] *Financial Times* (note 27).

[35] SIPRI (note 1), pp. 275–80.

[36] *Rheinischer Merkur/Christ und Welt*, 20 May 1983.

[37] H. Wulf, 'Kein Geld mehr zu verpulvern', *Die Zeit*, 18 November 1983.

[38] The GCC members are Bahrain, Kuwait, Oman, Qatar, Saudi Arabia and the United Arab Emirates. The GCC was originally intended to co-ordinate the economic, cultural, scientific, educational and health activities of the participating states. Defence co-operation, on internal security matters and against external threats, received increasing emphasis during 1982–83.

[39] *Asiaweek*, 4 November 1983, p. 24.

[40] The term 'major weapons' conforms with SIPRI's general practice of covering deliveries of aircraft, armoured vehicles including heavy artillery missiles and warships. 'Other support' includes deliveries of small arms, ammunition and spare parts, provision of financial aid, transit rights, military advisers or troops, and training. Excluded are deliveries of civilian ships and aircraft, so-called dual technology and industrial assistance.

[41] See, for example, *International Herald Tribune*, 29 July 1983.

[42] *Strategic Studies*, Vol. 7, 1983/84:1, p. 10.

[43] *Financial Times*, January 6, 1983; *Wehrtechnik*, No. 1, 1984, p. 104.

[44] *IDSA News Review—China*, New Delhi, January 1983, p. 622.

[45] *Der Spiegel*, 21 November 1983, p. 16.

[46] Howarth, H. M. F., 'The impact of the Iraq–Iran war on military requirements in the Gulf states', *International Defence Review*, No. 10, 1983, p. 1406.

[47] Wulf, H., *Developing Countries*, in Leitenberg and Ball (note 28), p. 336.

[48] *Times*, 11 October 1983.

[49] Blechman, B. R., Nolan, J. E. and Platt, A., 'Pushing Arms', *Foreign Policy*, No. 46, 1982, pp. 140–41.

[50] Independent Commission on International Development Issues, *North–South. A Programme for Survival* (MIT Press, Cambridge, MA, 1980), p. 117.

[51] European Trade Union Institute, *Disarmament and the Conversion of Arms Industries to Civil Production* (ETUI, Brussels, 1983).

[52] United Nations, *Study on the Relationship between Disarmament and Development*, A/36/356, 5 October 1981, pp. 172–76.

5. 'Deep strike': new technologies for conventional interdiction

PER BERG and GUNILLA HEROLF

Superscript numbers refer to the list of notes and references at the end of the chapter.

I. Introduction: strengthening conventional deterrence

In an area of nuclear weapon parity, threats of deliberate escalation beyond the nuclear threshold gradually diminish in credibility. NATO therefore feels the need to address the perceived conventional weapon imbalance.[1] There are several possible approaches to this credibility problem, such as rearmament, transarmament (alternative defence options), arms control and disarmament. NATO has, predominantly, chosen rearmament. One main effort has been to exploit emerging technologies for striking deep into enemy territory.

The proponents of 'deep strike'[2] maintain that the new conventional weapon technologies offer a solution to NATO's perceived inferiority in conventional weapons and a comparatively cheap way of raising the nuclear threshold and reducing reliance on nuclear weapons within the NATO doctrine of flexible response.

Sceptics have raised serious doubts, based on the technological difficulties that are likely to arise, particularly taking battlefield conditions and enemy technical and operational countermeasures into account. At their meeting in December 1983, the NATO defence ministers agreed to study the emerging technologies further, but the European NATO allies voiced concern about both total costs and the sharing of the lucrative industrial contracts that will result (the 'two-way street').[3]

Even if deep strike should prove technologically and economically feasible—at least some of the suggested weapons are likely to be developed —there are serious arms control implications. These technologies could prove destabilizing by enhancing the pre-emptive incentives on both sides, especially when combined with such offensive operational doctrines as the US 'AirLand Battle' and the Soviet 'operational manoeuvre groups' (OMGs). If, on the other hand, some of the deep strike technologies are used to reinforce and monitor less provocative defence postures, such as disengagement zones, their contribution could prove both security- and confidence-building.

II. Interdiction

To 'interdict' by NATO definition means "to isolate, or seal off an area by any means; to deny the use of a route or approach".[4] Interdiction therefore

126

aims at isolating the battlefield, thus preventing additional enemy forces from influencing the direct (close) battle. The entire arsenal of modern warfare may be applied to interdiction: conventional, chemical or nuclear munitions, electronic warfare, deception, naval or ground operations, and so on.

Although interdiction may be carried out by any means, it has been considered to lie mainly within the air force domain. The definition of air interdiction is: "Air operations conducted to destroy, neutralize, or delay the enemy's military potential before it can be brought to bear effectively against friendly forces, at such distance from friendly forces that detailed integration of each air mission with the fire and movement of friendly forces is not required." [5]

At the lower end of the range spectrum is close air support, which does require such "detailed integration" with one's own forces. The dividing line between air interdiction and close air support is not fixed, but could somewhat arbitrarily be put at the range of the weapons organic to the ground forces being supported, that is, some 30 km (the present range of field artillery and multiple rocket launchers). [6]

At the far end of the range spectrum, interdiction may reach deep into enemy territory, but it does *not* include attacks on the enemy's political, population or industrial centres, nor on its strategic arsenal. These targets are left to strategic bombardment.

The area of interdiction must be viewed as a continuum beyond about 30 km from the forward edge of the battle area (FEBA), and battle relevance is more important than battlefield proximity. [7] However, the depth of the interdiction has implications for both its potential payoff and costs.

The possible targets of interdiction are diverse. They may be soft or hard (from open-air fuel dumps to command and control bunkers and armoured vehicles), and they may be fixed (such as bridges, highway junctions or other permanent installations) or mobile (whether moving or stationary). Even more important is the function the target performs within the enemy force structure. The main categories of function are force (combat units), supply (logistical units and infrastructure), and command and control.

Airfields constitute a special class of target. Attacking them is part of the counter-air mission of tactical airpower, which includes both offensive (attacking an enemy's airpower over or on its own territory) and defensive operations. While not strictly part of interdiction, offensive counter-air missions are conceptually similar and will be treated as such. Airpower remains a key element in modern warfare, as illustrated by the wars in Lebanon and over the Falkland/Malvinas Islands. A very effective way of reducing enemy air sortie generation rates is by attacking airfields, best illustrated by events of the 1967 Middle East war. [8]

III. Technologies for conventional interdiction

A prerequisite for interdiction is to have the means to establish the position of the intended targets. Another condition is to have an efficient, unjammable C^3 (command, control and communications) system. Other vital elements are high-precision, long-range weapon systems.

Surveillance and target-acquisition systems

The location of such fixed targets as bridges, railway shunting yards and airfields is usually known in advance from maps, satellite photographs and other means. In order to be able to attack moving targets, however, a type of surveillance system which can track them and transmit the data in real time is needed. For example, information about a column of tanks moving along a road must be forwarded as the movement takes place since the targets may be far away from their original positions when the aircraft or missile attacks.

Since present radar systems lack the capability to discern moving targets, Joint Stars or JSTARS (Joint Surveillance and Target Attack Radar System) is currently being developed with the US Air Force as primarily responsible. The Army requirement is for a wide-area surveillance system able to identify moving ground targets. The Air Force requests a longer-range radar with both fixed and moving target indicators and a weapon guidance capability. Joint Stars was initiated in 1982 but builds on the technology of two earlier programmes: the SOTAS (Stand-Off Target Acquisition System) of the Army and the Pave Mover of the Air Force.[9]

The main application of Joint Stars will be the detection and transmission of information on such moving targets as armoured formations, but it will also be used for fixed targets such as ammunition storage areas and command and control centres. Information from the Joint Stars radar will be passed to a ground data-processing station, where it will be analysed to find potential targets. The weapon guidance function will also track missiles and aircraft moving toward the targets and provide guidance updates to correct their trajectories.

Joint Stars will be implemented in a step-by-step fashion. The first step will be to fill the requirements of the Army, these being the less demanding. The Initial Operating Capability (IOC) for the Army is scheduled for 1987. For the Air Force, where the data link for weapon guidance is an important element, the IOC will be a few years later.[10]

Aircraft carrying the Joint Stars radar will fly parallel to borders, at a distance of some 50 km to avoid fire while scanning the area on the other side. The range of the radar is usually quoted to be between 150 and

200 km. The Army will deploy the Joint Stars radar on its OV-1D aircraft. The Air Force prefers to deploy it on the C-18 aircraft, a derivative of the Boeing 707, but has been instructed by Congress and the Department of Defense to use the TR-1 instead.[11] The C-18 is large enough to permit some airborne data processing, while the smaller size of the TR-1 and the OV-1D necessitates data processing on the ground.

Other systems can also be used to perform tasks similar to those of the Joint Stars radar. The PLSS (Precision Location Strike System) is an airborne sensor system which will be mounted on TR-1 aircraft and co-ordinated with Joint Stars. This system can locate and identify radio-emitting sources, including jammers. It will have a range of about 130 km. When a strike is ordered the PLSS system would lead the aircraft to computed points, at which the weapons are released.[12] The AWACS (Airborne Warning and Control System) radar which is deployed on E-3A aircraft can give increased warning time of aircraft taking off from air bases on the other side of the border and can also establish the position of secondary air bases by tracking aircraft as they land. New types of electro-optical imaging cameras will be able to provide surveillance during daytime even through haze and smoke and over long distances. For areas closer to the front, remotely piloted vehicles (RPVs) can be used. An RPV can provide real-time information up to 50 km from its data-link terminal.[13]

Command, control and communications

The demands which the plan for attack into the rear area places on the C^3 structure are great. Information is created in vast amounts, emanating from different sources. The system must therefore be able to sort unimportant information from important information in order to provide a usable basis for decisions. These decisions must quickly reach the operators of the weapon systems, and feedback from operations must be given promptly. The task is also made more difficult by the necessary co-ordination within the NATO alliance. The ground and air forces will also have to co-ordinate their operations. Keeping C^3 invulnerable to enemy jamming is essential. The JTIDS (Joint Tactical Information Distribution System) has been adopted as the basis for communications throughout NATO. This system for data and voice transmission is claimed to be highly jam-resistant. Additionally, the space-based Milstar communications system is being developed to give long-range jam-resistant communications. It is estimated that this system will become fully operational in the early 1990s. Similarly, the opponent's C^3 installations are considered to be important targets not only for destruction but also for jamming. The EF-111A aircraft can be used for jamming at stand-off distances. The ALQ-99 jamming system of the EF-111A is claimed to blind hostile radars far behind enemy lines. Unattended expendable jammers (UEJ) can be dispersed into the deep attack area in a number of ways; they can be air-dropped, weapon-delivered or RPV-borne. They have the advantage, compared to the stand-off jammer, of interfering less with one's own communications.[14]

Weapons against fixed targets

Some fixed targets have been termed 'high-value, time-sensitive targets'. 'High-value' refers to their vital function for the outcome of a war. 'Time-sensitive' refers to the fact that the effect of an attack on them depends heavily on the timing. This group consists of main air bases as well as chokepoints and important underground constructions. Since very few of these targets are located close to the border, they can be attacked almost solely by long-range interdiction. With advance knowledge of the positions of these targets, attacks are not restricted to the area covered by a surveillance system.

Airfields

Among the fixed targets, main air bases have high priority. Apart from runways, they also include such targets as weapon and fuel depots, aircraft out in the open and hardened shelters for aircraft. The main WTO operating bases would be attacked before their aircraft returned from the first-wave attack; the aircraft would thus be forced to go to secondary operating bases. The resulting dispersal would degrade subsequent sortie rates. The aircraft would also be more vulnerable owing to the absence of strong air defence and hardened shelters. Since the location of these WTO dispersal bases would be identified by the AWACS system as the returning aircraft are directed to them, they could then be attacked by NATO aircraft.

The present strategy for attacking main air bases with conventional munitions is by aircraft alone. Attack by both aircraft and missiles is envisaged in the future. New efficient runway penetrators, as well as dispensers fitted to the aircraft and containing a great number of sub-munitions, will reduce the number of aircraft sorties considered necessary. Ballistic and cruise missiles have the advantages of being unmanned and able to carry sub-munitions.[15]

One method of attacking runways is to use a penetrator bomb such as the French Durandal. The weapon is released by the aircraft at a very low altitude and thereafter retarded by two parachutes until it assumes an angle at which it will not ricochet. A rocket booster is then ignited to give a high impact velocity to enable the bomb to penetrate the runway. It then explodes after a firing delay. This weapon, in full production since 1978, has been ordered by 10 countries, including the USA, which is deploying it in Europe.[16]

Another means of attacking runways is by dispensers such as the JP233. This weapon system, being developed in the UK, consists of two dispensers, carrying cratering sub-munitions and area denial mines. The SG357 runway-cratering bomblet incorporates two warheads, the primary one used for implanting the secondary one, which can detonate to produce a large crater. The HB876 area denial mine is released simultaneously in order to make post-attack clearance more difficult and time consuming. The JP233 is scheduled to enter service in 1985.[17]

The MW-1 (*Mehrzweckwaffe*), developed in FR Germany and scheduled to enter service in 1984, is a dispenser system similar to the JP233. The sub-munition is ejected sideways from 112 tubes. The runway-cratering Stabo (*Startbahn-Bombe*) uses a propelling charge which makes the warhead penetrate the runway, after which a second charge detonates. Other sub-munitions intended for attack on operating bases are the MUSPA (*Multi-Splitter Passiv und Aktiv*) area denial mine with a sensor which can tell when aircraft are taxiing or taking off, and the ASW (*Anti-Shelter-Waffe*) sub-munition. The ASW is designed to penetrate hardened aircraft shelters to destroy aircraft inside them. The ASW is at a less advanced stage of development than the other sub-munitions mentioned.[18]

JP233 and MW-1 are so-called captive systems, which means that the aircraft will have to pass over the target when releasing the sub-munition. To reduce the vulnerability of the aircraft, the development of smaller dispenser systems has been instigated which could be launched up to tens of kilometres from the target by adding an engine or wings.[19]

Cruise missiles for this application would have a range of several hundred kilometres. While the US MRASM (medium-range air-to-surface missile), which included an airfield attack version, was cancelled in 1983, a new long-range cruise missile is being developed by Lockheed. This programme is run by the Navy but the Air Force has agreed to be associated with it. Unlike the MRASM the new missile employs stealth technology, giving a smaller radar signature, thereby delaying discovery.[20]

In November 1983 the governments of the USA, FR Germany and the UK signed an agreement on the development of an LRSOM (long-range stand-off missile). The range of the missile will be at least 200 km, and it is scheduled to enter service in the 1990s. The current candidates appear to be a version of the British Sea Eagle missile and the Messerschmitt–Bölkow–Blohm (MBB)–McDonnell Douglas Stand-Off Missile (SOM) which is based on the MW-1.[21]

Ballistic missiles have certain advantages over other missiles for attack on main operating bases. They have greater speed, and their ballistic trajectory makes them less vulnerable to air defence. The US AXE project envisages the use of ballistic missiles in hardened sites to deliver sub-munitions on runways and other fixed high-value, time-sensitive targets.[22] Three missiles have been suggested, all based on existing missiles.

The first of these, the CAM-40, is a derivative of the US Pershing II missile. A two-stage version of the Pershing II is claimed to have a long enough range to reach all WTO main operating bases from anywhere in western Europe, and a one-stage version would cover 70 per cent of them. A radar area-correlation terminal-guidance system would be used. The re-entry vehicle would have two or three bays containing runway penetrators. With a re-entry velocity of Mach 12, they can penetrate the runway, after which the charge explodes. It is possible to time the fuse, so some penetrators will act as mines.[23]

Another candidate missile for the AXE project is the BOSS (Ballistic Offensive Suppression System). This is a delta-wing glider launched by the booster of a Trident missile into a ballistic trajectory, which in contrast to the CAM-40 is endo-atmospheric. The range of the missile would be about 650 km and the guidance is of the stellar inertial type, which sights a single star to provide mid-course updating. This system would give the BOSS a circular error probable (CEP) of only 30–45 m, depending on the distance to the target. The runway penetrators consist of eight clusters and penetrate the runway before exploding. A third candidate, proposed by the US Army, is the 'Incredible Hulk', also known as TABAS or TABASCO. This missile would use booster components from the Thor/Delta or Saturn space rocket. It would be able to carry a payload of 25 tonnes.[24]

Other missiles like the smaller T-16 and T-22 can also be used to attack runways and other fixed targets.

Chokepoints

Other fixed targets are chokepoints such as bridges, railway yards and highway junctions. If these are attacked at an early stage, the opponent's forward movement will be considerably slowed down. The crossing of the Elbe River by an army could, for example, take seven days instead of the normal two if all the bridges were destroyed.[25]

Laser-guided bombs and air-to-ground missiles such as the Maverick can attack these targets. The ballistic and cruise missiles mentioned above would, however, be preferred since they have sufficient range to allow for launch on the western side of the border coupled with high-precision terminal guidance. A missile attack on bridges would be followed by an aircraft attack on the provisional bridges which would be constructed as well as on the ground forces amassed at these points.

Underground constructions

The most efficient munition for destroying bunkers for C³ and storage of nuclear weapons and fuel would have a length/diameter ratio of 10:1 in order not to bounce up to the surface again. The Bunkered Target Munition (BTM) which is of this type is currently being developed in the USA.[26]

Ballistic missiles are best suited to carry this kind of munition. The same ballistic missiles envisaged for airfield attack could be used. The CAM-40, for example, could carry eight BTMs. Cruise missiles and aircraft would avoid radars by flying very low. A pop-up manoeuvre by the munition would then be necessary to attack the target at an angle of 60° to the ground. It would also have to increase its speed. Since cruise missiles could carry only about three BTMs, more missiles would be needed than if ballistic missiles were employed, the number depending on the size of the bunker area.[27]

Assessments

It is argued by proponents of new weapons for the interdiction mission that their use could considerably increase the effectiveness of interdiction. For example, four sorties of an aircraft such as the F-4 or F-111, carrying a bomb like the Durandal, would be sufficient to put a runway out of action. For aircraft fitted with MW-1 or SAW dispensers, only one or two sorties would give the same effect. However, attacking aircraft must be escorted by other aircraft to fight off the opponent's air defences. The anticipated attrition rate for such missions is 20–50 per cent. If, instead, missiles were used to attack these targets, five cruise missiles like the MRASM, two to three CAM-40s or one BOSS would be sufficient to put a runway out of use. One Incredible Hulk missile alone can even destroy a whole base. It has been estimated that 800 CAM-40s would be required to keep the 40 most important main air bases inoperable for three days. It would require around 300 CAM-40s to destroy some 100 choke-points.[28]

However, doubts have been raised as to the feasibility of carrying out deep strikes. It is claimed that more research is needed for the development of these weapons. For example, many of the components of the sub-munition would need to be miniaturized to make room for explosives. Also, the JP233, the STABO and other airfield attack sub-munitions which have two sets of explosives have not worked very well in tests. The same applies also to other types of sub-munition.[29]

The new weapons will also pose a number of problems for arms control. These problems are discussed in section VI.

Weapons against mobile targets

Mobile targets are the advancing forces and the tactical nuclear missiles and their support units. Mobile targets in the rear area can at present only be attacked by aircraft-launched weapons with limited stand-off capability. The introduction of dispenser-carried sub-munitions is supposed to give increased effect since it would reduce the number of aircraft sorties. Later on, further advantages would come from the introduction of missiles guided by Joint Stars and sub-munitions with terminal homing capability.

The West German MW-1 dispenser will employ the KB44 anti-armour bomblet which has an additional fragmentation effect against soft targets, the MUSA multi-splinter mine which is effective against semi-hard targets like truck convoys, and the MIFF anti-tank mine. The US equivalents are the CEM (cluster effects munition) and the Gator mine. The USA has also developed the AMIS (anti-material incendiary sub-munition) fire munition which could destroy light armoured vehicles.[30]

The most important US weapon for interdiction is the Joint Tactical Missile System (JTACMS).[31] This system would bring together the Army's CSWS (Corps Support Weapon System) and the Air Force's CSW (Conventional Standoff Weapon) programmes. The Army requirement was for a ground-launched weapon delivering a range of warheads, including nuclear and chemical warheads and terminal-guided sub-munitions. The Air Force requested an air-launched missile for attack of rear-area targets and for defence suppression. This missile would be capable of launch from aircraft ranging in size from the F-16 to the B-52. In 1982 these two programmes were merged into the JTACMS with the Army as primarily responsible.[32]

The requirement is for a missile that can be air- and ground-launched against targets deep behind enemy lines. The design parameters are expected to be determined by the Army and the Air Force in early 1984. The missile will draw heavily on the Assault Breaker which was a technology demonstration programme for non-nuclear attack of second-echelon forces. The Assault Breaker programme, which started in 1978 (and also included the SOTAS and the Pave Mover radars), made a number of tests using the Martin Marietta T-16, based on the Patriot ground-to-air missile, and the Vought T-22, based on the Lance missile. These two missiles are the main competitors for the contract for which also the T-19, a version of the SRAM missile developed by Boeing, is competing.[33]

Both the T-16 and the T-22 would use an inertial guidance system—the T-16 with a mechanical gyroscope and a stellar inertial unit, and the T-22 using the more accurate ring laser gyroscope. The missile selected will vary in range, payload and size according to its application. For Army use it will weigh up to 1 360 kg and have a range of up to 250 km. The Air Force request varies with the aircraft: the F-16 weapon would have a range of around 180 km, while the range of the B-52-launched missile would be considerably longer.[34]

The US Air Force is of the opinion that the T-16 and the T-22 might still be too heavy for fighter aircraft. Another design, the NV-150, suggested by Northrop, has aroused the interest of the Air Force. The NV-150 is a turbojet-propelled stealth cruise missile, with a range of more than 370 km, intended for inertial and global positioning system (GPS) guidance. The GPS consists of a number of satellites emitting time-synchronized coded signals which can be received by the missile. By noting the time of arrival of signals from the different emitters, the missile can calculate its own position. The manufacturing process of this missile would be extremely innovative, "stamping the missiles out like plastic toys," which is said to reduce the price of the missile considerably. The cruise missile advantages of long range and heavy payload in comparison to the weight of the weapon should also be weighed against the lesser vulnerability of the ballistic missile.[35]

Whichever proposal will be selected for the JTACMS, the initial missile to be fielded will probably be a weapon having inertial guidance without further aid from Joint Stars, the Precision Location Strike System or the Global Positioning System. Thus initially the JTACMS will only be able to attack fixed targets.[36]

The introduction of guided sub-munitions would also come at a further stage. The Army would, for the initial version, prefer to use the non-nuclear warhead of the Lance missile on the JTACMS. This warhead is used against unarmoured targets. The Vought Corporation claims that the destruction of the C^3 and logistics support of the opponent would be much more decisive for the outcome of the war than the destruction of a similar proportion of armoured vehicles. This type of target is not particularly mobile and a real-time capability is therefore not considered necessary.[37]

Two types of guided sub-munition were tested as part of the Assault Breaker programme. The terminally guided sub-munition (TGSM), after ejection from the missile, would use a parachute to retard its descent. At a predetermined height it would start to scan the surface in any of four patterns, which are either elliptical or circular depending upon the shape of the target. The instruction on which pattern to select is given to the missile in flight after analysis of information from the Joint Stars radar. The infra-red (IR) seeker, which has been tested on the TGSM, would be tuned to the heat emissions typical of a tank and would automatically home on such targets. When impacting, the shaped-charge warhead would form a jet of molten metal to penetrate the target's armour.

The Skeet sub-munition, also tested in the Assault Breaker programme, works in a similar fashion. Four Skeets are carried by an SDVA (Skeet delivery vehicle assembly), which is ejected by the missile, deploying a parachute and at a height of 30 m releasing the Skeets in pairs. The IR seeker (the same type as that tested on the TGSM) would scan the ground in a circular pattern. When the characteristic heat signature of a tank is detected, the detonation of the SFF (self-forging fragment) warhead is triggered. This detonation forms a heavy metal disc (of copper, tantalum or depleted uranium) inside the warhead into a streamlined projectile which travels at an extremely high velocity and thereby penetrates the target by its kinetic energy. If the intended target is not detected, the charge is detonated in a different way to produce a maximal effect against personnel and lightly armoured vehicles.[38]

At the 'lower end' of the interdiction spectrum, the MLRS (multi-launch rocket system) has been operational since 1983. It will soon be able to fire anti-tank mines to a distance of 40 km. The third phase is to equip it with terminally guided sub-munitions, probably using millimetre-wave radar guidance. This version will be operational in the late 1980s and have a range of more than 30 km.[39]

Assessments

The implementation of new methods for attacking second-echelon forces is seen by its proponents as a major step in increasing the capability to fight a conventional war.

The crucial task of surveillance and target acquisition is claimed to be less difficult because of the knowledge already acquired by observing exercises and studying topographic conditions and communications networks, on the basis of which probable patterns of movement could be predicted. The potential of the Joint Stars radar was demonstrated in a test in which it located a single tank at a range of more than 150 km.[40]

The effects of the weapons have been estimated. A Soviet division contains about 3 000 vehicles. It is believed that it would be replaced when 60 per cent of the division, that is, 1 800 vehicles, have been destroyed. For free-falling 250-kg bombs this is thought to require 2 200 aircraft sorties. With unguided sub-munitions only 300 sorties would be needed, and for guided sub-munitions the number is further reduced to some 50–60 sorties.[41]

There has also been much criticism of the second-echelon attack strategy. The estimates mentioned above for the effect of the weapons have been claimed to be largely incorrect, owing to technical inaccuracies and organizational misperceptions.[42] It is also claimed that the attack would probably not proceed as envisaged. Tests have been performed on components and some of them have been successful, but many others have failed. The tests also seem to have been performed under favourable conditions, such as with no countermeasures and in a type of terrain where tanks are highly visible. Above all there have as yet been no tests where all the components of the system—the airborne radar, the missile and the munition—have been successfully used together.

Doubts have also been voiced as to the capability of the Joint Stars radar. There have been problems with radars at much shorter ranges than those cited for this radar. Additionally, the size and complexity of data emanating from it are vast. Even without outside interference it is an extremely difficult task to carry out this process of collecting, evaluating and dispersing data. Since electronics now replaces human beings for several functions, the system is also bound to be less adaptive to new conditions. The centralized structure of the system makes it a high-priority target. Furthermore, the position of the aircraft makes the system vulnerable. The WTO would also have systems to home on to emitting sources for destroying and jamming. The survival of the whole system thus depends on staying one step ahead in technology.

IV. Current proposals

Despite the controversial December 1979 NATO decision to deploy new long-range theatre nuclear missiles in Europe, the main emphasis of current NATO rearmament is on conventional weaponry. Nine of the ten 'task forces' of the NATO Long Term Defence Programme (LTDP) concerned across-the-board improvements of the conventional force posture.[43] According to one of the key US officials behind President Carter's LTDP initiative, R. W. Komer, the tenth task force—TNF (theatre nuclear forces) modernization—was merely "an add-on designed to reassure our European friends that no 'gap' in the deterrent spectrum would be allowed to develop while we all focused on strengthening our conventional shield".[44]

Although improvement in conventional weapon technology was not accorded a separate task force as such, it was regarded as the implicit common denominator of the LTDP. The NATO summit meeting in Bonn in June 1982 stated that NATO would "explore ways to take full advantage both technically and economically of emerging technologies, especially to improve conventional defence".[45] This is known as the 'Weinberger initiative' since it was the US Secretary of Defense who suggested to the NATO defence ministers in May 1982 that the Alliance should study the use of emerging technologies for conventional defence. At the December 1982 NATO ministerial meeting, Weinberger presented a US proposal along these lines, focusing on the areas of defence against first-echelon attack, interdiction of Warsaw Treaty Organization (WTO) follow-on forces, improving counter-air capability, enhancing command, control, communications and intelligence (C³I), and disrupting WTO C³.[46]

The idea of exploiting emerging technologies for conventional interdiction has been pursued primarily by the US R&D communities in the military services, various civilian research institutions and the military industry.[47] At official NATO level, attention has focused on the two concepts of 'follow-on forces attack' (FOFA) and the US Army AirLand Battle doctrine (ALB).

The 'Rogers Plan' is the label put by the mass media on the call in the autumn of 1982 by US General B. W. Rogers, SACEUR (Supreme Allied Commander, Europe) for general improvements in NATO's conventional defence capabilities, including readiness, sustainability and new technologies. Development of the key concept of attacking WTO follow-on forces began in late 1979.[48] It was approved by the Military Committee in October 1981,[49] and the intra-Alliance decision-making process continues.

In a Congressional hearing last spring, Rogers described these plans:

Let me describe our concept of operations of which striking deep is a subconcept.

We charge our lead divisions, the divisions occupying our general defensive position, each to handle two enemy divisions opposite them. Those are the first and second tactical echelon divisions of the Warsaw Pact's first operational echelon.

Our second subconcept of operations calls for our reserves . . . to take care of the enemy's second operational echelon forces or any Operational Maneuver Groups—exploiting forces—which may have broken through.

Then our third subconcept calls for us to attack both mobile and fixed targets in the enemy's rear area.

What I am talking about is interdiction. We have had interdiction from time immemorial, but this will be very accurate and on specific targets which we would quickly locate, target, get the information to a joint tactical fusion center where human judgment is exercised by man and pass it to a weapon system to attack the target before it leaves.[50]

The FOFA concept apparently envisages interdicting the full range of targets—including airfields, combat and supply units, lines of communications, C³I installations, and so on.[51] Interdictive strikes will be carried out across the entire European battlefield, up to and including the three westernmost military districts (the Baltic, White Russian and Carpathian) of the Soviet Union.[52]

There are many similarities between the FOFA ideas and the new US Army AirLand Battle doctrine. AirLand Battle, as put forth in the new field manual on 'operations',[53] incorporates many changes compared with the previous doctrine of 'active defence'.[54] It incorporates concepts such as the 'extended' and the 'integrated' battlefield: extended in depth, time and range of assets; integrated since use of conventional, nuclear, chemical and electronic warfare is contemplated.

The links to the FOFA plan are obvious: lacking the necessary geographic depth to allow trading space for time, NATO should extend the battlefield into enemy territory. This is to be accomplished through 'deep attacks' on the enemy's follow-on echelons, thus preventing them from reinforcing the front line forces. There are, however, significant differences in how these second-echelon attacks are to be carried out, differences that NATO officials are understandably keen to point out.[55] The AirLand Battle doctrine implies deep attacks by counter-offensives on the ground, as well as integrated nuclear and chemical strikes. This of course raises serious arms control questions, which will not be discussed in this chapter. There has also been some confusion with the US Army futuristic AirLand Battle 2000, which discusses the battlefield of the period 1995–2015.[56]

As far as range is concerned, however, AirLand Battle is more modest in its approach than FOFA, although this may be due to division of responsibility between the armed services rather than to choice.[57] The main emphasis is on battlefield air interdiction,[58] the purpose of which is "to bring airpower to bear on those enemy forces not yet engaged but positioned to directly affect the land battle. To be more specific . . . enemy second echelon regiments or divisions, moving toward contact with friendly troops already engaged by enemy first echelon regiments/divisions."[59]

Battlefield air interdiction would mainly be applied to the area from close air support up to the corps' "area of influence",[60] that is, from 30 km to some 150 km.[61] Battlefield air interdiction is clearly aimed at 'force' rather than 'supply' interdiction, and in NATO it is considered part of offensive air support (also including close air support and tactical reconnaissance).

V. 'Defend forward' or 'strike deep'?

With finite and, even in the USA, increasingly constrained resources available for the military sector, defence planners will have to make a careful assessment of the costs and benefits involved when deciding on which doctrines and associated weapon systems to choose.[62]

Even if the technological problems discussed in section III are solved and realistic cost estimates made, several important questions remain to be addressed. Which targets should be attacked, and to what effect? Will the adversary devise appropriate technical and operational countermeasures? Empirical studies of the benefits of interdiction campaigns have concentrated on experience from World War II, the Korean War, and—although less relevant in a European scenario—the Viet Nam War. The

Rand Corporation has carried out a number of studies on interdiction. One report finds that:

The problem of the interdiction planner is to match his air resources (taking target acquisition, weapons, and delivery accuracies into account) against a set of targets which, if destroyed or damaged, will produce the most favourable *net payoffs* in the context of the particular operational situation. ... Attacks intended to delay supply buildup usually, and attacks against route structure often, require the continuous application of air resources over time. ... Moreover, even if supply interdiction is successful, the payoffs are often long deferred.[63]

Moreover, the supply interdiction campaign studies were almost invariably conducted with air superiority, a key factor in cost assessments. Under realistic central European battlefield conditions, with strong enemy air defences,[64] dense road networks and 'short war' postures (with significant supplies up front, organic to units), supply interdiction could prove even less cost effective.

For these reasons there is growing awareness that attacks against forces en route—against manoeuvre-unit vehicles—can be particularly attractive if the operational situation is suitable: the target is fleeting but usually concentrated compared with resupply convoys; only a short-term commitment of air resources is needed to earn some immediate dividends; and experience suggests that such dividends can sometimes be very high indeed.[65]

One of the first public signs of recognition that the US Air Force was (and had for a long time been) interested in interdiction against enemy combat forces—which could prove more lucrative than simply 'applying the tourniquet' to lines of communication—came in an article on 'tactical counterforce' in 1974. The definition offered was very similar to that of battlefield air interdiction:

Tactical Counterforce has as its objective the destruction or disruption of major ground forces that threaten, but are not engaged with, friendly ground forces. The targets are enemy firepower elements located beyond the forward edge of the battle area. Because it strikes directly at enemy land forces rather than at lines of communication, Tactical Counterforce differs from current perceptions and from the traditional emphasis of interdiction.[66]

Although attacking enemy combat units may be more attractive than severing the lines of communication, the costs involved may also be higher. The targets are hard (armoured) and mobile, thus increasing the requirements for real-time C^3 and target acquisition, as well as for accurate and lethal sub-munitions. Moreover, the targets are often dispersed, calling for area weapons. Some of these problems may be solved if one accepts simply stopping the vehicles temporarily rather than totally destroying them. Such counter-mobility interdiction could be carried out through remotely laid mines, which are relatively cheap, cover large areas, and have effects of longer duration (until they are cleared or self-destruct).[67]

Generally, the cost of each of the links in the interdiction chain—intelligence, surveillance and target acquisition; command, control and communications; delivery vehicles; and munitions—increases with range (with the possible exception of the munitions). Also, combat vehicles in the far rear area are less likely to suffer a 'catastrophic' secondary explosion, since they are not combat-loaded.[68] On the other hand, enemy air defences are likely to be stronger near the front.

The adversary can be expected to develop countermeasures against every link in the long and vulnerable chain of interdiction. Active countermeasures may be offensive, such as counter-air, or defensive, including air defence (possibly anti-tactical missile systems) and disrupting the different terminal guidance systems (flares against infra-red guidance, and chaff or electronic jamming against radar guidance; smoke optimalized against different parts of the electromagnetic spectrum). Among the passive countermeasures, there are various deception techniques such as dispersion, camouflage, and so on. Electronic warfare will be widely employed.

The fundamental threat assessment underlying the 'deep strike' concept is based on a rather stereotyped view of Soviet World War II operations —more specifically, the use of second echelons.[69] A second (or, rarely, a third) echelon is a portion (usually one-third to one-half) of a unit kept to the rear of the attacking first echelon. The purpose of this second wave is to keep up the momentum of the attack, either to achieve a breakthrough or to exploit it. The aim of 'deep strike' is to interdict such second echelons, thus keeping the force ratios at the front at manageable levels (no more than 3:1 in favour of the attacker). However, the second echelon assumption may be seriously flawed, on several accounts.

First, it is a question of on what levels of command the Soviet Union will choose two echelons rather than one. As is shown in figure 5.1, this has clear implications for the optimal range to seek for one's weapon systems.

At theatre level, the WTO second strategic echelon will consist mainly of forces in the western Soviet Union. Interdicting these formations as they move westwards is likely to have but marginal and delayed effects, owing to the long range and alternative routes.

The fronts (the largest Soviet military formation, usually consisting of four armies) of the first strategic echelon—the groups of Soviet forces in eastern Europe—are likely to deploy their armies in two echelons only if NATO defences are properly deployed; against weak and hastily prepared defences, a Soviet front might use only a single echelon of armies (up to 120 km), although with a strong operational reserve.[70] This seems to be accepted in the AirLand Battle doctrine, where the main emphasis is on battlefield interdiction (up to 150 km).

Figure 5.1. Artist's impression of Soviet military echelons, as seen by the USA

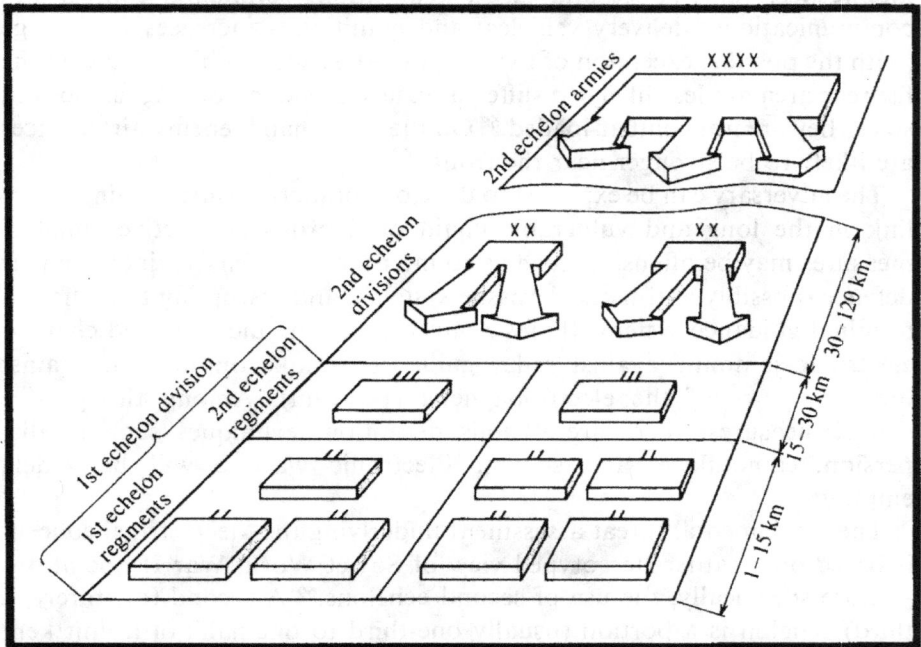

Whether the armies will deploy their (usually) four divisions in one or two echelons is once again dependent on the state of NATO defences, but the likelihood of second-echelon divisions is large enough to warrant devoting 'deep strike' resources to attacking them (at ranges of 30–120 km).[71]

Second, it is not only the depth to which the Soviet Union is likely to deploy its various units that is of importance, but also their intended functions. The US Army feels that this is of no major significance: "Whether our enemy is stylistically echeloned [as shown in figure 5.1] is not really critical, what is important is that superiority in numbers permits him to keep a significant portion of his force out of the fight with freedom to commit it either to overwhelm or bypass the friendly forces."[72] For the USSR, "The distinction of the second echelon from the reserve was that it was created ahead of time with a precisely defined mission—to intensify the force of attack of troops of the first echelon from a specific position and exploit success in depth."[73] Echelons would form in prearranged positions with pre-determined missions, thus becoming lucrative targets and being clearly relevant to the front-line battle. Reserves, on the other hand, would be smaller, dispersed, and would be used flexibly whenever need arose (that is, they would group for combat only when and if the first echelon fails or a breakthrough has been achieved). Once again, the status of NATO forward defences would be decisive.

This leads us to the third and most crucial conceptual flaw: the Soviet Union may penetrate NATO defences before they have been properly deployed. The USSR is believed to prefer that any war in Europe should be kept short, both in order to prevent NATO from bringing their globally superior resources to bear, and—most importantly—to avoid escalation to the nuclear level. This could be achieved through a surprise attack before NATO is fully mobilized or forward deployed, thus not requiring a second echelon or a breakthrough operation at all, rather imitating German infiltration tactics of World War I.[74] As soon as possible, preferably on the first day of the war, the USSR would hope to insert one or more operational manoeuvre groups behind NATO lines.

OMGs would be tank-heavy formations of divisional (at army level) or corps (at front level) size, organized on an *ad hoc* basis at very short notice (a few hours).[75] The OMGs would make a nuclear response by NATO less likely by rapidly crumbling NATO defences. This would leave NATO little time to decide on a first use. OMGs could destroy NATO tactical nuclear resources in deep raids, and would make less attractive nuclear targets through intermingling with NATO forces and population centres. Rogers seems to be aware of the dangers of OMGs,[76] but the reserves to stop them may not be there—they are another competitor for scarce resources.

It is a question of getting one's priorities right. NATO would have to create a credible, 'non-surprisable' defence up front in order to force the USSR to echelon; the two defence concepts are complementary, but without a strong NATO forward defence, there may be no second echelons to 'strike deep' into. Rogers pays lip service to this fact:

[T]his ability to strike deeply is not to be acquired at the expense of our ability at the FEBA. On the contrary, defending the FEBA and attacking the follow-on forces are complementary and mutually reinforcing facets of the ACE [Allied Command, Europe] concept of operations: defense at the FEBA protects our means to conduct attacks on the follow-on forces, and striking deep will keep the force ratios at the FEBA manageable.[77]

Once again, it is a question of a conscious choice of which military investments to make. The allocation of resources between the 'defence in contact' at FEBA and the 'deep strikes' depends on the kind of cost-benefit assessment discussed above. It is likely that costs will increase and benefits decrease with required range. Cost estimates of the different deep strike proposals are necessarily very sketchy, and probably over-optimistic. The technologies for attacks at shorter range, on the other hand, are already available, relatively cheap, and could be vastly improved by the sub-munitions and surveillance capabilities developed for deep strike. And, finally, the majority of enemy targets, and those with most direct influence on the battle, are at the front.[78]

VI. Arms control implications

The 'technological imperative' is commonly acknowledged to be one of the main driving forces behind the arms race. There is much industrial interest in the R,D&A (research, development and acquisition) aspects of deep strike technologies. Therefore, we may expect another turn of the arms race spiral if these new technologies are fully pursued.

However, fiscal restraints may impede the growth of deep strike. General Rogers has been quoted to the effect that the required conventional capabilities could be attained towards the end of this decade at a cost of about 4 per cent real increase per year in NATO military expenditures.[79] This might seem a small sacrifice. However, few NATO countries manage even to achieve the increase agreed to with the LTDP, the so-called '3 per cent solution'.[80]

Moreover, Rogers has clarified his points somewhat:

What I have actually stated is that the current force goals (1983–88) which NATO nations have accepted can be achieved with a 4% real increase in defense spending for each of those six years. Included in those force goals are some systems aimed at attacking follow-on forces; however, all of those systems needed are not available in the time frame of the 1983–1988 force goals and will be included in later iterations of the goals which are agreed on a biannual basis.[81]

It is clear that development of deep strike capabilities in full may eventually demand even larger resources. In real terms, the estimates of the cost of these new proposals are necessarily vague. The European Security Study puts it at $20 billion (± 50 per cent) over a 10-year period, which again "could be accommodated within a level of expenditure approximately 1 per cent higher than the current NATO norm of 3 per cent annual real growth".[82] The history of arms development advises us to treat such preliminary estimates with scepticism.

However, if deep strike capabilities are generally believed to enhance the credibility of the conventional component of NATO's flexible response posture, the public might prove willing to foot the high bill. The consensus on NATO policy has suffered considerably because of this lack of credibility; the dilemmas and untenability of an 'early-first-use' policy have dawned on the public much as a result of the peace education process that has taken place in the shadow of the euromissiles.[83]

Crisis stability

The surveillance technologies associated with deep strike could perform an important monitoring function during peace-time. The intelligence gathered could be used to verify compliance with arms control agreements, reduce the fear of surprise attack, as well as in preparation for such an attack. The net stabilizing effect is dependent on factors such as the vulnerability of the surveillance installations and platforms and on the overall force postures on both sides.

This also applies to the deep strike weapons themselves. If they are vulnerable to pre-emption, and at the same time are coupled to a strategy of forward deployment and ground counter-offensives, they may seriously decrease crisis stability. If the WTO felt that a war was inevitable, it is argued above that they might choose to strike first, before NATO forces are fully deployed. The incentives for pre-emption would be even greater if the USSR developed deep strike capabilities of its own: they would be eminently suitable for interdicting the forward movement of NATO reinforcements to the front. For instance, the Dutch corps on the north German plain will consist of 10 brigades when fully deployed. Of these, only one is permanently deployed in FR Germany (some 100 km from the border with the GDR); the other nine (of which four would have to be mobilized) must move an average of 300 km up to their general defensive positions.[84]

The destabilizing potential of counter-air strikes is particularly worrying. This is especially so for the ballistic missile option. The 'time urgency' in attacking enemy airfields depends on the scenario. Unless one aims at destroying the enemy air forces on the ground in a first strike, the short flight times of ballistic missiles are not needed (ballistic missiles have of course other factors in their favour, such as relative invulnerability).

The arguments made about surprise attacks and crisis stability point to one of the more fundamental dilemmas for Western defence planners—the stronger NATO's eventual, fully mobilized forward defences, the fewer resources remain for the standing forces and peace-time readiness, and the stronger will be surprise attack incentives for the WTO. The less confident the USSR is of eventual victory in a long drawn-out war, the stronger are Soviet pre-emptive inclinations if they believe war to be inevitable.[85]

No-first-use and the nuclear threshold

The overriding concern of our world today is avoiding a nuclear war. Once the nuclear threshold has been crossed, through the employment of nuclear weapons, the chances are that no intermediate halting line ('firebreak') may be established before the total, cataclysmic holocaust, threatening the extinction of the human race. The key issue is therefore to prevent nuclear weapons from being used in the first place, and there have been numerous calls for the adoption by the nuclear powers of no-first-use declarations.[86]

The decision on first use of nuclear weapons would be a grave one indeed. Apart from the fundamental moral aspects and the force of world opinion, the main factors influencing such a decision—and thus the level of the nuclear threshold—would be the likely enemy retaliatory measures, military utility and necessity, and collateral damage. Improvements in conventional military capabilities could raise the threshold by reducing the need for and offering alternatives to nuclear weapons.

Some of the problems of assessing the net impact of deep strike technologies in this context—in terms of technological problems, possible operational misperceptions and opportunity costs—are mentioned above. If deep strike does not work as planned, if fewer resources are devoted to NATO's standing forward defences, and the WTO adopts a more pre-emptive posture, the nuclear threshold may indeed be lowered.

Nevertheless, the idea that an improved conventional deterrent would raise the threshold and de-emphasize the role of nuclear weapons in NATO strategy is a basic premise of the Rogers Plan, although General Rogers himself explicitly rejects NATO adoption of no-first-use.[87] This aspect of deep strike has also been stressed by one of the most important supporters of the idea, Senator S. Nunn.[88] Together with Senator E. Kennedy, he introduced an amendment to the Senate defence appropriations bill that barred, for one year, expenditures on research, development, testing, evaluation or procurement for integration of a nuclear warhead into the joint tactical missile system. Kennedy voiced his concern that a basically conventional system should not be turned into a nuclear one: "We should not permit a system that is supposed to raise the nuclear threshold in Europe to be turned into a system that will lower this threshold".[89] Whether, in fact, a nuclear version of the JTACMS—if and when developed—will actually lower the threshold as compared to its current, shorter-range predecessor, the Lance, is open to debate. The conclusions on the threshold-raising qualities of conventional deep strike remain, however. When discussing deep strike and the nuclear threshold, it should also be remembered that the previous US Army doctrine stressed nuclear attacks on second-echelon and reserve forces.[90]

The counter-argument has been made that new deep strike technologies will lower the threshold through 'blurring' the distinction between nuclear and conventional weapons. This may be wrong. Comparisons between the destructiveness of low-yield (a few kilotons of TNT) nuclear warheads and conventional deep strike weapons are based on estimated destruction of point targets (say, a company of 10 armoured vehicles). There is no similarity in area of destruction. That a conventionally armed missile could destroy as many tanks as a low-yield nuclear missile, without corresponding collateral damage to civilians, could only serve to increase the inhibitions against—and reduce the need for—using the latter.[91]

As mentioned above, some of the deep strike weapons could be equipped with nuclear warheads. It has been argued that preparations for actual launch of such missiles could be interpreted by the opposite side as nuclear actions, leading to pressures for nuclear pre-emption or launch-on-warning. This is a fundamental dilemma of all dual-capable weapon systems, the problems being more severe the longer the range (and the more vital the installations that may be reached) and the shorter the flight time. Dual-capable systems would, on the other hand, be more numerous and thus less vulnerable than nuclear-dedicated systems. However, some of the dual-capable systems would have to be retained for nuclear eventualities, weakening conventional capabilities when most needed. The problem could best be addressed by maintaining a separate, dedicated, invulnerable retaliatory nuclear force, keeping the deep strike systems for a strictly conventional role.

'Deep strike' and LRTNF negotiations

Several proposed deep strike weapons are based on nuclear missiles with a range of more than 1 000 km, the lower limit of the adjourned LRTNF negotiations. Distinctions between the conventional missiles and their nuclear counterparts would be necessary in order to achieve a verifiable reduction in the numbers of nuclear missiles.

Various measures have been suggested to accomplish this distinction. Differences in deployment practices (like base security arrangements) can be observed by satellites and by other means. This method could be complemented by inviting on-site inspections. Physical differences between the nuclear and conventional versions are naturally also highly desirable. Neither this nor any of the other methods would, however, prevent the replacement of conventional with nuclear warheads immediately before an attack. To guard against this, conventional long-range missiles would also have to be included in the restricted numbers agreed upon.[92]

Since weapons of a lower range than 1 000 km have not been included in LRTNF negotiations, circumvention of an agreement can be achieved by forward basing of shorter-range systems. If the area of negotiations is extended down to a range of some 200 km, many of the proposed deep strike weapons would fall in this category. Such an extension could also be a dissuading factor against the development of dual-capable, nuclear warhead versions of deep strike missiles. Circumvention of an LRTNF agreement could also come about due to the non-inclusion in the negotiations of aircraft and sea-launched cruise missiles.[93]

Transarmament

A structural change of the armed forces, a transarmament process, could be used to produce a new type of defence—non-provocative defence. Transarmament would then have the same aim as disarmament measures —to reduce the risks of a war breaking out. The transarmament method has the advantage of not requiring negotiations before implementation. The two methods are, however, not mutually exclusive: transarmament might lead to disarmament measures.

A number of outlines for non-provocative defence systems have been presented. These usually envisage the employment of small mobile units equipped with portable short-range weapons. The units would attack enemy forces as they enter their assigned area, reducing the enemy's numbers and lowering his speed. In addition, artillery deployed at some distance from the border and border sensors are usually included in these outlines.

While the deep strike plans as currently envisaged do not fit into a non-provocative defence concept, several components could be incorporated to increase the efficiency of non-provocative defence without losing its defensive character. The incorporation of an efficient surveillance system would thus increase the time to prepare for an impending attack. Efforts made to create efficient unjammable communications systems could be taken advantage of. Much of the development in sub-munitions, guidance and warheads carried out for deep strike weapons would apply also to short-range weapons of the non-provocative defence concept.

Disengagement zones

From time to time, the idea has been put forward that a disengagement zone in central Europe could serve both to reduce the fears of surprise attack and to raise the nuclear threshold.[94] This zone could combine the withdrawal of battlefield nuclear weapons with the removal of major conventional weapons that are particularly suited for offensive use, and could cover some 100 km on each side of the inter-alliance border.[95]

Such zonal arrangements could combine disarmament, transarmament and rearmament measures. In the disarmament context, zones could be coupled to agreements in Vienna or, preferably, to all-European solutions incorporating graduated zones from the Atlantic Ocean to the Ural Mountains, with more severe restrictions of military activities and deployments closer to the central European dividing line. Whereas a mutually binding and verifiable agreement on such a zone would be preferable, its unilateral adoption by either side could well lead to increased security for both, thus enhancing their 'common security'.

Within this combined disengagement zone, defences could be 'trans-armed' along the lines discussed above. Such an arrangement would reduce tension because of its less offensive and non-provocative nature; in addition it would significantly reduce the opponent's possibilities and incentives for surprise attack. A potential aggressor would have to move his forces through a network of territorial defence units, which could reveal his main avenues of attack, slow him down by forcing him to deploy from road to battle formation, and inflict considerable attrition, especially on his vulnerable logistical tail. It would be very difficult to predict the total disruptive effects suffered by an invader within the zone, but this uncertainty would in itself contribute to deterrence, especially as the weakened invasion force would face the defender's fresh, fully mobilized counter-attack units once he has crossed the zone.

Deep strike weapons could enhance the credibility of such a defensive concept. The entire invasion force (both first and subsequent 'echelons') would be targetable, over a distance of at least 100 km (200 km if the zone, by agreement, extends bilaterally into enemy territory, banning the deployment of offensive combat units there). In order to keep up his momentum and speed, the invader would have to stay on the roads, offering ideal targets. In any war in central Europe, especially with offensive operational doctrines like AirLand Battle and the Soviet OMGs, there would rapidly develop a non-linear, intermingled battle. In such a mêlée, the light, unmechanized territorial defence units would have a decidedly different electromagnetic signature from that of the enemy's attacking armoured forces, so that the defender would need to show little self-restraint—that is, would not need to fear attacking its own troops—when firing deep strike weapons from the rear areas (where they are less vulnerable) into the zone. This is another reason why this suggested re-arrangement of NATO defences would be less vulnerable to the develop-ment of corresponding deep strike capabilities by the WTO. In addition, the vulnerable movement of NATO units from peace-time barracks to their wartime fighting positions would be reduced.

Notes and references

[1] See, for example, the European Security Study (ESECS), *Strengthening Conventional Deterrence in Europe: Proposals for the 1980s* (St Martin's Press, New York, 1983); North Atlantic Assembly, Military Committee, *Interim Report of the Sub-Committee on Conventional Defence in Europe* (K. Voigt, Rapporteur), AA191, MC/CD(83)4, November 1983.

[2] In this chapter 'deep strike' will be used in a broad sense for all the various suggestions for interdiction with conventional weapons, even though 'strike' has clear nuclear connotations in NATO. 'Deep attack' is a term defined in the US Army AirLand Battle doctrine.

[3] See Feazel, M., 'NATO ministers debate research costs', *Aviation Week & Space Technology*, Vol. 119, No. 24, 12 December 1983, pp. 18–19; Bloom, B., 'Nato holds back on advanced technology weapons', *Financial Times*, 7 December 1983.

[4] US Department of Defense, *Dictionary of Military and Associated Terms*, Joint Chiefs of Staff, Washington, D.C., 3 September 1974.

[5] US Department of Defense (note 4).

[6] Dotson, R. S., 'Tactical air power and environmental imperatives', *Air University Review*, July–August 1977, p. 29, footnote.

[7] Dews, E., *A Note on Tactical vs. Strategic Air Interdiction*, RM-6239-PR (The Rand Corporation, Santa Monica, Calif., 1970), p. v.

[8] Wikner, N. F., 'Interdicting fixed targets with conventional weapons', *Armed Forces Journal International*, Vol. 120, No. 7, March 1983, pp. 77–90.

[9] Boyle, D., 'Battlefield targeting, a requirement that won't go away', *Interavia*, September 1982, pp. 959–60.

[10] *Interavia*, April 1983, p. 285.

[11] *Defense Daily*, Vol. 131, No. 9, 14 November 1983, p. 70.

[12] *Flight International*, Vol. 125, No. 3897, 14 January 1984, p. 61.

[13] Wanstall, B. and Boyle, D., 'Attacking armour at long ranges', *Interavia*, August 1983, p. 828.

[14] Schlitz, W., 'C³ for the European air war', *Air Force Magazine*, Vol. 66, No. 6, June 1983, p. 65; Schultz, J. B., 'Milstar to close dangerous C³I gap', *Defense Electronics*, Vol. 15, No. 3, March 1983, p. 59; Ulsamer, E., 'New era in electronic warfare', *Air Force Magazine*, Vol. 64, No. 9, September 1981, p. 118; Gabbert, H., 'ECM for the extended battlefield', *Journal of Electronic Defense*, Vol. 14, No. 6, November/December 1981, pp. 27–32.

[15] Wikner, N. F., 'Neue konventionelle Technologien und Vorneverteidigung in Europa', *Europäische Wehrkunde*, 32 Jahrgang, No. 4, 1983, pp. 201–15.

[16] *Interavia AirLetter*, No. 10, 364, 19 October 1983, p. 4.

[17] *Armed Forces Journal International*, Vol. 120, No. 12, July 1983, p. 16.

[18] ' "Strike deep": a new concept for NATO', *Military Technology*, Vol. 7, Issue 5, 1983, pp. 38–60.

[19] The MW-1S and the SR-OM have originated in FR Germany as has the CWS, now merged with the French Apache. The Pégase is another French programme, while the LOC-POD is a NATO endeavour at an early stage of development. The SAW (derived from the Brunswick LADS programme), the TMD and the ND-7 are being developed in the USA. See *Military Technology* (note 18), p. 58; *Air et Cosmos*, No. 957, 4 June 1983, p. 107; *Air et Cosmos*, No. 954, 14 May 1983, p. 9; *Jane's Weapon Systems 1983–1984* (Macdonald & Co., London, 1983), p. 187; *Interavia Data, Aircraft Armament* (Interavia Data S.A., Geneva, Switzerland), July 1983, p. 429; Wikner (note 15), p. 204; Schemmer, B. F., 'NATO's new strategy: defend forward, but STRIKE DEEP', *Armed Forces Journal International*, Vol. 120, No. 3, November 1982, pp. 50–68.

[20] *Interavia AirLetter*, No. 10, 331, 1 September 1983, p. 3; Robinson, C. A., 'USAF studies new standoff weapons', *Aviation Week & Space Technology*, Vol. 119, No. 16, 17 October 1983, pp. 54–67.

[21] *International Defence Review*, Vol. 16, April 1983, p. 401; *Air et Cosmos*, No. 974, 5 November 1983, p. 48.

[22] *Air Force Magazine*, Vol. 65, No. 9, September 1982, p. 36.

[23] Ropelewski, R. R., 'Firm studies counter-airfield weapon', *Aviation Week & Space Technology*, Vol. 119, No. 9, 29 August 1983; Wikner (note 8), p. 87.

[24] 'Surface-to-surface missile recommended for NATO', *Aviation Week & Space Technology*, Vol. 116, No. 23, 7 June 1982, pp. 64–67; Schemmer, B. F., 'Tac Air, conventional force initiatives: airfield denial, runway attack and counter-air—planes or missiles?' *Armed Forces Journal International*, Vol. 120, No. 5, January 1983, pp. 48–54.

[25] *Military Technology* (note 18), p. 54.

[26] Wikner (note 15), p. 203.

[27] Wikner (note 8), p. 80.

[28] Wikner (note 15), pp. 213–14.

[29] Gordon, M. R., 'E.T. weapons to beef up NATO forces raise technical and political doubts', *National Journal*, Vol. 15, No. 8, 19 February 1983, pp. 364–69.

[30] *Military Technology* (note 18), p. 58.

[31] The development of another missile, the WASP, seems to have been halted. The range of 20 km would have given it insufficient stand-off capability. WASPs were, however, intended to get the capability of autonomously finding their targets guided by millimeter wave radar. When released in salvo the different missiles were also supposed to lock on to different targets. *Defense Daily*, Vol. 131, No. 17, 28 November 1983, p. 130.

[32] Clausen, P., 'Defence dept. joins army, air force missile projects', *Aviation Week & Space Technology*, Vol. 117, No. 18, 1 November 1982, p. 77.

[33] 'Vought competing on new missile system', *Defense Electronics*, Vol. 15, No. 11, November 1983, p. 43; Robinson, C. A. (note 20); Hewish, M., 'The Assault Breaker program, US

stand-off weapon technology of the future', *International Defense Review*, Vol. 15, September 1982, pp. 1207–11.

[34] Hewish (note 33); Sweetman, B., 'JSTARS and JTACMS', *International Defense Review* Vol. 16, November 1983, pp. 1552–53.

[35] Robinson (note 20).

[36] Sweetman (note 34).

[37] 'Improved Lance offered to NATO', *Flight International*, Vol. 122, No. 3829, 25 September 1982, p. 915.

[38] Hewish (note 33).

[39] *Jane's Defence Review*, Vol. 4, No. 9, 1983, pp. 857–58.

[40] Schemmer, B. F., 'Pave Mover—J/STARS', *Armed Forces Journal International*, Vol. 120, No. 5, January 1983, p. 39.

[41] Wikner (note 15), p. 204.

[42] Canby, S., 'The new technologies: technological brilliance or military folly?', paper prepared for SIPRI Workshop on 'Measures to Reduce the Fear of Surprise Attack in Europe', 1–3 December 1983, Stockholm, Sweden.

[43] *NATO Review*, Vol. 26, No. 3, June 1978, pp. 3–15.

[44] Komer, R. W., 'Europeans missing the irony in weapons dispute', *Boston Globe*, 1 January 1982, p. 16.

[45] *NATO Review*, Vol. 30, No. 3, 1982, p. 27.

[46] US Department of Defense, *Report of the Secretary of Defense Caspar W. Weinberger to the Congress on the FY 1984 Budget, FY 1985 Authorization Request and FY 1984–88 Defense Programs* (Annual Report to the Congress, Fiscal Year 1984), 1 February 1983, p. 275.

[47] The most comprehensive individual proposal is that of Cotter, D. R., 'Potential future roles for conventional and nuclear forces in defense of western Europe', in ESECS (note 1), pp. 209–53.

[48] *Atlantic News*, No. 1461, 22 October 1982, p. 2.

[49] *Atlantic News*, No. 1556, 21 September 1983, pp. 2–3.

[50] US Congress, Senate, Committee on Armed Services, *Department of Defense Authorization for Appropriations for Fiscal Year 1984*, Hearings, 98th Congress, 1st Session, on S. 675, Part 5: Strategic and Theater Nuclear Forces (US Government Printing Office, Washington, D.C., 1983), p. 2387.

[51] Rogers, B. W., 'Sword and shield: ACE attack of Warsaw Pact follow-on forces', *NATO's Sixteen Nations*, Vol. 28, No. 1, February–March 1983, pp. 16–26.

[52] '... die Sowjetunion hat mit alledem doch angefangen!' *Wehrtechnik*, Vol. 15, No. 5, 1983, pp. 14–18.

[53] US Department of the Army, *Field Manual 100-5, Operations* (Department of the Army, Washington, D.C., 20 August 1982).

[54] US Department of the Army, *Field Manual 100-5, Operations* (Department of the Army, Washington, D.C., 1 July 1976).

[55] Rogers, B. W., 'The "Strike Deep" initiative' (Letter to 'Defense Forum'), *Armed Forces Journal International*, Vol. 120, No. 5, January 1983, p. 5; see also Schulze, F-J., 'Wandlungen im NATO-Konzept? Ja—aber keine neue Strategie', *Wehrtechnik*, Vol. 15, No. 6, 1983, pp. 14–21, 94.

[56] US Department of the Army, Training and Doctrine Command (TRADOC), *AirLand Battle 2000* (TRADOC, Fort Monroe, Va., August 1982).

[57] The US Air Force already shows concern over the co-ordination problems involved, see Cardwell, T. A., III, 'Extending the battlefield—an airman's point of view', *Air University Review*, Vol. 34, No. 3, 1983, pp. 86–93.

[58] FM 100-5, 1982 (note 53), pp. 7–11.

[59] Alberts, D. J., 'An alternative view of air interdiction', *Air University Review*, Vol. 32, No. 5, July–August 1981, pp. 31–44.

[60] Deal, C. L., Jr., 'BAI—the key to the Deep Battle', *Military Review*, Vol. 62, No. 3, March 1982, pp. 51–54.

[61] US Department of the Army, TRADOC, *Operational Concepts for the AirLand Battle and Corps Operations—1986*, TRADOC Pamphlet No. 525-5 (TRADOC, Fort Monroe, Va., 1981).

[62] Based on World War II operations analysis, these assessments have become increasingly systematic and complex. For an introduction to such systems analysis, see Quade, E. S. (ed.), *Analysis for Military Decisions* (Rand McNally, Chicago, 1967). This chapter is confined to pointing out elements which might be included in such an analysis, with very limited opportunity cost speculations.

[63] Dews, E. and Kozaczka, F., *Air Interdiction: Lessons From Past Campaigns*, N-1743-PA&E (The Rand Corporation, Santa Monica, Calif., 1981).

[64] Rasmussen, R. D., 'The central Europe battlefield—doctrinal implications for counterair-interdiction', *Air University Review*, July–August 1978, pp. 2–20.

[65] Dews and Kozaczka (note 63), p. 14.

[66] Bray, L. W., Jr., 'Tactical counterforce', *Air Force Magazine*, Vol. 57, No. 6, June 1974, pp. 36–40.

[67] Walker, J. K., Jr., *Air Scatterable Land Mines As An Air Force Munition*, P-5955 (The Rand Corporation, Santa Monica, Calif., 1978).

[68] Canby (note 42).

[69] For a good introduction to the 'echelon' concept, see Vigor, P. H., 'Soviet army wave attack philosophy', *International Defense Review*, Vol. 12, No. 1, 1979, pp. 43–46.

[70] Hemsley, J., *Soviet Troop Control* (Brassey's, Oxford, 1982), p. 130.

[71] Echeloning seems to be rather standard practice up to divisional level (30 km); cf. Hemsley (note 70), p. 130. For an alternative view, that even divisions and regiments may deploy in single echelons, see Vigor, P. H., 'Soviet echeloning', *Military Review*, Vol. 62, No. 8, August 1982, pp. 69–74.

[72] US Department of the Army, TRADOC (note 61), p. 5.

[73] Sidorenko, A. A., *The Offensive* (Moscow, 1970), (Translated by the US Air Force, published by the US Government Printing Office), p. 97.

[74] Lupfer, T. T., *The Dynamics of Doctrine: The Changes in German Tactical Doctrine During the First World War*, Leavenworth Papers No. 4 (US Army Command and General Staff College, Fort Leavenworth, Ks., 1981).

[75] The best presentation of the OMG concept is Donnelly, C. N., 'The Soviet operational manoeuvre group—a new challenge for NATO', *International Defense Review*, Vol. 15, No. 9, 1982, pp. 1177–85. Some authors claim that Soviet forces in the GDR and Czechoslovakia are already prepared for OMG missions; see Dick, C. J., 'Soviet operational manoeuvre groups —a closer look', *International Defense Review*, Vol. 16, No. 6, 1983, pp. 769–76; Urban, M. L., 'Central group of forces', *Armed Forces*, September 1983, pp. 333–37. Others maintain that it is only a desirable option; see e.g. Lippert, G., 'Die "operativen Manövergruppen" der Sowjetarmee—eine neue Herausforderung für die NATO?', *Soldat und Technik*, Vol. 26, No. 11, November 1983, pp. 596–602; and, above all, that it should be considered in its broader context, cf. Hines, J. G. & Peterson, P. A., 'The Warsaw Pact strategic offensive—the OMG in context', *International Defense Review*, Vol. 16, No. 10, 1983, pp. 1391–95.

[76] US Congress (note 50).

[77] Rogers (note 51), p. 18.

[78] A Rand study on WTO rear area activities shows that daylight target opportunities in the first 30 km beyond FEBA could outnumber all those—day and night—at greater depth. Wise, R. A. *et al.*, *A Model of Vehicle Activity in the Warsaw Pact Tactical Rear During A Conventional Attack Against NATO*, N-1495-AF (The Rand Corporation, Santa Monica, Calif., 1980).

[79] *Atlantic News*, No. 1437, 7 July 1982, p. 2.

[80] See chapter 3.

[81] Rogers (note 55).

[82] ESECS (note 1), p. 35.

[83] International Institute for Strategic Studies, 'Defence and Consensus: The Domestic Aspects of Western Security', Parts 1–3, *Adelphi Papers*, Nos. 182–184 (IISS, London, 1983); see also appendix A.

[84] Rogers, B. W., Statement to the standing committees for foreign affairs and defence of the Second Chamber, The Netherlands Parliament, The Hague, 13 January 1983 (mimeo).

[85] Epstein, J. M., 'On conventional deterrence in Europe: questions of Soviet confidence', *Orbis*, Vol. 26, No. 1, spring 1982, pp. 71–86.

[86] Blackaby, F., Goldblat, J. and Lodgaard, S. (eds), *No-First-Use*, SIPRI (Taylor & Francis, London, 1984).

[87] Rogers, B. W., 'Greater flexibility for NATO's flexible response', *Strategic Review*, Vol. 11, No. 2, spring 1983, pp. 11–19.

[88] Nunn, S., *NATO: Can the Alliance Be Saved?* Report to the Senate Armed Services Committee (US Government Printing Office, Washington, D.C., 1982).

[89] US Congress, *Congressional Record*, Senate CR S15584, 7 November 1983.

[90] Doughty, R. A., *The Evolution of US Army Tactical Doctrine, 1946–76*, Leavenworth Papers No. 1 (US Army Command and General Staff College, Fort Leavenworth, Ks., 1979).

[91] However, 'blurring' the distinction from the other direction by making less destructive and more selective 'mini-nukes' (less than 1 kt) or warheads with special 'tailored' effects, could indeed lower the threshold by decreasing the inhibitions against their employment. This is one of the arguments behind the increased deterrent effects attributed to the neutron bomb, with its enhanced radiation/reduced blast effects. Will the threshold on the WTO side then not be correspondingly lowered, as they see decreasing chances of conventional victory? The near certainty of NATO retaliation and eventual escalation to the strategic level will remain; in effect, one may say that the 'conventional war threshold' is raised.

[92] Wit, J. S., 'Deep Strike, NATO's new defense concept and its implications for arms control', *Arms Control Today*, Vol. 13, No. 10, November 1983.

[93] Lodgaard, S., in SIPRI, *World Armaments and Disarmament, SIPRI Yearbook 1983* (Taylor & Francis, London, 1983), p. 4.

[94] Lodgaard, S. and Thee, M. (eds), *Nuclear Disengagement in Europe*, SIPRI (Taylor & Francis, London, 1983); for the historical background see Paper 1 of their book, by M. Saeter, 'Nuclear disengagement efforts 1955–80: politics of *status quo* or political change?' pp. 53–69.

[95] Lodgaard, S. and Berg, P., 'Disengagement and nuclear weapon-free zones: raising the nuclear threshold', Paper 5 in *Nuclear Disengagement in Europe* (note 94), pp. 101–14.

6. Ballistic missile defence

BHUPENDRA JASANI

Superscript numbers refer to the list of notes and references at the end of the chapter.

I. Introduction

The 1972 bilateral ABM Treaty limits land-based ABM systems and bans the development, testing or deployment of ABM systems or components which are sea-based, air-based, space-based or mobile land-based. However, there is a certain amount of ambiguity introduced in the Agreed Interpretations and Unilateral Statements regarding the ABM Treaty. For example, in Paragraph D of the Agreed Interpretations it is stated that "the Parties agree that in the event ABM systems based on other physical principles and including components capable of substituting for ABM interceptor missiles, ABM launchers, or ABM radars are created in the future, specific limitations on such systems and their components would be subject to discussion". Moreover, in Article II of the Treaty it is stated, "For the purpose of this Treaty an ABM system is a system to counter strategic ballistic missiles or their elements in flight trajectory, currently consisting of . . .". This could be interpreted as a ban on ABM systems that existed in 1972 and before. This article and paragraph D of the Agreed Interpretations would allow the development, testing and deployment of high-energy beam systems as well as some conventional ones which use optical sensors instead of radars together with non-nuclear interceptors.

In the early 1970s the significance of the Treaty was seen to lie in the fact that both sides had in effect agreed to maintain mutual vulnerability. The current interest in BMD is thus of special concern because it reflects a change of doctrine away from deterrence.

II. Conventional BMD systems

The essential elements of any BMD system are target-detection, -recognition, -tracking and -destruction systems. At present these tasks are being performed by ground-based radar sensors and by target interceptors armed with nuclear warheads. However, considerable efforts have been devoted to R&D on new concepts of a BMD system. While much can be learnt from the open literature about US thinking on BMD, an equal amount of information is not available from the Soviet Union. Thus, the following discussion is confined to the US programmes.

Since the de-commissioning of the US Safeguard ABM system in 1975, research and development funding has continued under two BMD programmes known as the Advanced Technology Program (ATP) and the Systems Technology Program (STP). Funding for these R&D programmes prior to fiscal year 1981 was nearly \$2.5 billion while for fiscal years 1982, 1983 and 1984 (requested) it was just over \$462 million, \$519 million and \$709 million, respectively.[1] The near doubling of funding in the figures of the past two years reflects the increased importance attached to these programmes.

Under the ATP, considerable emphasis has been placed on the development of non-nuclear kill warhead technology. In fact, of the total 1984 budget of \$709 million, \$170 million is for the ATP. Some 60 per cent of this is for development of the NNK warhead and optical sensor.[2] The technology is being developed for both endo- and exo-atmospheric applications using a long-wavelength infra-red optical sensor (mounted either on an aircraft or on board a missile), NNK warheads and micro-data processing of target-acquisition and -tracking information. Advanced radars are also being investigated. This investigation includes shorter wavelength (millimetre-range) radars to increase resistance to blackouts owing to nuclear explosions. Such radars may also increase the resolution and accuracy of measurements of the range, angle and speed of targets.

Passive optical sensors using long-range infra-red signals to detect and discriminate large numbers of objects in space are being investigated under the Designating Optical Tracker (DOT) programme. The device would be launched by a sounding rocket and would be operated when above the atmosphere. A DOT device has been tested on four occasions: in December 1978, February and September 1979, and June 1981.

Another development under way within the ATP is the so-called Forward Acquisition Sensor System (FASS). The purpose of FASS is to demonstrate the use of a long-range missile-borne target acquisition sensor which might be used in a BMD and in an early-warning system.

The STP is concerned with the integration of systems developed under the ATP and other programmes in a workable BMD system. At present, under the STP two BMD concepts are being considered: Low Altitude Defense (LoAD, designed for defence—below 9 km—of missiles in fixed silos); and Overlay Defense. The use of these two concepts either individually or combined in a layered defence is being considered (see figure 6.1).

At the lowest level, layered defence envisages low-altitude defence at heights of up to 9 km and terminal defence at an altitude of between 9 and 45 km using radar sensors, data processors and interceptor technology being developed under the LoAD programme. The mid-course defence ranges from altitudes of about 45 km to 90 km, and exo-atmospheric

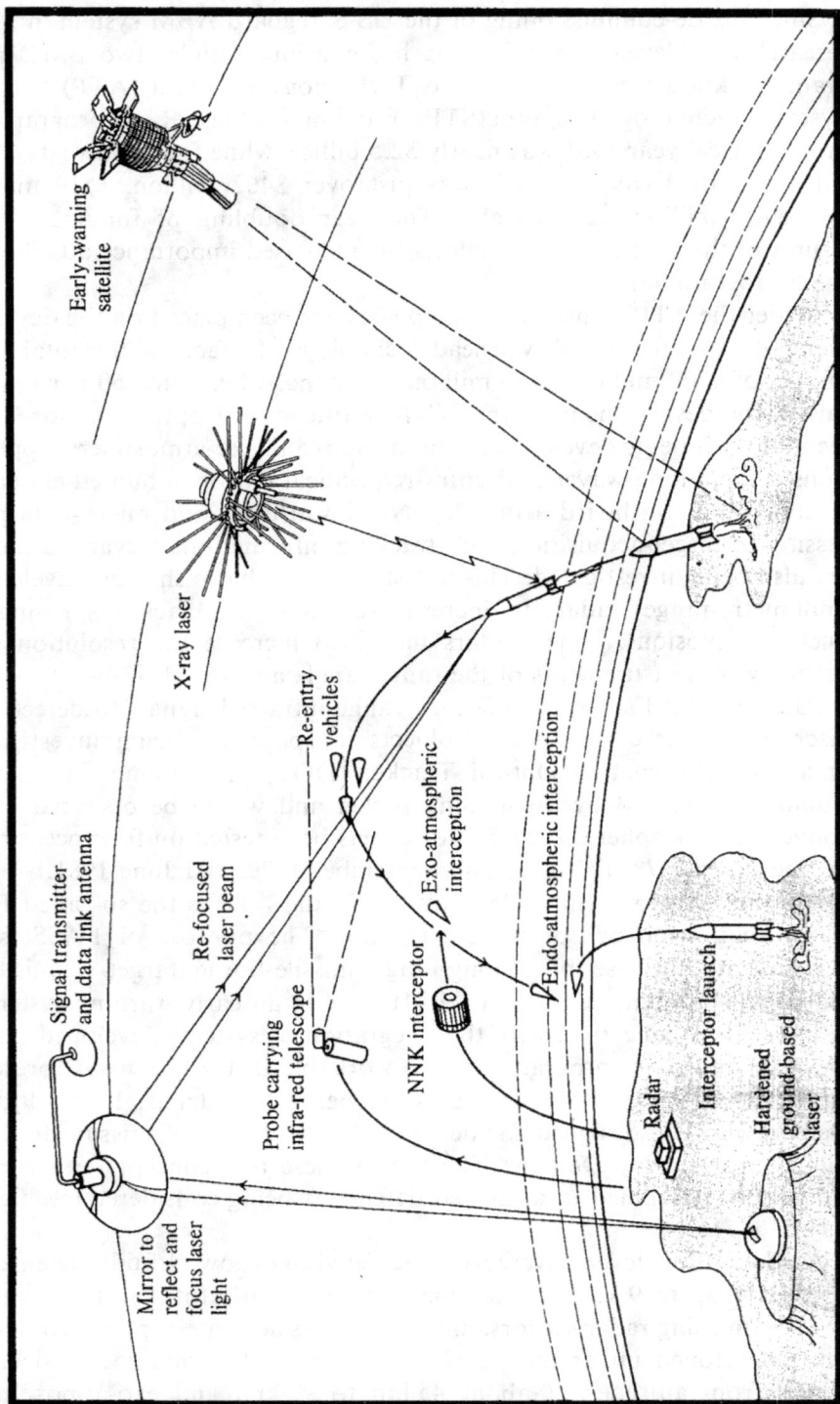

Figure 6.1. Drawing of a concept of the layered BMD system

Early-warning satellite

X-ray laser

Signal transmitter and data link antenna

Re-focused laser beam

Re-entry vehicles

Mirror to reflect and focus laser light

Probe carrying infra-red telescope

Exo-atmospheric interception

NNK interceptor

Endo-atmospheric interception

Radar

Interceptor launch

Hardened ground-based laser

defence is envisaged above 90 km. At high altitudes the defence would consist of long-range interceptors with NNK warheads and optical, terminal-homing guidance systems to intercept incoming warheads above the atmosphere.

Once warning of an attack is received either from an early-warning satellite or from forward acquisition systems such as ground-based early-warning radars, a sounding rocket would be launched. Optical sensors on board such a rocket would locate and track the warheads and transmit their trajectory data to interceptors.

Under the layered defence programme, the Homing Overlay Experiment (HOE) has been designed to investigate the NNK system and optical guidance. One of the aims of HOE is to demonstrate the intercept capability of a single NNK warhead using a long-wavelength infra-red terminal guidance system. A Minuteman I ICBM is launched, followed by the launch of an infra-red telescope to detect and track the target and then the NNK interceptor to kill the target (see figure 6.1). The infra-red telescope and its onboard data processor are planned eventually to replace large ground-based radars and computers for acquisition, assessment, tracking and discrimination of the target.

In another system, the NNK interceptor, instead of destroying the target by collision, ejects metal pellets in a controlled sequence so as to place them in concentric circles in the path of the incoming target warheads. These pellets would then destroy them on impact.[3]

Some four tests were planned under the HOE programme.[4] Two of these were completed on 7 February and 28 May 1983.[5] In both tests, the missiles failed to intercept their targets. It is interesting to note that such activities are permitted, even with the 1972 ABM Treaty. This is because, for example, the Treaty bans the use of radars in the ABM mode while an ABM optical sensor, which is based on a "different physical principle" but performs the task of a radar, is allowed according to the Agreed Statements of the Treaty.

It is also interesting to note that even as early as the late 1960s and early 1970s, the concept of layered defence was evident in US thinking on ABM systems. A further dimension seems to have been added now, as suggested by President Reagan's 23 March 1983 speech.

The BMD concepts described above do not include methods of early-trajectory or boost-phase interception of offensive missiles. High-energy laser devices or other directed-energy weapons are thought to be particularly applicable as BMD non-nuclear interceptors of ICBMs during their boost phase (see figure 6.1).[6]

III. Space-based BMD systems

There are three concepts under consideration as space-based BMD systems. The first is that in which high-energy lasers are orbited. High-energy lasers are those which have an average power output of more than 20 kilowatts (kW) or a single pulse energy of at least 30 kilojoules (kJ). For beam weapon applications laser energies range from a few hundred kilowatts to a few megawatts.

In the laboratory environment, a 10-kW laser can easily penetrate a few centimetres of steel in a fraction of a minute while, theoretically, a 5-MW hydrogen fluoride laser (power density about 2 kJ/cm²) can make a hole through steel 0.2 cm thick in less than 10 seconds from a distance of 1 000 km.[7] In the latter case it is assumed that the target surface is non-reflective and has not been hardened in any way and that the laser beam has been focused to a minimum radius of about 1 metre.

For industrial use 20-kW lasers are available, while the military has plans for lasers with a power output of between 2.5 MW and 5 MW.[8] The US Air Force has an Airborne Laser Laboratory (ALL) equipped with a 400-kW carbon dioxide gas dynamic laser. The laser emits light at an infra-red wavelength of 10.6 micrometres (μm). In early February 1981, the US Air Force tested its ALL system at full power on the ground.[9] On 1 June, the ALL was tested against an air-launched AIM-9L Sidewinder air-to-air missile. The beam hit the target, but it did not destroy it.[10] Two days later a second test was carried out against an AIM-9L missile. It was able to lock on to the target for a long period.[11] More recently, it was reported that in July 1983 the laser beam engaged five Sidewinder missiles and managed to change their course.[12]

The US Navy, under a programme called Sea Lite, is investigating a more powerful chemical laser. The Defense Advance Research Project Agency (DARPA), under the DARPA Triad programme, is investigating the use of a ground-based chemical laser device to demonstrate the feasibility of a laser suitable for deployment in outer space.[13]

The Triad consists of three elements, code-named Alpha, under which the feasibility of generating a 5-MW infra-red chemical high-energy laser is being investigated; LODE (Large Optics Demonstration Experiment) under which a large mirror, 4 metres in diameter, is being developed to steer and centre the laser beam; and Talon Gold under which the target-acquisition, -tracking and precision-pointing technologies are being investigated.[14]

Prior to 1983, the USA had already spent nearly $2 billion on high-energy lasers.[15] For fiscal year 1984, the final budget for the space weapons amounts to $1 195 million. Of this amount, $467.9 million is for directed energy weapons, $501.9 million for BMD and $225.5 million for ASAT weapons.[16]

Several types of high-energy lasers have been proposed for weapon applications. However, in order to keep the beam divergence and the size of the optics to a minimum, short-wavelength lasers are preferable. Moreover, since beam–target coupling strongly increases with decreasing wavelength, the need for short-wavelength lasers is further emphasized. Nonetheless, considerable effort has been devoted to research on long-wavelength laser devices. For example, the US Air Force ALL is equipped with a gas dynamic laser (GDL) which uses carbon dioxide. The laser radiates at 10.6 μm. In a GDL, the rapid expansion of a gas provides the inverted distribution of excited molecular energy states necessary for laser beam emission, while in a chemical laser, the corresponding conditions are obtained by means of chemical reactions. The most commonly used chemical reactions for the latter type of laser are between hydrogen and fluorine emitting radiation at 2.7 μm or deuterium and fluorine radiating at 3.8 μm. The main characteristics of these high-energy lasers are summarized in *SIPRI Yearbook 1984*. It is useful to note here that, over a 10-km path, a high-power hydrogen/fluorine laser beam is very poorly transmitted through the atmosphere while deuterium/fluorine, carbon dioxide and some short-wavelength laser beams (operating in the range between 0.3 and 2 μm) have transmittance approaching 100 per cent.

In the electric discharge laser (EDL) the lasing material is excited by collisions with the electrons of an electric discharge. Another type of EDL is called the excimer laser which uses noble gases (such as xenon or argon) and operates in the visible and near ultraviolet wavelengths. This latter laser type has produced high-power bursts at short wavelengths in the laboratory.

A relatively new and, in principle, different and tunable laser type is the free-electron laser (FEL). It might be developed to exhibit very high efficiency in converting electrical energy to laser energy. Theoretical predictions suggest that power in the megawatt range could be produced from such a laser.[17] In an FEL, an alternating magnetic field interacts with a beam of relativistic electrons causing emission of coherent radiation. The wavelength can, in principle, be selected from a range between microwave and the ultraviolet. While theoretically with the existing accelerator technology, 10–20 kW (or 10–20 kJ/s) laser light in the visible wavelength could be produced, a room-sized electron accelerator costing up to about $1 million could produce a laser light of 10–100 W (10–100 J/s) power in the infra-red wavelength range.[17]

Other potential devices which have entered the high-energy laser weapon debate are the gamma-ray laser or 'graser' and the X-ray laser. These have been the subject of theoretical analyses both in the USA and the USSR

159

for more than a decade.[18] In contrast to optical lasers which derive their beam energy from the stimulated release of energy stored in excited atoms or molecules, the radiative energy emitted by a graser or X-ray laser originates from excited states in the shell structure of the nuclei of atoms or excited states in the high-energy K and L shells of atoms. The pumping of X-ray lasers requires very intense radiation, like that emitted in a nuclear explosion.[19]

An X-ray laser can in principle be pumped by a high-intensity flash of X-rays from a conventional X-ray source. However, these are generally not intense enough to achieve the required gain, except for the possibility of optical resonances existing in the nuclei of some isotopes.[20]

X-rays can be neither reflected by mirrors nor refracted in prisms. The normal laser technique to create and sustain an inverted population of energy states in the lasing material by repeated reflections between mirrors can, therefore, not be used in X-ray lasers. Moreover, the X-ray laser radiation cannot be focused using mirrors and lenses as is done in other types of lasers. In addition, the lifetime of a high-energy excited state is very short compared with normal excited atomic states. All these factors necessitate the use of copious radiation from a nuclear explosion as the pumping source of the X-ray laser. This means that such an X-ray laser operates as a single laser pulse device. Its beam properties, particularly the beam divergence, are therefore determined by the geometry of the lasing medium, normally taken as long rods (see figure 6.1) pumped end-on by the nuclear explosion. It was reported in 1981 that the Lawrence Livermore Laboratory tested the concept of the X-ray pumped laser during an underground nuclear explosion.[21]

Thus, while the US Department of Defense has so far concentrated on the chemical laser for a possible space-based system, owing to the limitations of such a laser, the emphasis seems to be shifting towards free-electron, excimer, graser and X-rays lasers. The chemical lasers have a chemical to laser energy efficiency of at most a few hundred kilojoules per kilogram of fuel.[22] This means that a very large amount of fuel is needed which must be transported to the orbital laser platform. Moreover, the wavelength of such lasers tends to be too long for them to be efficient weapons.

There are two other important questions of a technological nature which remain to be solved. One is the need for a compact power source to supply input energy for a laser. The Soviet Union has been orbiting small 10-kW(e) nuclear power reactors for the past decade or so and the USA has a plan to orbit a 100-kW(e) reactor in the very near future.[23] In any case, if graser and X-ray lasers are made to work, they may derive their energy from small nuclear explosions. The other problem is that of acquisition of, aiming at and tracking a target. Some of these problems are common to other areas as well—for example, the NASA space telescope and space-surveillance and anti-satellite activities. Once these problems are solved the techniques will, no doubt, be applied to laser weapons as well.

The second concept in the space-based BMD scheme is that proposed by the High Frontier Group. In this concept, it is envisaged that 432 satellites, each armed with 40–45 missile interceptors, be permanently placed in orbit round the Earth.[24] The interceptors, each capable of obtaining a velocity of about 90 km/s relative to the carrier satellite, would be guided by infra-red sensors to home in on enemy missile boosters and destroy them by colliding with them at high speed. Owing to the vulnerability of the above space-based systems, a third concept has been put forward.

The third BMD concept, which is partly space-based, is that supported by US presidential science adviser George A. Keyworth. This system would consist of several hundred lasers each operating at or near the visible light spectrum. The lasers would be dispersed throughout the US land mass and would be fired at large Earth-orbiting mirrors launched in great numbers on warning of an attack by enemy missiles. The laser light would be reflected off and refocused by these mirrors on targets. While this scheme is at a conceptual stage, it is difficult to see how problems such as launching and placing the mirrors in their correct orbital positions could be solved in time for enemy missiles to be intercepted by the reflected laser beam. The total time taken by a missile to reach its target is not much longer than 30 minutes and in many instances even shorter. Thus, the mirrors have to be in placed in orbit in a considerably shorter time than 30 minutes. Moreover, the laser beam must strike the ICBMs during their boost phase, which lasts at most 300 seconds.[25]

Another method which could be classified under the third BMD concept is known as the 'pop-up' system. Anti-missile rockets would be kept ready for immediate launching carrying either conventional or nuclear explosives or X-ray laser devices. The latter would have to be a nuclear explosive laser since the pop-up rocket has to be launched with high acceleration, which could be achieved only if a relatively light payload is used. For boost-phase interception, such a pop-up system would suffer from the same objection as mentioned above (i.e., the time factor). The interception of the warheads could be made once they are released after the boost-phase but a laser may be ineffective against hardened warheads.

The technological problems involved in the sum total of the systems required for an adequate BMD are very large indeed. Many outside experts regard them as virtually insoluble, even if funds were available. An active group of leading scientists in the United States have declared their opposition to the programme. For example, Professor Hans Bethe, Chief of the Theoretical Physics Division of the Manhattan Project during World War II and a Nobel Prize Winner in physics in 1967, has stated:

... the technologies required for a defense of our population against nuclear-armed ballistic missiles are far beyond the state of the art, and in most instances are unlikely ever to work effectively. In contrast to this, countermeasures that are cheap and already known to work exist in abundance.... If it is really our objective to reduce the exposure of our population to nuclear weapons, we must avoid a commitment to global BMD, for that will produce precisely the opposite result: a large expansion of nuclear forces aimed against us, combined with a vastly complex defensive system whose performance will remain a deep mystery until the tragic moment when it will be called into action. It is difficult to imagine a more unstable and hazardous confrontation. And it is also puzzling why anyone should believe that that is the road to a less dangerous world, for a direct, cheap, and safe road is known to exist: negotiated and verifiable deep, deep cuts in strategic offensive forces, and non-nuclear alternatives to our excessive reliance on nuclear weapons.[26]

Even within the Administration there is clearly some scepticism. Richard D. De Lauer, Under-Secretary of Defense for Research, has testified that the directed-energy weapons for the proposed BMD system posed several serious technical problems and would involve "staggering costs". Each problem, he said, would require a mobilization of science and engineering as great or greater than that required to land men on the Moon.[27]

IV. Implications of BMD

Even though the technological problems relating to a space-based BMD laser weapon system may not be solved in the foreseeable future, the proposed application of high-energy laser beams raises considerable difficulties from the point of view of arms control. For example, the possible use of high-energy beam weapons as a ballistic missile defence system may have a destabilizing effect on the relationship between the two superpowers. If one side acquired such a weapon, it might then be tempted to strike first against the other, probably using tactical nuclear weapons, believing that it could still defend itself against the opponent's ICBMs, the release of which might result in escalation from tactical to strategic nuclear weapons. This is to be viewed particularly in the light of the availability of such small-yield, highly accurate nuclear weapons.

Moreover, a very important consequence would be for both the USA and the USSR to embark on yet another round of arms competition. Not only may there be a laser BMD race, but the two sides would multiply manyfold their offensive nuclear arsenals to ensure that despite the opponent's BMD systems some nuclear weapons would reach their targets. This would accelerate the nuclear arms race rather than check it.

Perhaps a more serious implication of such a development lies in the fact that it violates the spirit of the 1972 ABM Treaty. The two parties should begin discussion of the limitation of these new systems. The Treaty provides for such discussions.

The second difficulty the new technology raises—and which has been discussed very little so far—is that if X-ray or gamma-ray lasers are deployed, this may jeopardize the 1963 Partial Test Ban Treaty (PTBT), which bans nuclear weapon tests in the atmosphere, in outer space and under water. As mentioned above, an X-ray and gamma-ray laser can be produced using small thermonuclear explosions or small fission or neutron bombs. X-ray lasers will not be deployed before considerable testing, thus violating the PTBT. Certainly the deployment of such systems will violate the 1967 Outer Space Treaty, which prohibits orbiting nuclear weapons and other weapons of mass destruction. In any case, the Outer Space Treaty will be violated in spirit since orbiting any BMD system cannot be regarded as a peaceful activity (it can also be used as an ASAT weapon) and the Treaty requires parties to use outer space for peaceful purposes only.

However, perhaps a very important problem raised by the development and possible eventual deployment of beam weapons is that relating to a possible anti-satellite treaty. Both the United States and the Soviet Union began talks on the control of their anti-satellite activities during 1978 and 1979. These did not progress very far, and, in fact, the discussions ceased in 1979. As a result of the first Soviet draft treaty proposal, in 1981, the discussion has been referred to the Committee on Disarmament in Geneva. However, the CD is finding it difficult even to establish a working group to consider the issue of the arms race in space. The possible deployment of a ballistic missile defence system which can also be used as an anti-satellite weapon will complicate discussions at the CD even more.

Notes and references

[1] *Department of Defense Authorization for Appropriation for Fiscal Year 1984, Hearings before the Committee on Armed Services*, Part I, US Senate, 1 February 1983 (US Government Printing Office, Washington, D.C., 1983), p. 337.

[2] Tate, G. D., Jr, *Department of Defense Authorization for Appropriation for Fiscal Year 1984, Hearings before the Committee on Armed Services*, Part 5, US Senate, March, April, May 1983 (US Government Printing Office, Washington, D.C., 1983), pp. 2681–85.

[3] Barasch, G. E., Cooper, N. and Pollock, R., 'Ballistic missile defense—a quick-look assessment', *Los Alamos Scientific Laboratory Report No. LA-UR-80-1578*, 1980; Aldridge, R. C., *First Strike! The Pentagon's Strategy for Nuclear War* (Southend Press, Boston, Mass., 1983), p. 201.

[4] 'Ballistic missile defense', *Fiscal Year 1983 Arms Control Impact Statements*, March 1982 (US Government Printing Office, Washington, D.C., 1982), pp. 128–45.

[5] 'Ballistic missile interception test', *Interavia Air Letter*, No. 10197, 21 February 1983, p. 1; 'HOE fails to intercept target in second test', *Defense Daily*, Vol. 128, No. 23, 2 June 1983, p. 179; 'Interceptor HOE', *Air et Cosmos*, No. 961, 2 July 1983, p. 38; 'Second HOE test fails', *Interavia Air Letter*, No. 10268, 3 June 1983, p. 4.

[6] See note 3; and Barasch, G. E., Kerr, D. M., Kupperman, R. H., Pollock, R. and Smith, H. A., 'Ballistic missile defense: a potential arms-control initiative', *Los Alamos Report No. LS-8632 UC-2*, January 1982; Lamberson, D. L., *Department of Defense Authorization for Appropriations for Fiscal Year 1984, Hearings before the Committee on Armed Services*, Part 5, US Senate, March, April, May 1983 (US Government Printing Office, Washington, D.C., 1983), pp. 2646, 2650–54.

[7] Harrack, J. J., 'Analytical solutions for laser heating and burn through opaque solid slabs', *Journal of Applied Physics*, Vol. 48, No. 6, June 1977, pp. 2370–83.

[8] 'Lasers light up the battlefield', *High Technology*, Vol. 1, No. 2, November–December 1981, pp. 76–81.

[9] 'USAF tests high-energy laser weapon', *Flight International*, Vol. 119, No. 3744, 7 February 1981, p. 334.

[10] 'Laser fails to destroy missile', *Aviation Week & Space Technology*, Vol. 114, No. 23, 8 June 1981, p. 63.

[11] 'Second laser laboratory test', *Interavia Air Letter*, No. 9778, 26 June 1981, p. 8.

[12] 'Airborne laser lab downs missiles', *Laser Focus/Electro-Optics*, Vol. 19, No. 9, September 1983, p. 82.

[13] Lamberson (note 6).

[14] 'DoD's space-based laser program—potential progress and problems', *General Accounting Office Report No. C-MASAD-82-10*, 26 February 1982.

[15] *Research and Development, Hearings on Military Posture, Department of Defense Authorization for Appropriations for Fiscal Year 1983*, Committee on Armed Services, House of Representatives, Part 5, March 1982 (US Government Printing Office, Washington, D.C., 1982), p. 558.

[16] Pike, J., 'Space policy update', *Federation of American Scientists Special Interest Report*, 9 September 1983, p. 3.

[17] 'Free electrons make powerful new laser', *High Technology*, Vol. 3, No. 2, February 1983, pp. 69–70.

[18] Douglas, J. H., 'Russian progress on the nuclear laser', *Science News*, Vol. 105, 5 January 1974, pp. 8–9; Baldwin, G. C. and Khokhlov, R. V., 'Development of a "graser" may be possible if ways can be found to achieve Mössbauer transitions and population inversion simultaneously in nuclear isomers', *Physics Today*, February 1975, pp. 32–39.

[19] Winterberg, F., 'Nuclear and thermonuclear directed beam weapons', *Fusion*, August 1981, pp. 52–54.

[20] 'New hope for gamma-ray lasers', *Laser Focus*, Vol. 18, No. 10, October 1982, pp. 14–15; Chapline, G. and Wood, L., 'X-ray lasers', *Physics Today*, June 1975, pp. 40–48.

[21] Robinson, C. A., Jr, 'Advance made on high-energy laser', *Aviation Week & Space Technology*, Vol. 114, No. 8, 23 February 1981, pp. 25–27.

[22] Henderson, W. D., 'Space-based lasers—ultimate ABM system?', *Astronautics & Aeronautics*, May 1982, pp. 44–53.

[23] Angelo, J. P., Jr and Buden, D., 'Shielding considerations for advanced space nuclear reactor systems', *Los Alamos Report No. LA-UR-82-2002*, 1982.

[24] Graham, D. O., *High Frontier—A New National Strategy* (High Frontier, Washington, D.C., 1982), pp. 119–28.

[25] The trajectory of an ICBM can be divided into three parts: the boost phase, during which time the ICBM is most vulnerable since it is easily detectable by observations of the exhaust flame from the booster and the missile structure is under considerable mechanical strain; the mid-course phase, during which the missile releases its warheads or warheads; and the re-entry phase, during which the warheads enter the atmosphere.

[26] Statement by Hans A. Bethe, *A Hearing of the House Armed Services Committee, Subcommittee on Investigations and Research and Development*, H.R. 3073, The People Protection Act, 10 November 1983.

[27] Wilford, J. N., 'Group of top scientists close to government fighting space weapons plan', *New York Times*, 16 November 1983, p. A8.

7. Negotiations on chemical disarmament

JULIAN PERRY ROBINSON (section I) and
JOZEF GOLDBLAT (section II)

I. Introduction and summary

SIPRI Yearbook 1984 records developments in the field of chemical and biological warfare (CBW) since the review published in *SIPRI Yearbook 1982* and its update in *SIPRI Yearbook 1983*. It concentrates on developments bearing directly upon the prospects for effective CBW disarmament. The perspective continues to be that of a Western observer.

At the time of writing (December 1983), chemical weapons have gained a new prominence from the apparent breakdown of the nuclear weapon talks in Geneva (START and INF) and the force reduction talks in Vienna (MBFR), for they are now the subject of the only intergovernmental arms negotiations involving both superpowers for which a definite date of recommencement has been set. The CW talks are taking place within the CD/CW—the *Ad Hoc* Working Group on Chemical Weapons of the multilateral Committee on Disarmament (CD) in Geneva—which reconvenes on 16 January 1984. It may turn out that the present confrontational attitudes of the superpowers will damage the CD, too, when it reconvenes, as the Conference on Disarmament, on 7 February 1984. In that event, even if the CD/CW is remandated for the year, it may prove a largely empty shell. But there are several factors, including the US Presidential and Congressional elections, militating against this, so that the substantial achievements of the CD/CW during 1983 may still begin to bear some fruit in 1984.

It cannot be said that CW is the most pressing of the security problems currently confronting the international community, yet the manner in which it is finally brought under control could have major implications for arms control in more important areas. The objective that has formally been accepted in the CW talks is not a mere ceiling or set of limitations but comprehensive disarmament, with all that would imply for the relative status of brute military power as determinant of national security. Further, the peculiarities of CW technology, and of the industrial base which provides it, require verification and other confidence-building measures of an exceptionally innovative kind if the chemical weapons convention that is being sought is to have lasting security value. Should that goal be achieved, obstacles to worthwhile agreement on nuclear and even conventional armaments would be diminished, and the prospects for constraining the overall arms race correspondingly enhanced.

The chief developments bearing upon CBW arms control during 1983 may be reviewed under three main headings: the progress made in the CD towards CW disarmament, concurrent moves in the field of CW armament and rearmament, and the reports alleging violations of the existing CBW arms control agreements.

Developments within the CD are reviewed in section II. Here in summary are the main points. In February 1983 the Vice-President of the United States informed the CD that the USA "would like to see ... negotiations undertaken on a treaty" banning chemical weapons, and six days later the US delegation submitted a long paper setting out its views on what exactly such a treaty should provide. The Administration of President Reagan had thus, for the first time, disclosed in detail its attitudes towards CW arms control. These attitudes did not differ in any major degree from those of the previous Administration. The CD already had before it the Soviet 'Basic Provisions' of June 1982, a similar though less detailed outline-treaty paper which envisaged, for the first time in any specific Soviet disarmament proposal since the days of the League of Nations, some application of *systematic* international on-site inspection. What had thus at last taken shape within the CD were outer bounds within which a potentially worthwhile compromise might be negotiated. The gap between the US Detailed Views and the Soviet Basic Provisions was not small, but, although the USSR continued to attract criticism from Western and non-aligned countries for withholding clarification of key features of its position, the concessions it had made by the end of the summer session of the CD had slightly narrowed the gap. However, neither the USSR nor its closest Warsaw Treaty Organization (WTO) allies accepted the invitation extended by the USA to CD members to visit, in November 1983, the CW stockpile location in Utah at which a demilitarization facility for CW agents and munitions was to be displayed for the purposes of a workshop on the verification of CW stockpile destruction. Prominent in the background to the CD's proceedings was the drive by the US Administration to modernize US CW capabilities, most evident in the unprecedented intensity with which the White House was again seeking to persuade the Congress to fund procurement of new nerve-gas munitions. The high point of the CD's work in 1983 came with the adoption of a report from the CD/CW setting out clearly the state of both agreement and disagreement on more than 100 of the subordinate issues on which consensus must be reached before the projected chemical weapons convention can be concluded. This document displays the full magnitude of the task ahead, but it also provides both a constructive framework and a new degree of obligation upon the participating states for proceeding with that task.

Developments during 1983 in armaments and use-allegations are reviewed more fully in *SIPRI Yearbook 1984*. With regard to armaments they were marked by two contradictory actions of the US Congress. The first, coming immediately after the September 1983 shooting down of the jumbo jet on Korean Air Lines flight 007, was legislation authorizing full-scale production of binary nerve-gas munitions. The second, six weeks later, was legislation expressly denying funding for that purpose during the 1984 fiscal year. As to armament developments in other countries, the USSR continued to maintain its silence on its own programmes. So did France. Information purporting to describe Soviet programmes was, however, released in new detail by the US Defense Department. Reports that certain countries outside the main superpower alliances are now arming with CBW weapons acquired, in some cases, new credibility during the year, but no definite substantiation. Iraq must now be added to the list of alleged possessor states.

With regard to allegations of use of CBW weapons, there were further developments concerning the Yellow Rain and related reports, none of which make it easier, however, for objective observers to judge whether toxic weapons really have or have not been used in Afghanistan and South-East Asia on the scale portrayed by the US government. What has become clearer is that most—maybe all—of the publicly disclosed evidence pointing to use of toxic weapons in Laos and Kampuchea does not in fact exclude the possibility of natural causation for the reported death and disease. Meanwhile, the Group of Consultant Experts convened by the UN Secretary-General in accordance with a resolution of the 37th General Assembly has made an interim report on the types of machinery and procedure that should be available if there are any further allegations of toxic-weapon employment. In December 1983 just such a complaint was lodged with the Secretary-General by Iran against Iraq.

II. Chemical disarmament

In 1983 the *Ad Hoc* Working Group of the CD which deals with the ban on chemical weapons, a priority item on the CD's agenda, continued its work. The three most comprehensive papers before the Group were the 1980 joint US–Soviet report on the bilateral negotiations on the prohibition of chemical weapons; the "basic provisions" for a chemical weapons convention, proposed in 1982 by the USSR; and the "detailed views" on the contents of such a convention, submitted in February 1983 by the USA. The problems most extensively discussed in the CD are reported in this section along with the points made and specific proposals put forward by individual delegations. (A complete list of official documents and working papers related to chemical weapons, produced in the course of the 1983 session of the CD, can be found in the CD report of 1 September 1983.)

Destruction/elimination of stockpiles

The USA proposed that the convention prohibiting chemical weapons should cover supertoxic lethal, other lethal, and other harmful chemicals, such as incapacitating chemicals (a classification based on the criterion of toxicity), as well as the precursors (chemicals used in their production), but not riot-control agents or herbicides. Toxins (synthetically produced) would be included implicitly since they are toxic chemicals. The reason given for the omission of riot-control agents and herbicides was that these chemicals would remain available in significant quantities for legitimate purposes.

The process of eliminating chemical weapons by destroying them should begin not later than six months after the convention has entered into force, and be completed not later than 10 years after that date. It should be carried out according to an agreed schedule, employing procedures which permit systematic international on-site verification. Such verification would have to take place on a continuous basis until destruction was completed. The depositary of the convention would be notified annually about the implementation of the parties' plans for elimination of chemical weapon stocks; the parties would also have to certify to the depositary that their stocks had been eliminated, not later than 30 days after the elimination process had been completed.

In a working document of July 1983, the USA emphasized that verification procedures for destruction of declared stocks should be designed to confirm the identity and quantity of the materials destroyed, and to confirm that the materials had actually been destroyed. The principles defined by the USA to guide verification of chemical agent destruction include: a detailed engineering review of the disposal facility by international verification personnel, including on-site inspection, before destruction operations begin; continuous inspection during periods in which destruction operations are under way; confirmation by the inspectors of the validity of all data used for verification purposes; minimizing interference with the operation of the destruction facility, while providing effective verification; and close co-operation between international verification personnel and host state operating personnel.

To facilitate verification, Yugoslavia proposed that a declaration of existing stocks of chemical warfare agents and chemical weapons should be made immediately or as soon as possible after the entry into force of the convention, say within 30 days. The declaration should specify the existence and location of stocks and the type and quantity of agents and weapons, and should contain proposals regarding the manner in which the stocks were to be destroyed and information about when the destruction would begin and how it would be verified. At this stage, the parties would also have to declare stocks of precursors.

The Soviet Union proposed that the parties should declare, also within 30 days after the convention entered into force, their stocks of chemical weapons, both filled and unfilled, their precursors and the components of binary weapons, by their chemical names and by the toxicity of the chemicals, in metric tons, and their stocks of chemical munitions by types and calibres. It considered, however, that the requirement to declare locations of the stocks was unrealistic, because it did not take into account the possible general use of such places where chemical weapons were kept and might affect defence interests not connected with chemical weapons. Instead, the USSR suggested that provision should be made for the creation of store-houses at the specialized facilities for the destruction of these stocks, the location of which would be declared concurrently with the declaration of the destruction facilities. At such places of storage, international verification would be permitted on a 'quota' basis, that is, through an agreed number of annual international inspections. The frequency of inspection visits would depend on the quantity of the stocks to be destroyed at a facility, the capacity of the facility, the toxicity of the chemicals and other relevant factors.

The German Democratic Republic suggested that binary chemical weapons be destroyed first. Their destruction should start within six months of the convention entering into force, and be completed within two years, while the destruction of other chemical weapons should begin within eight years and be completed within 10 years after entry into force of the convention. The GDR also reiterated the Warsaw Treaty Organization's proposal for a Europe free of chemical weapons and expressed readiness to enter into negotiations with states interested in creating a chemical weapon-free zone in central Europe.

The United States considered the proposal to single out binary chemical weapons for special treatment as "extraordinarily one-sided", and as intended to preserve Soviet chemical weapon capabilities while eliminating those of the USA. As regards chemical weapon disengagement in Europe, the opinion of the Federal Republic of Germany was that removal of chemical ammunition would not protect the European zone from being attacked with the same kind of ammunition from the outside, by ordnance or from aeroplanes.

Italy requested that the destruction of stocks of chemical weapons should be accompanied by extensive environmental and security measures, which could affect both the methods of destruction and the duration of the operations in question. In this connection, it suggested that a clause be included in the convention permitting the transfer of stocks of chemical weapons for purposes of destruction under appropriate international control. This would be, in the opinion of Italy, the most reliable way of eliminating certain stocks.

Agreement could not be reached on the following questions:

1. Should the location of chemical weapon stocks be declared as part of the initial declaration?

2. What information should be provided about the stocks in such a declaration?

3. Should the declared stocks be subject to prompt and systematic international on-site inspections and, if so, on what basis?

4. Should the declared stocks be subject to systematic international on-site monitoring until they are eliminated and, if so, on what basis?

5. Could some stocks, as an alternative to their destruction, be eliminated by being used for non-hostile purposes and, if so, which chemicals could be so used, in which quantities, and under which verification provisions?

6. What specific measures are required for systematic international on-site verification?

7. What should be the deadline for beginning the elimination of stocks?

8. How should the general schedule for stockpile destruction be defined?

9. What should be the nature of the provisions regarding transfer of declared stocks from one party to another for the purpose of destruction, and regarding chemical weapons found after the initial declaration has been made?

Destruction/elimination of the means of production

According to a US proposal, each party should cease immediately all activity at any chemical weapon production or filling facility; close each facility according to agreed procedures which would render the facility inoperative; permit systematic international on-site inspection promptly after declaration, and subsequently at agreed intervals until the facility is destroyed; permit the monitoring of each facility by appropriate types of sensor; destroy each facility by razing it, employing agreed procedures which permit systematic international on-site verification; begin destruction of the chemical weapon production and filling facilities not later than six months after the date on which the convention entered into force and complete the destruction not later than 10 years after that date; permit systematic international on-site verification of the destruction of such facilities; undertake not to construct any new facilities, or modify existing ones, for purposes proscribed by the convention; annually notify the depositary of the convention regarding implementation of the plan for the destruction of facilities; and certify to the depositary that the facilities have been destroyed, not later than 30 days after the destruction process has been completed. A chemical weapon production or filling facility could be temporarily converted for destruction of chemical weapons, but it would have to be destroyed as soon as it was no longer in use.

According to a Yugoslav proposal, the declaration of production facilities should specify the location of the facility and its owner; complete documentation on the technological processes, the facility's capacity and the raw materials used, apparatus, measuring instruments, ventilation systems, etc.; as well as include a proposal for the destruction of the facility. In the case of production facilities for precursors, the declaration should also describe the technological process, capacity and technical documentation, and contain a proposal for destroying or dismantling the facility. Filling facilities for chemical weapons should be similarly declared and closed within 30 days of the entry into force of the convention. The declaration of these facilities should specify their location and capacity; the agents used for filling, and the type and kind of the weapons produced; measuring instruments; as well as plans for destruction.

The Soviet Union proposed that elimination of chemical weapon production facilities should start not later than eight years after the convention has entered into force, and that the declaration of their location should be made one year before that date. Consequently, the initial declarations of the parties would refer only to the existing capacities for the production of chemical weapons.

Thus, the differences which remained concerned the contents and the timing of the declaration of chemical weapon plants and the specification of their location, as well as the methods of their elimination and verification.

Non-production of chemical weapons in the chemical industry

To make sure that the substances listed as key precursors were not being used for the production of chemical weapons, it would be necessary, in the view of the United Kingdom, to subject to inspection the facilities which produce these substances. An appropriate verification regime for declared facilities would comprise the following components: (*a*) declarations of facilities producing chemicals specified in an agreed list, and of facilities designed, constructed or used for such purposes in the past; (*b*) periodic random selection of a number of such declared facilities for on-site inspections; and (*c*) on-site inspections by a team of inspectors. The objectives of on-site inspection would be to ensure that the quantities of a particular substance being produced at the facility under inspection were compatible with the declared use; that any stockpiling was carried out in a manner and quantity compatible with the declared civil use; and that the production facilities had not been modified in such a way that they could be used to produce chemical warfare agents. All such measures would apply to key precursors for supertoxic chemicals. As regards dual-purpose chemicals which have a wide civil use but are also important in chemical warfare, there would have to be a requirement for a declaration of all facilities producing these chemicals above a pre-determined quantity, and of their civil uses. In the opinion of the United Kingdom, inspections would affect few facilities and could be so designed as to cause as little disruption as possible to the chemical industry; the number of routine inspections would be kept to a minimum and the inspection procedures could be both simple and confidential; they would not involve intrusion into research activities or into the details of production.

Sweden noted that routine monitoring of non-production of supertoxic lethal chemicals and key precursors on the basis of agreed on-site visits according to a random selection system would help to avoid the "politically cumbersome" verification by challenge. Also, the Netherlands and the United Kingdom thought that routine monitoring would be preferable, because it may be difficult to acquire enough information to justify a request for a challenge inspection, and because a challenge could create distrust and lead to recriminations. Nevertheless, in the opinion of Sweden, verification by challenge would be necessary when the destruction period had expired and when the parties could not resolve a controversy through consultations. Since verification can be arranged in such a way as to preclude disclosure of unrelated sensitive information to the challenging party, turning down a request for on-site inspection would be perceived as a tacit admission of violation. However, the Soviet Union expressed the view that one cannot demand from a state to which a request was addressed that it should automatically accept verification.

Yugoslavia suggested that the production of key precursors for chemical weapons should be prohibited along with the weapons themselves. If their application in civilian industry were proven, their production should be carried out under strict control. States producing precursors for chemical weapons should be obliged to submit an annual report on the capacity of their production and on the further processing of these chemicals.

Important differences remained with respect to possible restrictions on supertoxic chemicals for permitted purposes. These are defined as industrial, agricultural, research, medical and other peaceful purposes, as well as law enforcement and protective purposes, and military purposes (such as the use of chemicals as rocket fuels) which are not related to chemical weapons. In particular, there were no identical views on whether there should be a limit on the amount of supertoxic lethal chemicals and key precursors which a party might have for all permitted purposes, including protective purposes and, if so, what the agreed amount should be and what the agreed production/capacity limit of a small-scale facility producing supertoxic lethal chemicals for permitted purposes should be. Neither was there agreement on the development of lists of chemical substances meeting the criteria of key precursors. The topics to be further discussed in order to develop procedures for verifying non-production of key precursors for chemical weapon purposes include information to be exchanged concerning the production facility location and capacity, the production level, civil use, and so on.

Prohibition of transfer

In the view of the United States, not only transfer of chemical weapons but also transfer to anyone "other than another party" of supertoxic lethal chemicals or key precursors produced or otherwise acquired for protective purposes should be prohibited. Permitted transfers would be limited to a maximum of 100 grams in any 12-month period. Advance notification of any transfers of such supertoxic lethal chemicals or key precursors would be necessary.

There was agreement that transfers, except for elimination purposes, would be restricted, but the allowable circumstances and amounts for such transfers required further consideration.

Verification institutions

It is generally assumed that a consultative committee will be established by the parties to the chemical weapons convention. The tasks of the committee, as viewed by the USA, would be: to develop and revise, as necessary, provisions for exchange of information, declarations and technical matters related to implementation of the convention; to review new scientific and technical developments which could affect the operation of the convention; to provide a forum for timely discussion of questions regarding compliance; to conduct systematic on-site inspections of the declared stockpiles, of the destruction of stocks, of the closure and destruction of declared production and filling facilities, of permitted small-scale production and facilities for supertoxic lethal chemicals for protective purposes, and of production for permitted purposes of specified types of chemicals which are deemed to pose a particular risk; to conduct *ad hoc* on-site inspections for fact-finding purposes; and to participate in such inspections agreed between two or more parties, if requested to do so by one of the parties involved. The consultative committee should not take any decision as to whether or not a party was in compliance with the provisions of the convention.

In order to facilitate prompt implementation of the provisions of the convention after its entry into force, the USA proposed that a preparatory commission should be set up soon after the convention was opened for signature. The commission would prepare studies, reports and recommendations for consideration by the consultative committee, and would remain in existence until the first meeting of the committee.

Within 30 days after entry into force of the convention, the depositary would have to establish a fact-finding panel. This panel would conduct a prompt fact-finding inquiry, including any necessary *ad hoc* inspections, make appropriate findings of fact, and provide expert views on any problem referred to it by the depositary upon request by a party. The fact-finding panel would be composed of not more than 15 members representing the parties.

It was emphasized by the Federal Republic of Germany that national technical means were insufficient for verifying a chemical weapon ban and that, consequently, "decisive" importance was attached to an international committee of experts with autonomous competence, including the right to carry out on-site inspections. Indeed, on-site inspection, possibly strengthened by remote sensors, is considered by many states to be the key to achieving a chemical weapons convention.

Brazil insisted that the composition of the international body charged with verification should not be discriminatory. Nor should the solution of disputes concerning compliance be referred to the UN Security Council whose rules permit a few parties to block all action. To inspire confidence in the credibility of the convention, and to encourage thereby the largest possible number of states to accede to it, Egypt suggested that, in addition to a stipulation concerning the convening of the consultative committee to consider matters relating to a violation of the convention, specific provision should be made for a commitment on the part of all parties to assist any state whose security was endangered or which was otherwise prejudiced as a result of the violation.

Non-use of chemical weapons

A number of countries, especially the non-aligned, have for many years insisted on the necessity to incorporate in the future chemical weapons convention a prohibition on the use of these weapons. Such a clause, it was argued, would make the convention truly comprehensive; it would also strengthen the 1925 Geneva Protocol which had banned the use of asphyxiating, poisonous and other gases, but allowed for ambiguity on the chemicals covered, left open the possibility of recourse to chemical weapons under certain circumstances, was applicable to "war" rather than to any armed conflict, and did not provide for verification. As a matter of fact, it was mainly because of the need for a provision to investigate the alleged use of chemical weapons that the proposal was made to include the prohibition of use in the convention.

The Soviet Union and its allies strongly opposed this proposition, claiming that it would prejudice the 1925 Geneva Protocol rather than strengthen it. But in 1983 they finally agreed to extend the scope of the negotiated convention, and suggested that the procedures to verify compliance with a no-use provision should envisage the use of the verification mechanism of the convention, including on-site inspection on a voluntary basis. Should any state not become party to the convention, it would not be released from its obligations under the Geneva Protocol, while the parties to the convention would be bound by the obligation not to use chemical weapons under both international agreements.

In the discussions that followed, Belgium made a reservation as to the appropriateness of including the Geneva Protocol prohibition in the convention under consideration. One question raised was whether such a prohibition, repeated solely in the context of chemical weapons, would not create a lacuna with regard to bacteriological weapons, which were equally prohibited by the Protocol. Nevertheless, a convergence of views seems to have emerged on the following issues: the contemplated prohibition clause should apply with respect to use against all states, not only parties to the convention; the prohibition should also apply in *any* armed conflict (to be further defined in an agreed understanding); verification of alleged use of chemical weapons should be provided for in the convention; there should be a clause of non interference with the relevant international treaties; the convention should contain the 'traditional' withdrawal clause; and there should be a reference to the obligations set forth in the 1925 Geneva Protocol.

Consensus could not be reached on whether the prohibition on use should apply to riot-control agents and herbicides; a solution will obviously depend on the definitions to be formulated in the convention. Neither was it possible to agree on how to uphold in law the deterrence value of remaining stocks of chemical weapons in the period preceding their destruction, or how states could preserve, should they choose to do so, the right to retaliate during this period. There was no common view as to the extent to which the 1925 Geneva Protocol had been subsumed in customary international law and how this should be reflected in the convention.

It will be recalled that in 1982 France suggested that "provisional" procedures for the verification of compliance with the Geneva Protocol should be worked out to apply until the conclusion of the chemical weapons convention. The United Nations then adopted a resolution requesting the UN Secretary-General to investigate, with the assistance of qualified consultant experts, information brought to his attention concerning activities that may constitute a violation of the Geneva Protocol, or of the relevant rules of customary international law. Procedures for the timely and efficient investigation of such information were to be devised. The Soviet Union refused to co-operate with the Secretary-General in this work because, in its view, a mechanism for the verification of compliance with the Geneva Protocol should be elaborated by the parties to the Protocol, on the basis of consensus, and not by the United Nations. However, France maintained that the aim of the resolution was to establish speedily a means of investigation in order to uphold the authority of, and to ensure respect for, the Geneva Protocol pending future commitments. (For a discussion of the recommended procedures, see *SIPRI Yearbook 1983*.)

In October 1983 a group of experts, set up in pursuance of the mentioned UN resolution, submitted its report. It suggested that, in deciding whether or not to initiate an investigation, the Secretary-General should be guided by the following criteria: (*a*) Has the state, which is reporting information concerning a possible violation, requested an investigation? (*b*) Does the report allege that chemical or biological warfare agents have been used, or that there has been an incident involving the use of a substance that can be construed as being a chemical or biological agent? (*c*) Does the report allege that the use occurred in the course of armed conflict or that the agent was used in a deliberately hostile manner? (*d*) Does the report contain sufficient information and was it submitted promptly enough, so that there is a good possibility that evidence of value to an investigation remains? Information contained in the allegation should include a description of the event with such details as the means of delivery, duration of the attack, effects on humans, animals and plants, and physical evidence, as well as the exact time and location of the alleged use.

Once the above criteria have been met, investigation should be initiated as rapidly as possible, ideally within 24 hours. If access to the territory of the country where the incident reportedly occurred is not possible, either because the government of that country will not permit it or because the security of the team and/or the necessary logistic support cannot be assured, or if any other obstacles to the investigation should arise, a neighbouring country or countries would be selected where evidence may be available through refugees or other persons crossing the border, and which would permit access to the team. If no possibility exists for visiting either the country where the incident reportedly occurred or a neighbouring country, the Secretary-General, with the assistance of experts, will evaluate such evidence as may be available while continuing to seek opportunities for conducting on-site investigation in the region where the alleged attack occurred. He will report to the UN member states and to the General Assembly when the analysis of the available information has been completed.

The report contains guidance for the conduct of an investigation, including guidance for the UN Secretariat for the grouping of experts according to their field of expertise, and for the classification of laboratories according to the type of analyses they can conduct. It also specifies the standards concerning the collection and handling of samples. An illustrative list of types of equipment to be stockpiled by the Secretariat and to be made available to the investigating team includes such items as protective equipment, kits for detection of chemical and biological warfare agents, sampling and packing equipment, and medical supplies for members of the team. Furthermore, criteria have been formulated for selection of members of the team to carry out fact-finding and evaluation. Methods have been prescribed for preservation of samples, and procedures have been recommended for the transmission and analysis of samples. On-site investigation itself would include a meeting with the local authorities to establish the programme of inspections and arrangements for logistic support and security for the team, examination of the site of the alleged attack, interviews with and medical examination of alleged victims, interviews with eyewitnesses, and interviews with military personnel, civil defence staff and social workers who participated in relief activities following the alleged attack.

The report of the team of experts should indicate the extent to which the alleged events have been substantiated, and possibly assess the probability of their having taken place. Individual opinions dissenting from the majority would also be recorded.

Because of the complexity of the subject matter and the shortage of time, it was not possible for the group to review thoroughly such aspects as the legal problems involved in the transportation of samples, requirements for logistic support and security arrangements, and materials needed in the course of an investigation. Neither was the group in a position to proceed with the assembling and systematic organization of documentation relating to the identification of signs and symptoms associated with the use of prohibited agents, as requested by the UN resolution.

Although consensus was reached in the CD that the negotiated convention prohibiting chemical weapons should include procedures to verify the ban on the use of such weapons, the interest in establishing an investigation mechanism within the framework of the United Nations, as a transitional measure, did not subside. Consequently, by a resolution adopted with 97 votes against 20, with 30 abstentions, the General Assembly asked the Secretary-General to pursue his action and to complete during 1984 the task entrusted to him under the terms of the 1982 resolution.

Conclusion

In 1983, consideration of the question of chemical weapons prohibition helped to reduce the points of disagreement among states on a number of technical matters as well as on certain procedures for verification. The remaining divergencies are not without significance, but the area of converging views now seems to be sufficiently wide to render possible the drafting of actual treaty provisions. This is the view of the overwhelming majority of the United Nations, which in the General Assembly resolutions of 20 December 1983 urged the CD to intensify negotiations on a chemical weapons convention, and to proceed immediately to drafting such a convention. Indeed, the very process of drafting, which implies trade-offs among the negotiators, may be conducive to overcoming the outstanding obstacles.

Further discussion of technical details, especially when they are of secondary importance and are related to obligations which have not yet been agreed upon, can hardly speed up progress. In any event, it is impossible to foresee all eventualities and formulate a treaty text accordingly. This is especially true of a chemical weapons convention in view of the complexity of the issues involved. It is therefore of paramount importance that an efficient mechanism be set up under the convention to deal, on a continuous basis and through consultations among the parties, with all the controversies that may arise. For the signing of the convention would merely mark the beginning of a lengthy process of chemical weapons elimination, which itself may create new problems.

8. US and Soviet allegations of breaches of arms control agreements

JOZEF GOLDBLAT

Superscript numbers refer to the list of notes and references at the end of the chapter.

Allegations of breaches of arms control agreements have been made repeatedly in the past 10 years, especially since 1980 when East–West cold war rhetoric became particularly shrill. They coincided, significantly enough, with the interruption or suspension of a series of important US–Soviet negotiations. But it was only at the beginning of 1984 that the United States and the Soviet Union decided to draw up comprehensive lists of their complaints against each other and make the lists public. This section summarizes the allegations put forward by the two powers as well as their responses. An attempt is also made to evaluate the charges.

I. US allegations

A report sent by President Reagan to the US Congress on 23 January 1984 lists seven cases of alleged non-compliance by the Soviet Union with its obligations under arms control agreements.[1]

1. The USSR maintains an "offensive" biological warfare programme and capabilities, and is involved in the production, transfer and use of toxins and other lethal chemical warfare agents that have been used in Laos, Kampuchea and Afghanistan. It has therefore violated its legal obligations under the 1972 Biological Weapons Convention and customary international law as codified in the 1925 Geneva Protocol.

2. The notification of the Soviet military manoeuvre *Zapad-81*, which took place on 4–12 September 1981, was "inadequate". The USSR therefore violated its political commitment under the Document on confidence-building measures, included in the 1975 Final Act (Helsinki Declaration) of the Conference on Security and Co-operation in Europe (CSCE).

3. The USSR is building near Krasnoyarsk in central Siberia a large phased-array radar. This is "almost certainly" a violation of the Soviet legal obligations assumed under the 1972 ABM Treaty, which limits the location and orientation of such radars with the view to precluding a territorial anti-ballistic missile defence.

4. The USSR has engaged in encryption of missile test telemetry (radio signals sent from a missile to ground monitors) deliberately to impede

verification. This practice constitutes a violation of the 1979 SALT II Treaty, under which the parties shall not deny telemetric information whenever such denial impedes verification. (Although the SALT II Treaty did not formally enter into force, the signatories were obligated under international law not to take action during the pre-ratification period, which would defeat the object and purpose of the unratified agreement; in 1981, after the USA had made clear its intention not to ratify the Treaty, the signatories assumed a 'political' commitment, as distinct from a 'legal' obligation, to refrain from actions contrary to its provisions.)

5. The USSR has tested a 'second new' type of ICBM (the SS-X-25). While the evidence is "somewhat ambiguous", such testing is a "probable" violation of the Soviet political commitment to observe the 1979 SALT II Treaty, which limits each party to 'one new type' of ICBM in order to constrain modernization and proliferation of more capable types. Even if the Soviet assertion were accepted that the SS-X-25 was not a prohibited new type of ICBM (the USSR stated that the SS-X-24 was its allowed one new type of ICBM), the USSR still acted contrary to the SALT II Treaty provision which prohibits an ICBM of an existing type, and equipped with a single re-entry vehicle, to be flight-tested with a re-entry vehicle the weight of which is less than 50 per cent of the throw-weight of that ICBM in order to bar the possibility that single warhead ICBMs could be quickly converted to MIRVed (multiple independently targetable re-entry vehicles) systems. Encryption on this missile impeded verification by the USA.

6. The USSR has deployed the SS-16 ICBM. While the evidence is "somewhat ambiguous" and no definitive conclusion could be reached, the Soviet Union's activities at Plesetsk (a missile test range) are a "probable" violation of its legal obligation (prior to 1981) and of its political commitment (after 1981) under the 1979 SALT II Treaty not to deploy the SS-16 nor to produce the third stage and the re-entry vehicle of that missile in order not to leave open the possibility of converting land-based launchers of ballistic missiles which are not ICBMs into launchers for ICBMs.

7. The USSR has conducted nuclear tests having a yield in excess of the agreed threshold. While the evidence is "ambiguous" and no definitive conclusion could be reached, the Soviet nuclear testing activities for a number of tests constitute a "likely" violation of the legal obligations under the 1974 Threshold Test Ban Treaty (TTBT), which prohibits the carrying out, as from 31 March 1976, of any underground nuclear weapon test having a yield higher than 150 kt. (The TTBT is not formally in force, but since neither party has indicated an intention not to ratify it, both the USA and the USSR are obligated under international law to refrain from acts which would defeat its object and purpose.)

The Soviet response to US allegations

The USSR characterized the US allegations as lies. It rejected, in particular, the accusation that it had transferred to others, or had used itself, chemical weapons in Laos, Kampuchea and Afghanistan. Regarding the Soviet military manoeuvre *Zapad-81*, the USSR stated that it had provided in advance all information required under the 1975 Helsinki Declaration. It also stressed its strict observance of the nuclear arms limitation agreements, including the 1972 ABM Treaty and the 1979 SALT II Treaty. It said that the charges against the Soviet Union were aimed at diverting attention from the USA's own violations of arms control agreements.[2]

II. Soviet allegations

At the end of January 1984, the Soviet Embassy in Washington transmitted to the US Department of State an aide-memoire listing cases of alleged non-compliance by the USA with its obligations under arms control agreements.[3]

1. The USA is engaged in a strategic programme of unprecedented dimensions with the avowed aim of achieving military superiority over the USSR. The USA, which is responsible for the unilateral interruption of the talks on a nuclear test ban, the Indian Ocean, anti-satellite systems, and others, has also blocked and wrecked the Geneva negotiations on nuclear arms. Such activities clearly contradict the US–Soviet accords stipulating that neither side shall strive for military superiority and that, in their mutual relations, the USA and the USSR will be guided by the principle of equality and equal security. Neither is the US position in line with the 1968 Non-Proliferation Treaty, under which the parties are obliged to pursue negotiations in good faith on effective measures relating to cessation of the nuclear arms race at an early date and to nuclear disarmament.

2. In refusing to carry the 1979 SALT II Treaty into effect, the USA has rendered impossible the development of mutually acceptable solutions in respect of long-range sea- and land-based cruise missiles, as specified in the Protocol to the Treaty, in order to be free to deploy such missiles on a massive scale. This does not accord with the US stated intention to refrain from acts undermining the existing agreements on strategic arms.

3. By deploying in western Europe the Pershing II ballistic missiles and long-range land-based cruise missiles, capable of reaching targets on the territory of the USSR, the USA has violated the provision of the 1979 SALT II Treaty which prohibits circumvention of the Treaty through any other state or states, or in any other manner, as well as the undertaking not

to assume international obligations conflicting with the Treaty. The deployment in western Europe of nuclear weapons, which obviously complement the strategic offensive arsenal of the USA, is not in conformity with the US commitment to refrain from actions undermining the SALT II Treaty.

4. The USA has been using shelters to cover launchers of Minuteman II and Titan II intercontinental ballistic missiles. This practice is contrary to the provisions for effective verification, as contained in the 1972 SALT I Agreement. (The SALT I Agreement expired on 3 October 1977, but the USA and the USSR formally stated that they intended to refrain from any actions incompatible with its provisions or with the goals of the current talks on a new agreement.) Of particular concern are shelters over silos for Minuteman II launchers which are being refitted. Since the refitted launchers of Minuteman II differ in no practical terms from launchers of Minuteman III, one can make a 'supposition' that it is the Minuteman III missiles, equipped with MIRVs, that are actually deployed in the silos in question. If this is so, the evident failure of the USA to observe the verification provisions of the SALT I Agreement constitutes at the same time a failure to respect one of the main obligations under the SALT II Treaty—the limitation on the number of MIRVed ICBMs.

5. The US intention to build two new types of ICBM—the MX and the Midgetman—does not conform with the task of limiting strategic arms, as reflected in the US–Soviet agreements.

6. The USA has deployed a large radar on Sheyma Island, using for its construction radar components tested for ABM purposes; it used shelters over silos containing ABM missile launchers; it develops mobile ABM radars and space-based ABM systems; it tests Minuteman I missiles to give them a capability to counter missiles; it develops multiple warheads for ABM missiles; "and so on". All these activities are clearly in conflict with the 1972 ABM Treaty.

7. The USA is deploying on the Atlantic and the Pacific coasts, as well as in the south, new large PAVE PAWS radars. This deployment runs counter to the obligation under the ABM Treaty not to deploy an ABM system for the defence of the territory of the whole country, nor to provide a base for such a defence.

8. The deployment of large-scale ABM systems, the development of which was formally announced by the USA in March 1983, would undermine the ABM Treaty.

9. The USA systematically violates the agreed principle of confidentiality of discussions in the US–Soviet Standing Consultative Commission.

10. There have been repeated instances of US nuclear explosions exceeding the 150-kt yield limit fixed by the 1974 TTBT.

11. There have also been instances when, as a result of US underground nuclear explosions, radioactive debris was found outside the territorial

limits of the USA. This is a violation of the 1963 Partial Test Ban Treaty (PTBT).

12. Each year, the USA organizes in Europe military exercises on such an enormous scale that it is becoming increasingly difficult to distinguish them from actual deployment of armed forces for war purposes. Mere notification of such exercises does nothing to remove the danger.

The US response to Soviet allegations

The USA dismissed the Soviet allegations as "groundless". In response to specific charges it gave the following explanations.[4]

Regarding the use of shelters over ICBM launchers: During the initial Minuteman missile launcher construction, as well as the Minuteman silo upgrade programme during the mid-1970s, environmental shelters were employed to protect construction at the launchers from the weather. The facts concerning the activities being carried out at the launchers were provided and explained to the USSR, and were also available to the public. In response to Soviet expressions of concern, the shelters were modified and their use was discontinued after the completion of the Minuteman silo upgrade programme in early 1979. In the case of the Titan II silo, a cover was used to protect it from the weather during repair work on damage due to an accident. It was specifically designed to avoid any impediment to national technical means of verification, and was removed promptly after the need for it ceased.

Regarding the charge that by not ratifying the 1979 SALT II Treaty, the USA has not fulfilled the provisions of the Protocol to the Treaty concerning the development of solutions for long-range sea- and land-based missiles: The SALT II Protocol would have expired on 31 December 1981, even if the SALT II Treaty had been ratified and had entered into force. The USA made it clear at the time the SALT II Treaty was signed that the Protocol would not be extended. The subsequent NATO decision to deploy land-based longer-range intermediate nuclear force (INF) missiles in Europe was made in response to Soviet SS-20 deployments. The USA remains willing to negotiate on all such systems, including ground-launched cruise missiles.

Regarding the Sheyma Island and PAVE PAWS radars: The Sheyma Island radar in the Aleutians is for national technical means of verification, and the PAVE PAWS radars are ballistic missile early-warning radars located on the periphery of the national territory and oriented outward, as specifically permitted by the 1972 ABM Treaty.

Regarding the circumvention of the SALT II Treaty: The USA made it clear to the Soviet Union during the SALT II negotiations, and subsequently stated publicly following the signature of the Treaty, that the SALT II non-circumvention provision would not alter existing patterns of co-operation with its allies or preclude transfer of systems and weapons technology. The only provision of SALT II which would have applied to longer-range INF systems was contained in the Protocol to the Treaty. The Protocol limited deployment until 31 December 1981 of cruise missiles capable of a range in excess of 600 km on sea- or land-based launchers. However, that provision would have expired in 1981. The Pershing II and the ground-launched cruise missiles (viewed as strategic by the Soviet Union) do not circumvent the 1979 SALT II Treaty, because the Treaty defines land-based strategic ballistic missiles as those having a range of 5 500 km or more. The US INF systems do not fall into that category. Moreover, in signing the SALT II Treaty, the USA stated explicitly that any future limitations on US systems principally designed for theatre missions would have to be accompanied by appropriate limits on Soviet theatre systems like the SS-20.

Regarding the yield limit of nuclear explosions: Since the effective date of the 1974 TTBT and the 1976 Peaceful Nuclear Explosions Treaty (PNET), the USA has conducted no nuclear tests having yields which exceeded the 150-kt threshold fixed in these treaties.

Regarding the conversion of Minuteman II into MIRVed Minuteman III: The Minuteman II silos were not converted to Minuteman III launchers. The Soviet Union has been informed that any launchers of Minuteman II ICBMs converted to launchers of Minuteman III ICBMs would be made distinguishable on the basis of externally observable design features, as required by the 1979 SALT II Treaty.

Regarding the confidentiality of the Standing Consultative Commission (SCC): The USA continues properly to discharge its obligations and responsibilities under the Regulations of the SCC. The US government is not making public the proceedings of the SCC; the appearance of stories in the press about the SCC and possible subjects under discussion there does not reflect a change in that policy.

Regarding the Helsinki Declaration: The USA is in compliance with all the undertakings contained in the Helsinki Declaration, and its military activities are completely in accordance with the provisions of that Declaration. The USA and its allies notify all exercises which exceed the threshold of 25 000 troops established by the Declaration, and often notify smaller-scale military manoeuvres as a voluntary effort to strengthen mutual confidence.

Regarding the radioactive fall-out from nuclear tests: Both the USA and the USSR have encountered some difficulty in totally containing all their underground nuclear tests. The USA, however, has had only a few problems in the past with the venting of radioactive debris from underground tests at the Nevada test site. As more experience was gained with the containment of underground tests, venting from US tests became even more rare. Over the past decade there has been only one incident of local and minor venting. The Soviet Union had not raised its concerns about US venting with the USA since 1976 until the latest reference to it.

Regarding space-based ABM systems: The 1972 ABM Treaty does not prohibit research, and both sides have had research programmes since the signing of the Treaty. Soviet research and development efforts in the ABM field have been continuous and more extensive than those of the USA. The US programme calls only for enhanced research in this area. As stated by the US President in his March 1983 speech, US activities in this area will be consistent with US treaty obligations.

III. Conclusions

The recent allegations of breaches of arms control agreements made by the USA and the USSR may be said to fall roughly into two categories: those relating to the general spirit of the agreements, and those dealing with specific provisions.

The charges belonging to the first category have been put forward mainly by the USSR. The Soviet Union gave a subjective interpretation of such controversial notions as military superiority versus equal security, or strategic versus non-strategic weapon missions in the European context. It also presented its own understanding of the duties of states under signed but unratified agreements, including non-circumvention of the treaty provisions. However, failure to share Soviet perceptions of the goals pursued in the arms limitation exercise can hardly be labelled a violation of treaty obligations.

The charges belonging to the second category have been put forward by both the USA and the USSR. Most of them are vague and conjectural. In some cases, the charges may be the result of a lack of sufficiently precise definitions. For example, the complex language of the ABM Treaty is far from unequivocal as to what is actually prohibited. The SALT II Treaty, banning encryption of telemetry which would impede verification, fails to indicate what kinds and amounts of information are needed to ensure verification.

In other instances, suspicions of breaches may have arisen because the relevant treaties have not entered into force. Thus, for example, the parties have accused each other of exceeding the 150-kt yield threshold for nuclear explosions set by the unratified 1974 TTBT, while the exchange of data necessary to establish a correlation between yields of explosions at specific sites and the seismic signals produced, as envisaged in the TTBT, is being held up pending ratification of the Treaty. It may be added that the parties themselves had recognized that predicting the precise yield of nuclear weapon tests was associated with uncertainties; upon signing the TTBT they reached an understanding that one or two breaches per year would not be considered a violation. Equally, had the SALT II Treaty formally entered into force, there most probably would have been fewer problems regarding compliance, because the envisaged regular and obligatory exchange of data on strategic arms possessed by each side would have facilitated a uniform interpretation of the Treaty provisions as well as their verification.

At least in two cases, old controversies which were practically resolved have been dug out, it can be suggested, merely to inflate the list of grievances. Thus, because it is impossible to contain radioactive material that has vented from an underground nuclear test to the surface entirely within the boundaries of the testing state, both powers decided years ago to consider sporadic radioactive leakages spreading outside their territories as no more than 'technical' violations. Also, the placement of shelters over ICBM silos was discussed as early as the mid-1970s, and the matter appeared already then to have been adequately explained.

The bulk of the remaining charges concern issues of relatively minor military significance. For example, one fails to see how the construction of a radar or radars, whatever their size, could render more effective the existing systems of ballistic missile defence (that is, those subject to limitation under the ABM Treaty), which are widely considered to be patently inadequate for preventing nuclear warheads from reaching the target. It is difficult to understand how a notification of a military exercise, which is less than "adequate", could affect the security of other states. The intentions (expressed or presumed) to deploy new weapon systems, to which both sides referred in their indictments, may well sound ominous, but cannot be censured as breaches of contracted commitments.

The most serious charges concern (a) the use of chemical and biological weapons by the USSR, and (b) the testing and deployment of strategic missiles prohibited by the treaties by both the USA and the USSR. But, as regards the first charge, no fresh evidence was provided to invalidate the statement made in 1982 by a group of UN experts that the allegations had not been proven. On the contrary, since that time, various scientific reports have lent weight to the suggestion that the phenomenon of 'Yellow Rain', the centrepiece of the US CBW accusations, is of natural origin. As regards the second charge, the US allegations were admittedly based on "somewhat ambiguous" evidence, while the Soviet allegation was based on a mere "supposition". One wonders how assertions challenging the good faith of governments, and therefore fraught with grave political conse-quences, can be made so lightly and on such loose grounds. The fact that the consultative bodies provided for in the arms control treaties, such as the Standing Consultative Commission, set up under the SALT agreements, had not been exhaustively used testifies to the propagandistic nature of the US and Soviet recriminations.

It goes without saying that agreements, such as the 1925 Geneva Protocol, that have no provision for verification, facilitate unsubstantiated charges. But even with the most elaborate safeguards against cheating, there will always be problems with the implementation of treaties, especially those dealing with arms control. This does not mean that the existing treaties should be undone, or that efforts to reach new agreements should be abandoned as some have suggested. But effective mechanisms to clarify suspicions regarding compliance and to protect parties against ill-considered allegations of violations are indispensable, if there is to be progress in arms control negotiations.

Notes and references

[1] US Information Service, Document Foreign Policy EUR-114, 23 January 1984, US Embassy, Stockholm.
[2] *Pravda*, 3 February 1983.
[3] *Pravda*, 30 January 1984.
[4] US Information Service, Document Foreign Policy EUR-116 and 117, 30 January 1984, US Embassy, Stockholm.

9. The Conference on Confidence- and Security-Building Measures and Disarmament in Europe

DAVID BARTON

Superscript numbers refer to the list of notes and references at the end of the chapter.

I. Introduction

The Conference on Confidence- and Security-Building Measures and Disarmament in Europe, of which the Stockholm Conference is the first phase, opened in Stockholm, Sweden on 17 January 1984. The conference was convened by the 35 states participating in the Conference on Security and Co-operation in Europe (CSCE).[1]

The Conference in Stockholm opened amid a flourish of diplomatic activity. A meeting between US Secretary of State Shultz and Soviet Foreign Minister Gromyko and numerous bilateral meetings between foreign ministers took place during the opening ceremonies. European security and the nuclear and conventional arms control negotiations were obvious topics of discussion. One of the only immediately evident and tangible results from this initial diplomatic activity was the fact that Soviet Foreign Minister Gromyko let it be known to the foreign ministers with whom he met that his country would return to the Mutual (Balanced) Force Reduction (MBFR) talks in Vienna in mid-March 1984.

II. Background—CSCE, Stockholm, confidence-building measures

The Stockholm Conference is part of the CSCE process which was started in 1973 and which completed its first phase when the Final Act was signed in Helsinki in 1975. The Final Act is meant to govern the co-existence of European states, and of Canada and the USA. The 35 states were to implement the Final Act provisions by finding ways to normalize and ameliorate their political, economic, social, human, cultural and military relations. The idea of holding a separate conference focused on disarmament in Europe was most notably suggested by France, as early as 1978 at the First Special Session on Disarmament at the UN, and in 1980 at the CSCE meeting in Madrid by France, Poland, Romania, Sweden and Yugoslavia. The neutral and non-aligned group of CSCE states worked hard at the Madrid review meeting between 1980 and 1983 to secure a consensus agreement to hold the Conference and to draft a mandate acceptable to all states yet meaningful in establishing a framework for agreement on steps to lessen the military confrontation and promote disarmament in Europe.

The Swedish Foreign Minister Ola Ullsten offered to host the Conference in Stockholm in a speech in November 1980 in which he said: "If we are to reach an agreement on the convening of a European disarmament conference, it will be necessary to devise a mandate which combines elements of common interest to all CSCE states. It is also essential that we strive for concrete and substantive results rather than propagandistic ones ... Europe needs disarmament, not just a disarmament conference."[2]

In Helsinki in 1975 the 35 CSCE states decided to notify each other of large military manoeuvres. The purpose of these notifications was to reduce the danger of armed conflict by sharing among the participating states timely and clear information about military activities which might, under certain circumstances, appear provocative and cause misunderstanding. The notifications were to provide information about the military manoeuvres such as their designation, purpose, duration, area, numbers of troops and composition of forces. One of the original ideas was to provide a more conducive setting for substantive arms control and disarmament by undertaking political and military measures which would strengthen trust among the participating states.

Since 1975 all 35 states have in general respected the provision which obliges them, on a voluntary basis, to provide a 21-day advance notification of their major military manoeuvres involving 25 000 troops or more (although there have been a few complaints of inadequate notification by the USSR). There have been in all some 130 notifications of 100 manoeuvres involving several million troops during this nine-year period. Observers were invited to almost all NATO manoeuvres and to about one-half of those of the Warsaw Treaty Organization (WTO) and neutral and non-aligned states. Some countries announced manoeuvres below the 25 000 specified troop level and others gave more than 21-days' notice.[3]

This good record on notifications is a positive sign for future compliance with new measures by these states. After all, each notification expresses a political willingness, not a legal obligation, by that state to comply with a process of building confidence. The problem is that this process has not been expanded. Neither air and naval manoeuvres nor regular military movements (troop rotations, alerts, and so on) have been notified. The treatment of observers and their access to witness the full scope, duration and variety of the military exercises conducted during manoeuvres have varied. One of the tasks of the Stockholm Conference will be to expand the existing set of confidence-building measures in ways which fulfil the mandate by being "militarily significant, politically binding, and adequately verifiable".

III. The Stockholm Conference mandate

The mandate for the Stockholm Conference is contained in the final document of the CSCE review meeting in Madrid which was finally signed in September 1983 after nearly three years of discussions. The general aim of the whole process of the negotiations—including the second phase envisaged after 1986—is stated as follows: "to undertake, in stages, new, effective and concrete actions designed to make progress in strengthening confidence and security and in achieving disarmament, so as to give effect and expression to the duty of States to refrain from the threat or use of force in their mutual relations". But, despite this overall aim to achieve disarmament measures and despite strong public sentiment in favour of disarmament in several European states, most of the 35 governments have limited their expectations for the conference to the detailed mandate set at Madrid for the first phase in Stockholm "devoted to the negotiation and adoption of a set of mutually complementary confidence- and security-building measures designed to reduce the risk of military confrontation in Europe." These confidence- and security-building measures (CSBMs) "will cover the whole of Europe as well as the adjoining sea area [including ocean areas adjoining Europe] and air space . . . will be of military significance and politically binding and will be provided with adequate forms of verification which correspond to their content".[4] Most of the participating states interpret this first phase as meaning the expansion of the existing set of notifications of military manoeuvres established when the CSCE Final Act was signed nine years ago in Helsinki. Those confidence-building measures do not attempt to limit or reduce military forces in Europe.

The mandate also states that the results of the Stockholm Conference will be assessed by the participatory states at the next review meeting of the CSCE in Vienna in November 1986 before proceeding to the next stage. This raises the question of just how far the first stage of the conference can go in the direction of disarmament, since many interpretations separate out specific consideration of disarmament from the first stage of the conference.[5]

Therefore, it seems safe to predict that between the opening of the conference in 1984 and the review of the first stage, in Vienna in November 1986, there will be several years in Stockholm of posturing, shuffled proposal papers, and discarded compromises. Perhaps the most that can be expected from the Stockholm Conference is a modest expansion of the existing set of confidence-building measures, some declaratory statements, and some fertile groundwork such as establishing a compliance committee which would be needed for these first-stage measures. It could then be built on for the second stage, which could undertake actual disarmament steps

190

and expand or incorporate progress achieved in any of the other conventional and nuclear arms negotiations.

IV. Opening positions

According to the CSCE rules of procedure the negotiations in Stockholm should take place outside the framework of the military alliances. However, in reality, consensus has usually been sought between three groupings of states—NATO, WTO, and neutral and non-aligned—and it has normally been each grouping which presents a common position or proposal. In past experience with the CSCE process it has frequently been the neutral and non-aligned group which has played the mediating role.[6]

NATO position

The NATO group was first to table a specific proposal, on 24 January 1984.[7] The NATO position stresses the importance of achieving greater transparency, openness and predictability for military activities and military forces in Europe. It seeks an exchange of military information relating to the structure of air and land forces in the geographical area of application and an annual preview of all military activities which should be notified in advance. The NATO position states that if the new set of measures is implemented and verified and if other international commitments are respected by all the CSCE states then that could open up prospects for new progress in disarmament, but only after the Vienna review meeting in 1986.

NATO wants notifications to be issued 45 days in advance for out-of-garrison activities involving over 6 000 troops or a specified number of armoured vehicles, mobilizations of more than 25 000 troops or three divisions, and amphibious exercises involving over 3 000 troops or more than three battalions. NATO also wants observers, inspections and other forms of verification to be used in order to ensure direct observation of all pre-notified military activities and compliance with the new notification requirements. In addition, NATO recommends inspection on request and national technical means as verification tools. The NATO position also suggests that the means of communication between the 35 states be improved, especially for crisis contingencies.

The criteria "formally established" at Madrid as US pre-conditions for the Conference give an indication of some of the negotiating problems ahead. These criteria were: (a) that the conference must remain an integral part of the CSCE process in order to maintain the appropriate balance between human rights and security concerns; (b) that the first stage would be limited to CSBMs which do not directly affect the size, weaponry, or structure of a state's military forces, and that, as France proposed, nuclear issues would not be negotiated at the conference; (c) that the conference must not interfere with any other arms control negotiations; and (d) that the CSBMs must be militarily significant, politically binding, verifiable, and applicable to the whole of Europe from the Atlantic Ocean to the Ural Mountains.[8]

Ambassador James Goodby, chief US delegate to the Stockholm Conference, has stressed these pre-conditions. He has also expressed the view that CSBMs should precede any declaratory measures, and that declaratory measures are meaningless when not accompanied by actions.[9] NATO will therefore probably not wish to consider any regional arrangements for CSBMs, or any constraints on nuclear weapons—even tactical battlefield nuclear weapons.

In addition, the US and NATO stress on transparency and verification may throw up one of the most difficult and traditional stumbling blocks to negotiations with the USSR and the WTO. The USSR and the WTO have come to accept inspections in addition to national technical means when actual reductions are involved.[10] However, the NATO position foresees reduction measures only in the second stage. Certainly the NATO stress on transparency may have provoked the comment in Foreign Minister Gromyko's speech to the Conference that "any attempts at the conference to advance unacceptable demands right from the start and, rather than build confidence, look for a crack in the fence to peep at one's neighbors could only impede its productive work."[11] Also, Ambassador Goodby has suggested that all disarmament measures be delayed until after a full review meeting in Vienna and that continuation of the Conference be contingent on a judgement at Vienna of how the Soviet and other WTO states have performed on other provisions of the Helsinki Final Act, such as those concerned with human rights.[12] Human rights debates in past CSCE meetings have delayed consideration of other issues. Therefore, judging from past experience, there might be a significant delay in consideration of disarmament measures if the view prevails that the Conference must wait for a full review in Vienna before entering into the disarmament stage.

WTO position

In the early weeks of the Stockholm Conference the WTO group had not tabled a specific proposal. Romania tabled its own proposal on 25 January 1984, but that proposal does not adequately represent the WTO position.[13] When questioned about the WTO position the member states, with the exception of Romania, pointed to the speech of Foreign Minister Gromyko at the Stockholm Conference opening ceremonies, the speech of President Brezhnev on 6 October 1979 in Berlin and recent WTO declarations. These speeches and declarations do outline a position which gives clear priority to pledges, and to "declaratory measures" of no-first-use of nuclear weapons and of non-aggression. Further development of CSBMs is mentioned but seems to have a low priority. This low priority seems also to be evidenced by the fact that the WTO has not tabled a proposal despite decisions taken at the Helsinki preparatory meeting, held from 25 October to 11 November 1983, urging the participatory states to introduce CSBM proposals as early as possible after the opening of the Conference in its first session.[14]

At the opening of the Conference, Gromyko stated that his country's priority was to prevent nuclear war and that the most important measures for the Conference to undertake would be pledges of no-first-use of nuclear weapons and of mutual non-use of conventional and nuclear military force in addition to a pledge to halt the arms race and achieve disarmament. He also mentioned his country's desire to see initiatives taken in Stockholm to make northern Europe a nuclear weapon-free zone and to make all of Europe nuclear- and chemical-weapon free.[9]

Gromyko also stated his country's willingness to consider a wide spectrum of new CSBMs with more scope and significance than the existing useful CBMs. He stated the Soviet desire to see agreements on new measures not only concluded but implemented before the Vienna review meeting in 1986. The specific improvements he mentioned for CSBMs were development of the use of prior notification, addition of military movements and redeployments to the notification procedures which apply now only to manoeuvres, and inclusion of air and naval manoeuvres in the sea, ocean and airspace adjoining Europe. It must be assumed that these and perhaps other expansions of the existing set of CBMs will form part of the WTO position, when and if it is tabled, in addition to a priority emphasis on the declaratory measures. However, in order for progress to be achieved in the work of the Conference the WTO should table a proposal of CSBMs and it would be helpful if it included suggested parameters for the new measures. Insistence that there should first be an agreement on declaratory measures and unwillingness to table a specific CSBM proposal will certainly block progress.

Romania tabled a proposal on 25 January which suggested geographical and numerical limits on military forces, armaments and activities, a nuclear weapon-free corridor between East and West, nuclear weapon-free zones in northern Europe and the Balkans, and a freeze on foreign troops, foreign bases and military expenditures in Europe. Such far-reaching proposals are unlikely to become part of a general WTO proposal.[13]

Neutral and non-aligned position

During the opening weeks of the Stockholm Conference it became clear that the neutral and non-aligned states would be obliged to continue the mediating role that they have played successfully in the past. They maintain a strong commitment to make the CSCE process work. But, they also presented their own proposals on 9 March 1984.[21]

Early working papers prepared by Sweden, Switzerland and Yugoslavia formed the basis for the eventual neutral and non-aligned proposal which is rather more ambitious than the NATO proposal. They suggest an enlargement of the existing set of confidence-building measures but they also underline a new factor in the mandate: security-building measures which seek to actually constrain military activities and capabilities including troop deployments and military equipment. While they appear to accept that disarmament measures will be first considered in a second stage after the Vienna review meeting in 1986, they also envisage a broad range of new CSBMs in the first stage to prepare fertile ground for that next stage of disarmament measures.[15]

The neutral and non-aligned position, as suggested in these working papers, seeks to expand the existing set of confidence-building measures by including smaller military manoeuvres, amphibious and airborne manoeuvres, and major military activities in the air and at sea which affect European security, troop movements and troop mobilizations. It also recommends the exchange of an annual listing of planned major military activities, the sharing of information on the current location of major military units, the improvement of the notified manoeuvre descriptions, the invitation of observers to all notified manoeuvres, and the drafting of guidelines for those observer missions. It will be difficult for the neutral and non-aligned states to define clearly all of the military activities involved and to reach a common understanding in their joint proposal, but such background work will assist them in achieving a final consensus and common interpretation of the new CSBMs.

The new measures mentioned in the neutral and non-aligned proposal are measures to place ceilings on the total number of troops involved in manoeuvres and in amphibious and airborne exercises, and to constrain the deployment in certain areas of troops or equipment with durable offensive capabilities. In both the expanded set of old CBMs and the new measures, the neutral and non-aligned states have not, so far, specified numbers for the size of the military manoeuvres and movements. They have only indicated parameters. This is probably designed to assist in the final negotiations to achieve consensus.

In addition, the neutral and non-aligned proposal suggests adequate arrangements to facilitate the exchange of information and verification. It also suggests that CSCE states share information on their military expenditures according to United Nations guidelines. The three working papers differed somewhat in their approach to declaratory measures but a similarity emerges in their proposal which reaffirms declarations either in the UN Charter or the Helsinki Final Act.

The final neutral and non-aligned proposal differs only slightly from the working papers. The shared ideas prevailed and the differences were reconciled.

V. Bridging differences

One of the most important differences which must be bridged is the emphasis the NATO position places on transparency of military activities and the priority the WTO position gives to declaratory measures. Each side has chosen to stress a subject which it knows the other side dislikes. Nevertheless, compromise is always possible and the neutral and non-aligned proposal clearly indicates possible solutions in their support for reaffirming certain declarations in the Helsinki Final Act and the UN Charter which deal with the mutual non-use of military force for aggressive and threatening purposes.[15] Such repetitions of existing declarations should not be too painful for the NATO side if some movement were to result in other areas. For example, it should be possible to bridge the gap between the 1983 statements by the WTO and NATO on the non-use of military force.[16] The Swedish working paper includes a suggestion for the military information and verification concerns. It proposes a consultative committee. This might facilitate the information exchange and any verification needs other than national technical means by having a CSCE committee which could be a non-intrusive repository for military information, a coordinator for observer missions, a processor of complaints, and perhaps even eventually a monitor of inspection on request to verify shared military information and compliance with CSBMs. However, there is a good chance that these particular WTO and NATO positions will remain hardened at least until after the US presidential election in November 1984.

Proposals for broadening the current criteria for notifications include decreasing the size specification of major military manoeuvres below the 25 000 level, expanding the types of military activity covered to include such activities as out-of-garrison movements and routine troop rotations, extending the notifications to all mobilizations of reserves including emergency or alert exercises, lengthening the notification period beyond the current 21 days, formalizing the exchange of observers with guidelines to allow them comprehensive access to manoeuvres and movements of troops and equipment, and expanding the mandate for notifications to cover air, naval and amphibious manoeuvres.

Judging from the past history of the CSCE notifications, the opening positions of the 35 states at the Stockholm Conference and their opinions on CBMs expressed to the Secretary-General of the UN and elsewhere, it is possible to envisage a consensus agreement among the 35 states to expand the existing system of notifications. When the Secretary-General of the UN received reports he solicited from European states on suggestions for CBMs most of the states stressed the need for improvements in the existing CSCE system of notifications. They gave priority to notifications of smaller military manoeuvres, movements, and air and naval manoeuvres. For example, five WTO states recommended prior notification of major air and naval manoeuvres.[17]

Naval and air manoeuvres have not been notified under the CSCE system. The treatment of observers to manoeuvres has also been judged by several states as unsatisfactory. These are just two of several areas which could become the focus for the Stockholm Conference. The working groups could propose guidelines for observer missions and for notifications of air, naval and amphibious manoeuvres. The presence of military expertise can assist the groups in successfully negotiating specific parameters and limits for the proposed expansion of the existing set of CBMs. Since there appears to be some basic agreement on the direction in which changes should be made, agreement on specific details should not be impossible.

There are other issues which may pose more serious problems, such as the ceiling on the size of manoeuvres, desired by the WTO states and opposed in the past by the NATO states, the inclusion of amphibious manoeuvres, which the WTO states have not yet mentioned, and the exact definition of when air and naval manoeuvres are to be included. But, again, compromise is always possible. For example, military manoeuvres and movements could be limited to 60 000 troops with an escape clause which would permit larger manoeuvres if a special notification were made perhaps at least 90 days in advance, or if they are part of the annual preview of military activities proposed by NATO. After all, in the nine-year history of CSCE notifications of 100 manoeuvres, only five NATO manoeuvres and one WTO manoeuvre have exceeded the 60 000 troop level.[5]

When amphibious manoeuvres have been part of major land manoeuvres they have been included in the notifications. It is when they are conducted independently that there is still some concern about their offensive nature even at levels of a few thousand troops. The neutral and non-aligned states are particularly interested in including the amphibious exercises and they have presented previous proposals at the Belgrade and Madrid review meetings to include them.[18] The working papers also contain some specific guidelines which could form the basis of an agreement.[15]

196

It seems that all three groups would like to include air and naval manoeuvres when they are connected to land manoeuvres. The difficulty will be agreement on when and how to include air and naval exercises when they are conducted independently of land exercises but do affect European security. Again, it would seem that most exercises conducted in European air, sea and ocean space do involve European security and the Conference should be able to deal with this matter even though definitions of European sea and ocean space may be difficult to agree upon.

Another problem has arisen about the geographical area of applicability. The CSCE agreed to extend the area of applicability from the Atlantic to the Urals thereby including more territory of the USSR. But now, some interpretations of the mandate seem to indicate that any new CSBMs considered at Stockholm must be applicable to all of Europe. Narrow interpretation of this criterion could eliminate all serious consideration of zonal or sub-regional arrangements such as thinning out conventional or nuclear forces along certain East–West borders, and nuclear weapon-free areas in the Baltic, northern Europe, the Mediterranean and the Balkan states. Several CSCE states view zonal arrangements as critically important to their security—so much so, for example, that Malta blocked the final consensus in Madrid in order to extract some concession to focus attention on the Mediterranean. Mediterranean non-participating states were invited to present their views and proposals for CSBMs in the Mediterranean during the second week of the conference.

Therefore, a new set of CSBMs should be within reach of the Stockholm Conference if the neutral and non-aligned states continue to play a unified and skilful mediating role, if the conference can solve the detailed problems of limits and parameters for the new measures and set guidelines for the inclusion of new manoeuvres and movements, and if a consultative committee can be established to set guidelines, monitor and serve as an intermediary for the exchange of information, verification and observation missions.

VI. Conclusions

The achievement of results at the Stockholm Conference will be a difficult task. Political leadership and skilful mediation will be required from the neutral and non-aligned states and also from the European states within the NATO and WTO groups to pressure both the USA and the USSR to step away from their recently soured bilateral nuclear arms negotiating experience. The USA brings to the Conference a set of pre-conditions "formally established" in its position in Madrid which could hinder progress in Stockholm.[19] The USSR brings to the Conference bilateral arms negotiations grievances, undoubtedly a set of pre-conditions for the resumption of those negotiations in Geneva, and a reluctance to exchange military information and to begin negotiating new CSBMs. These hidden and extracurricular agendas must be set aside. Differences cannot be bridged and working groups cannot be established until all the main proposals are tabled and until there is some agreement on the main items to appear in the final document.

The narrow interpretations of the mandate for the Conference given by many of the 35 states help to explain the pessimism of many observers. To spend two or three years achieving at best only a modest expansion of the existing CBMs would hardly be a major achievement. There are a number of ideas for 'second-generation' confidence-building measures which deserve examination—much fuller examination, of course, than can be given here. There is the suggestion of border zones with thinned-out military forces, other force limitations and reductions, and the rear-basing of certain types of military equipment. There is the idea of establishing verification and inspection systems modelled after either the successful Quadripartite Agreement implementation or the Sinai early-warning, monitoring and verification system. An experimental early-warning, inspection and verification zone in central Europe could be the central feature of a new approach which, by demonstrating practical improvements in European security in an experimental setting, might encourage the 35 states to adopt more ambitious CSBMs and disarmament measures.[20]

Agreement in Stockholm on a new set of CSBMs, even though modest and fairly insignificant militarily, would be better than no agreement at all, particularly since there are few signs of progress in other arms control negotiations. Also, the establishment of effective working groups and a consultative compliance committee would be good groundwork accomplishments that would be very useful for the second stage of the conference. The results of the first stage will be assessed at the CSCE Vienna review meeting starting in 1986. Judging from past experience that review meeting might easily last two or three years because it will also evaluate all the other elements of the CSCE process—human rights, economic, social and international problems. It would be very unfortunate if, as a result of the Vienna review, there was a hiatus of two or three years in which no further progress was made towards the consideration of actual disarmament proposals. A way might possibly be found by which the Conference on Confidence- and Security-Building Measures and Disarmament in Europe could move on to the second stage while the Vienna review was proceeding. In that second stage there would be a much greater need than in the first for co-ordination with other negotiations, such as the MBFR negotiations at Vienna.

Notes and references

[1] There are three groups of CSCE states: (NN) neutral and non-aligned states; (W) Western states, members of NATO and/or the European Community; and (E) Eastern states, members of WTO. They are Austria(NN), Belgium(W), Bulgaria(E), Canada(W), Cyprus(NN), Czechoslovakia(E), Denmark(W), Finland(NN), France(W), German DR(E), FR Germany(W), Greece(W), Holy See, Hungary(E), Iceland(W), Ireland(W), Italy(W), Liechtenstein(NN), Luxembourg(W), Malta(NN), Monaco, the Netherlands(W), Norway(W), Poland(E), Portugal(W), Romania(E), San Marino(NN), Spain(W), Sweden(NN), Switzerland(NN), Turkey(W), UK(W), USA(W), USSR(E), Yugoslavia(NN).

[2] Lindskog, L., *Facts about the Stockholm Conference*, paper published by the Swedish Institute of International Affairs, Stockholm, Sweden, December 1983.

[3] See tables and notifications of military manoeuvres in compliance with the Final Act of the CSCE, in SIPRI, *World Armaments and Disarmament, SIPRI Yearbooks 1975 . . . 83* (Almqvist & Wiksell, Stockholm, 1975 . . . 77, and Taylor & Francis, London, 1978 . . . 83).

[4] For the text of the mandate see *SIPRI Yearbook 1984*, appendix 15A.

[5] Opening statements by foreign ministers of the 35 CSCE states presented during the first week of the Stockholm Conference in January 1984.

[6] See the proposal submitted by the delegations of Austria, Cyprus, Finland, Liechtenstein, San Marino, Sweden, Switzerland and Yugoslavia in 1981, in SIPRI, *World Armaments and Disarmament, SIPRI Yearbook 1983* (Taylor & Francis, London, 1983), p. 609.

[7] *Confidence- and Security-Building Measures (CSBMs)*, Proposal submitted by the delegations of Belgium, Canada, Denmark, France, Federal Republic of Germany, Greece, Iceland, Italy, Luxembourg, Netherlands, Norway, Portugal, Spain, Turkey, UK and USA, 24 January 1984.

[8] *Conference on Disarmament in Europe*, GIST, Bureau of Public Affairs, US Department of State, January 1984.

[9] Goodby, J., Three-part interview with Ambassador James Goodby, chief US delegate to the Conference on Confidence- and Security-Building Measures and Disarmament in Europe. USA Document, US Information Service, 8 December 1983, Stockholm, Sweden.

[10] Barton, D. and Pöllinger, S., 'Negotiations for conventional force reductions and security in Europe', in *SIPRI Yearbook 1983* (note 6), pp. 595–608.

[11] Statement by Andrei A. Gromyko, Member of the Politbureau, CPSU Central Committee, First Deputy Chairman, USSR Council of Ministers, Minister for Foreign Affairs of the USSR at the Conference on Confidence- and Security-Building Measures and Disarmament in Europe, Stockholm, 18 January 1984, p. 15.

[12] See note 9, particularly Part I, pp. 6–8.

[13] *Confidence- and Security-Building Measures (CSBMs)*, proposal submitted by the delegation of Romania, Stockholm, 25 January 1984 (see appendix 15D for full text); Statement by the Minister for Foreign Affairs of the Socialist Republic of Romania, Mr Stefan Andrei, at the Conference on Confidence- and Security-Building Measures and Disarmament in Europe, Stockholm, Sweden, 20 January 1984.

[14] Helsinki Preparatory Meeting document CSCE/HPM/1/Rev. 1, 11 November 1983.

[15] Swedish working paper, 31 January 1984, presented to neutral and non-aligned group; Swiss working paper, 6 February 1984; Yugoslav working paper, 29 December 1983. It should be noted that the assessments of negotiating positions in this chapter are taken as of March 1984.

[16] Political Declaration of WTO States, Prague, 5 January 1983; NATO Defense Ministers Communique, Brussels, 2 June 1983.

[17] Report to the UN General Assembly, 34th Session, General and Complete Disarmament, Confidence Building Measures, Report to the Secretary-General A/34/416, 5 October 1979. Reports on confidence-building measures to the Secretary-General of the UN were mandated by UN Resolution 33/91B of 16 December 1978.

[18] See the proposal submitted to the Madrid Conference by the delegations of Austria, Cyprus, Finland, Liechtenstein, San Marino, Sweden, Switzerland and Yugoslavia on Confidence-Building Measures on 12 December 1980, in SIPRI, *World Armaments and Disarmament, SIPRI Yearbook 1981* (Taylor & Francis, London, 1981), pp. 498–500.

[19] See notes 8 and 9.

[20] For further information about the Quadripartite Agreement and its applicability for CSBM use in central Europe see: Krause, C., 'How effective are military confidence-building measures?', paper for Friedrich Ebert-Stiftung, Bonn, July 1982.

[21] *Confidence- and Security-Building Measures*, Proposal submitted by the delegations of Austria, Cyprus, Finland, Malta, San Marino, Sweden, Switzerland and Yugoslavia, 9 March 1984.

INDEX

Radar:
jammers, 129, 130
ranges, 128–9
trade in, 102, 103, 105, 115
USA:
Joint Stars, 128–9, 134, 135, 136, 137
Pave Mover, 128, 134
PAVE PAWS, 182, 184
USSR, 180
see also under Aircraft
Rand Corporation, 54, 140
Rapier Missiles, 104
Reagan, President Ronald:
arms exports, 91, 123
BMD, 10, 157
chemical weapons and, 166, 179
military build-up and, 13, 60, 65, 66
military expenditure and, 58, 65
military objectives, 63–4
Rivlin, Alice, 62
Rogers, General Bernard, 56, 57, 144, 146
Romania, 76, 77, 188, 192, 193
Rostow, Eugene, 40
RPVs (remotely piloted vehicles), 129, 130

SALT I:
ABM Treaty (1972), 11, 154, 157, 163, 180, 181, 182, 183, 184, 185, 186
Interim Agreement on Certain Measures With Respect to the Limitation of Strategic Offensive Arms (1972), 23, 39, 182
SALT II, 39, 44, 180, 181–2, 183, 184, 185, 186
Satellites, 135, 157, 160
Saudi Arabia, 94, 95, 100, 101, 103, 108–9, 113, 114
SAW dispensers, 133
Schlesinger, James, 35
Schmidt, Chancellor Helmut, 58
Scowcroft Commission, 35–8, 60
Sea Eagle missile, 131
Sea Lite programme, 158
Shahine missile, 103
Shemya Island, 182, 184
Ships, trade in, 97, 100, 103, 104, 106, 115
Shultz Report, 188
Singapore, 101, 106
Skeet sub-munition, 136
Small arms, trade in, 107

SNIAS–Aérospatiale, 102
Somalia, 96
SOTAS, 128, 134
South Africa:
arms exports, 112, 113, 114
arms imports, 102, 105
military aggression, 98
South America, 52, 88
South Asia, 52, 88, 93
Space programmes, 10–11
Spain, 17, 18, 19, 67, 69, 90, 113, 114
Spinney, Franklin, 60–2
Stabo (runway bomb), 131, 133
START (Strategic Arms Reduction Talks), 5, 6, 7, 37–9, 42–4, 46–7
Stockholm Conference *see* Conference on Confidence- and Security-building Measures and Disarmament in Europe
Submarines:
cruise missiles on, 28, 32, 45
production, 116
trade in, 97, 109
UK, 105
USA, 4, 23, 29, 30, 36
USSR, 5, 23, 28
Sub-munitions, 131, 133, 134, 135, 136
Sudan, 113
Sweden:
arms exports, 116, 119, 120
disarmament issues and, 10, 172, 188, 189, 194, 195
military expenditure, 69, 75
Switzerland, 69, 113, 194
Syria, 91, 94, 95, 100, 112, 113, 114

T-16, T-19, T-22 missiles, 132, 134, 135
TABAS/TABASCO missile, 132
Taiwan, 95, 100–1, 112, 113, 114
Talon Gold programme, 158
Tanks:
trade in, 100, 103, 108, 109, 114, 115, 116, 117
US, 61, 67
Thailand, 100, 106
Thatcher, Margaret, 104
Third World:
arms exports, 92, 94, 95
arms imports, 13–14
debts, 13, 53, 90
military expenditure, 53
Thomson–CSF, 102
Transarmament, 148, 149
Turkey, 55, 109

World Armaments and Disarmament
SIPRI Yearbook 1984

Those chapters and appendices marked with an asterisk are included in this paperback.